Developing and Evaluating Quality Bilingual Practices in Higher Education

BILINGUAL EDUCATION & BILINGUALISM

Series Editors: **Nancy H. Hornberger** *(University of Pennsylvania, USA)* and **Wayne E. Wright** *(Purdue University, USA)*

Bilingual Education and Bilingualism is an international, multidisciplinary series publishing research on the philosophy, politics, policy, provision and practice of language planning, Indigenous and minority language education, multilingualism, multiculturalism, biliteracy, bilingualism and bilingual education. The series aims to mirror current debates and discussions. New proposals for single-authored, multiple-authored or edited books in the series are warmly welcomed, in any of the following categories or others authors may propose: overview or introductory texts; course readers or general reference texts; focus books on particular multilingual education program types; school-based case studies; national case studies; collected cases with a clear programmatic or conceptual theme; and professional education manuals.

All books in this series are externally peer-reviewed.

Full details of all the books in this series and of all our other publications can be found on http://www.multilingual-matters.com, or by writing to Multilingual Matters, St Nicholas House, 31–34 High Street, Bristol BS1 2AW, UK.

BILINGUAL EDUCATION & BILINGUALISM: 128

Developing and Evaluating Quality Bilingual Practices in Higher Education

Edited by
Fernando D. Rubio-Alcalá and Do Coyle

MULTILINGUAL MATTERS
Bristol • Blue Ridge Summit

DOI https://doi.org/10.21832/RUBIO3699
Library of Congress Cataloging in Publication Data
A catalog record for this book is available from the Library of Congress.

Names: Rubio-Alcalá, Fernando D. - editor. | Coyle, Do - editor.
Title: Developing and Evaluating Quality Bilingual Practices in Higher
   Education/Edited by Fernando D. Rubio-Alcalá, Do Coyle.
Description: Bristol, United Kingdom; Blue Ridge Summit, PA: Multilingual
   Matters, 2021. | Series: Bilingual Education & Bilingualism: 128 |
   Includes bibliographical references and index. | Summary: "This book
   provides an overview and evaluation of the quality of bilingual
   education found in internationalised higher education institutions. Its
   authors focus on the multifaceted roles that language(s) play in these
   growing multilingual spaces and analyse and identify the many factors
   that account for quality multilingual degree programmes"-- Provided by
   publisher. Identifiers: LCCN 2020044034 (print) | LCCN 2020044035 (ebook) | ISBN
   9781788923682 (paperback) | ISBN 9781788923699 (hardback) | ISBN
   9781788923705 (pdf) | ISBN 9781788923712 (epub) | ISBN 9781788923729
   (kindle edition)
Subjects: LCSH: Education, Bilingual. | Education, Higher. | Language and
   education. Classification: LCC LC3727 .D484 2021 (print) | LCC LC3727 (ebook) | DDC
   370.117/5--dc23 LC record available at https://lccn.loc.gov/2020044034
LC ebook record available at https://lccn.loc.gov/2020044035

British Library Cataloguing in Publication Data
A catalogue entry for this book is available from the British Library.

ISBN-13: 978-1-78892-369-9 (hbk)
ISBN-13: 978-1-78892-368-2 (pbk)

Multilingual Matters
UK: St Nicholas House, 31–34 High Street, Bristol BS1 2AW, UK.
USA: NBN, Blue Ridge Summit, PA, USA.

Website: www.multilingual-matters.com
Twitter: Multi_Ling_Mat
Facebook: https://www.facebook.com/multilingualmatters
Blog: www.channelviewpublications.wordpress.com

Copyright © 2021 Fernando D. Rubio-Alcalá, Do Coyle and the authors of individual chapters.

All rights reserved. No part of this work may be reproduced in any form or by any means without permission in writing from the publisher.

The policy of Multilingual Matters/Channel View Publications is to use papers that are natural, renewable and recyclable products, made from wood grown in sustainable forests. In the manufacturing process of our books, and to further support our policy, preference is given to printers that have FSC and PEFC Chain of Custody certification. The FSC and/or PEFC logos will appear on those books where full certification has been granted to the printer concerned.

Typeset by SAN Publishing Services.
Printed and bound in the UK by the CPI Books Group Ltd.
Printed and bound in the US by NBN.

Contents

	Contributors	vii
	Foreword. Quality in Multilingual Higher Education: From Supra-National Strategies to Institutional Realizations *Emma Dafouz*	xv
	Introduction *Fernando D. Rubio-Alcalá and Do Coyle*	1
1	Internationalization, Quality and Multilingualism in Higher Education: A Troublesome Relationship *Patrick Studer*	9
2	Building a Language Policy for Quality Multilingualism in Higher Education: From Theory to Practice *Inmaculada Fortanet-Gómez*	31
3	Glocalization and Internationalization in University Language Policy Making *Kyria Finardi, Pat Moore and Felipe Guimarães*	54
4	From EME to SDG: The Journey of a Medical University *Karin Båge and Jennifer Valcke*	73
5	The Role of Languages in the Internationalization of Higher Education: Institutional Challenges *Víctor Pavón Vázquez*	96
6	A Key Development Indicator Matrix for Systemizing CLIL in Higher Education Environments *David Marsh and Wendy Díaz Pérez*	115
7	AGCEPESA Project: Designing a Tool to Measure the Quality of Plurilingual Programmes in Higher Education *Javier Ávila-López, Francisco Rubio-Cuenca and Rocío López-Lechuga*	137
8	Team Teaching: A Way to Boost the Quality of EMI Programmes? *David Lasagabaster*	163

9   Understanding the Affective for Effective EMI in Higher
    Education   181
    Maria Ellison

Index   201

Contributors

Editors

Fernando D. Rubio-Alcalá, PhD, is a Senior Lecturer at the University of Huelva, Spain (2000–) and Head of Language Policy. He was also Associate Dean of International Relations and Plurilingualism (2006–2018). His main research field is foreign language acquisition, paying particular attention to bilingualism in tertiary education and the influence of affective factors in foreign language teaching and learning. He is the Head Researcher in the project 'Analysis of quality in bilingual programmes in Andalusian universities' (2014–2018, €91,935, Government of Andalusia, Spain), and was the President of the International Conference on Quality of Bilingual Programmes in Higher Education (Huelva, Spain, May 2018). Fernando co-edited the monograph *Addressing Bilingualism in Higher Education: Policies and Implementation Issues* (with Moore & Pavón Vázquez, 2018, Porta Linguarum), edited the volume *Self-esteem and Foreign Language Learning* (2007, Cambridge Scholars Publishing), and has contributed book chapters to two volumes published by Multilingual Matters: 'The links between self-esteem and language anxiety and implications for the classroom' (in Gkonou, Daubney & Dewaele, 2017, *New Insights into Language Anxiety: Theory, Research and Educational Implications*) and 'Self-esteem and self-concept in foreign language learning' (in Mercer & Williams, 2014, *Multiple Perspectives on the Self in SLA*). He was also a Visiting Professor at the University of Virginia (2007, 2008, 2011) and a Visiting Scholar at the University of Texas (2005). Fernando has participated in over 100 academic events in Europe and North, Central and South America.

Do Coyle has worked at the University of Edinburgh since 2017. Her specific research interests lie in plurilingual learning and cross-disciplinary networks, as well as professional learning in schools, visual learning (including the role of video conferencing and digital communication) and community sustainability through technological advancement. She is involved in a wide range of European initiatives and has published extensively in the field of content and language integrated learning (CLIL), including the 4Cs conceptual framework and the English national guidelines for CLIL. Her other publications focus on transforming pedagogies in the field of modern language education, bilingual education and teacher education, especially in technology-enhanced environments. Her work has enabled her to co-research with bilingual and CLIL teachers and learners across the world. She sits on advisory panels at local, regional, national and international levels and is a regular keynote speaker at international conferences. Do's recent publications include a widely acclaimed book on CLIL published by Cambridge University Press (with Hood & Marsh, 2010). Her current research involves teacher–learner networks for analysing effective CLIL practice using digital tools and virtual spaces, as well as carrying out collaborative research in Austria and Italy to investigate pluriliteracies in CLIL settings. She has several funded research projects which include: investigating motivation and achievement in CLIL classrooms in the UK (Esmée Fairbairn Foundation); creating innovative distributed professional learning communities connected through practice-based evidence of effective learning (Scottish Government); and investigating sustainable rural communities through transforming natural resources into business opportunities (LEADER). While at the University of Aberdeen, Do has led the university's e-learning and e-research strategies and currently directs the CASS Connected Communities Cross-Disciplinary Research network. She has set up the new MEd in plurilingual education and currently supervises nine doctoral students in the field of teacher professional learning, CLIL, modern language classrooms and new technologies.

Authors

Patrick Studer is a university researcher, lecturer and teacher trainer at ZHAW, Switzerland. Patrick teaches applied linguistics to undergraduate and graduate students in the School of Applied Linguistics, Winterthur. In his research, Patrick focuses on language sociological questions, especially on English language use and competence in higher education. His recent book-length editions include *Internationalizing Curricula in Higher Education: Quality and Language of Instruction* (2018, Swiss Journal of Applied Linguistics), *Ideological Conceptualizations of Language: Discourses of Linguistic Diversity* (2013, Peter Lang) and *Linguistic Diversity in Europe: Current Trends and Discourses* (2012, de Gruyter Mouton).

Inmaculada Fortanet-Gómez is a Full Professor and researcher at Universitat Jaume I, Castellón, Spain, where she has coordinated the Group for Research on Academic and Professional English (GRAPE) for the last 20 years. Her research interests are related to content and language integrated learning in higher education and to multimodal discourse analysis. Inmaculada is the author of *CLIL in Higher Education:*

Towards a Multilingual Language Policy (2013, Multilingual Matters). She is a founding member of ICLHE (Integrating Content and Language in Higher Education) and has sat on its Executive Board since its creation. She has published articles in *English for Specific Purposes*, *Journal of English for Academic Purposes*, *Discourse Studies* and *ESP across Cultures*, among other journals.

Kyria Finardi has a CNPq/PQ research scholarship and is a Senior Lecturer in the Department of Languages, Culture and Education (DLCE) and a researcher in the postgraduate Programmes of Education (PPGE) and Linguistics (PPGEL) at the Federal University of Espírito Santo (UFES), Brazil. At undergraduate level, her teaching focuses on preservice English language teacher development, and at postgraduate level it focuses on aspects related to language, education and internationalization. She has an extensive list of publications and co-authored and edited the books English in Brazil and English in the South. She was the President of the Brazilian Association of Applied Linguistics ALAB (2018-2019) and co-founded and co-coordinates the AILA's regional Ibero-America Association of Applied Linguistics (AIALA).

Pat Moore is a Senior Lecturer in the Department of Languages and Translation at the University Pablo de Olavide, Spain, where both her teaching and research revolve around questions of language education. Nowadays most of her teaching is at postgraduate level, with pre-service and in-service teacher development, and her research is centred on various facets of bilingualism – from both the perspective of bilingual education (teachers) and emerging bilinguality (students). Pat recently co-edited a monograph devoted to tertiary bilingual education for the Spanish journal *Porta Linguarum* and published an article in the *ELT Journal* discussing the idea of bilinguality as the goal of EFL. She is also a co-editor of *Conceptualising Integration in CLIL and Multilingual Education* (2016, Multilingual Matters). Prior to Sevilla, Pat worked at universities in the UK, China and Brazil – where she spent some time at UFES – thereby laying the seeds for the international collaboration behind her contribution to this volume.

Felipe Guimarães has earned his PhD in the postgraduate programme of Linguistics (PPGEL) at the Federal University of Espirito Santo (UFES, Brazil), in cotutelle with the programme of Humanistic Studies & Languages (DHH) at the Pablo de Olavide University (UPO, Spain), jointly supervised by the two preceding authors. His research topics include language policies, internationalization, intercultural education and multilingualism for higher education. Felipe also holds a master's degree in Public Administration. He was the Coordinator of the 'Languages without Borders' (LwB) programme at UFES in 2015, and was awarded by the

Brazilian Ministry of Education (MEC) for his work in LwB. He also works as a translator-interpreter at UFES, developing joint research with UPO.

Víctor Pavón Vázquez holds a PhD in modern languages and is a Senior Lecturer at the University of Córdoba, Spain. He is a member of the Committee for Linguistic Accreditation within the CRUE (the national association of Rectors of Spanish Universities), Head of the Department of English and German Philology and President of the Language Policy Commission at the University of Córdoba. As an author, researcher and lecturer, Victor is active in education development programmes in Europe and beyond. His current interests focus on research and development for capacity building and subsequent competence building of staff, to support the implementation of bilingual education programmes. Victor has recently published articles in the *Journal of English Studies* and *Porta Linguarum* and contributed a chapter to *Integrating Content and Language in Higher Education: From Theory to Practice* (Wilkinson & Walsh, 2015, Peter Lang).

Karin Båge holds an MA in visual and media anthropology at the Freie Universität, Berlin, Germany and a BA in anthropology and international relations from the University of Sussex, UK, 2007. Karin is an educational developer with expertise in global health, and works at the Global and Sexual Health research group in the Department of Public Health Sciences at Karolinska Institutet (Stockholm, Sweden).

Jennifer Valcke is an educational developer at Karolinska Institutet (KI) in Stockholm, Sweden. Her role includes teaching, training and advising on issues related to international/intercultural education and CLIL. Jennifer supports and prepares teaching staff for multilingual and multicultural learning spaces and provides support for educational leaders to implement KI's internationalization strategy.

David Marsh, PhD, has professional experience in over 40 countries, has contributed to over 150 publications and has received five degrees from the UK, Finland and Spain. In recent years his work on transforming education has ranged from designing blueprints for new schools and developing teaching and learning processes through to analytic and research tasks. Special focuses of interest are on the impact of languages on the mind and brain, building positive school ecosystems and adjusting educational practices to accommodate the needs of digitally astute young people. Having co-launched content and language integrated learning (CLIL) under the auspices of the European Commission, David currently works on developing education primarily in Finland, Mexico and Vietnam. His current work in progress is *The Children of Cyberspace: Towards a New Understanding*, due for publication in 2021.

Wendy Díaz Pérez, PhD, is the coordinator of the Foreign Languages Institutional Program and Professor in Public Policy at the University of Guadalajara, Mexico, and has experience of higher education in Spain, Japan and the USA. Having specialized in Asian and Pacific Rim studies, she now focuses on the internationalization of higher education through the activation of language policies and strategy. She is co-author of *Teaching through English in Higher Education: Realizing Internationalization in Practice* (2017, Inter-American Organization for Higher Education).

Javier Ávila-López, PhD, teaches at the University of Córdoba, Spain, and has been a visiting scholar at Prague University and other institutions. He is currently the main editor of *CETA* (Cordoba English Teachers' Association) magazine. His research interests are in the field of bilingual education and the affective component in language learning. Javier has been involved in research projects on bilingualism and CLIL and has published numerous articles in different scholarly journals such as *International Journal of Bilingual Education and Bilingualism* and *Porta Linguarum*. He has also co-edited a book on CLIL, *Didactic Applications for Content Integrated Language Learning* (in Spanish).

Francisco Rubio-Cuenca, PhD, is an Associate Professor in the Department of French and English Philology at the University of Cadiz, Spain. He teaches theoretical linguistics and instrumental English in the Faculty of Arts. Following his 20 years' experience as an English for Specific Purposes (ESP) teacher in the School of Engineering, University of Cádiz, Francisco joined the School of Education, where he became a member of the coordinating team developing the School's Plurilingual Education Program. Currently, he is Head of the coordinating team of the Plurilingual Education Program in the School of Engineering under the CLIL teaching approach. As a teacher-trainer and teaching innovator, Francisco has been the coordinator of many teacher training and innovation projects. He has been a research member of the AGCEPESA project, an Excellence Project promoted and financed by the Andalusian government with the aim of improving plurilingual teaching and learning by promoting high-quality research. Finally, he has been an active participant in the working groups collaborating in the design of the CRUE's framework document on language policy and internationalization of Spanish higher education institutions (approved in 2017). Currently, his main research interests are bilingual teaching, CLIL, higher education language policy and the implementation of plurilingual education programs in higher education institutions.

David Lasagabaster is Professor of Applied Linguistics at the University of the Basque Country, Spain. He has published on second/third language acquisition, English-medium instruction (EMI), content and language integrated learning (CLIL), attitudes and motivation, and multilingualism.

He currently coordinates a research project on team-teaching at university level in which seven European universities are involved. David has published widely in international journals (*Applied Linguistics, Language Teaching, International Journal of Bilingual Education and Bilingualism, The Modern Language Journal, Studies in Higher Education, Language Teaching Research, Language and Education, TESOL Quarterly*, etc.), books and edited books. Among others, he co-edited *CLIL in Spain: Implementation, Results and Teacher Training* (with Ruiz de Zarobe, 2010, Cambridge Scholars Publishing), *English-Medium Instruction at Universities: Global Challenges* (with Doiz & Sierra, 2013, Multilingual Matters), *Motivation and Foreign Language Learning: From Theory to Practice* (with Doiz & Sierra, 2014, John Benjamins) and *CLIL Experiences in Secondary and Tertiary Education: In Search of Good Practices* (with Doiz, 2016, Peter Lang).

Maria Ellison is Assistant Professor of Didactics in the Faculty of Arts and Humanities at the University of Porto (FLUP), Portugal. She holds a PhD in didactics of languages from FLUP. Her doctoral research focused on CLIL as a catalyst for developing reflective practice in foreign language teacher education. She teaches about CLIL within doctoral and pre-service master's degree programmes in teaching foreign languages and in-service teacher development courses. Maria has experience of coordinating and monitoring CLIL projects in primary, secondary and higher education in Portugal. She has designed EAP courses for faculty teaching staff at the University of Porto and has conducted research into teachers' perception of need in EAP and ICLHE contexts. Maria is the coordinator of the recently established Working CLIL network in Portugal through the Centre for English, Translation and Anglo-Portuguese Studies (CETAPS), which connects communities of researchers and teachers of CLIL across the country.

Rocío López-Lechuga, PhD, works as a researcher and lecturer in the Behavioural Sciences Department at the University of Huelva, Spain. She has a bachelor's degree in psychology and another bachelor's degree in humanities. She also has a MSc (health psychology) and two MAs (functional applied analysis and university lecturing). Rocío was hired as an expert research methodologist for the AGCEPESA project (2014–2019) and has co-authored 'A systematic review on evidences supporting quality indicators of bilingual, plurilingual and multilingual programs in higher education' (with Rubio-Alcalá, Arco-Tirado, Fernández-Martín, Barrios & Pavón-Vázquez, 2019, *Educational Research Review*).

Emma Dafouz is an Associate Professor in the Department of English Studies at Complutense University of Madrid, Spain. For over two decades she has researched on English-medium education in higher education and

CLIL and published extensively in international journals. Her most recent publication is a co-authored book entitled *ROAD-MAPPING English Medium Education in the Internationalised University* (with Ute Smit) published in 2020 by Palgrave Macmillan. Emma served as Policy Advisor for curricular internationalisation at her university from 2014–2019.

Foreword. Quality in Multilingual Higher Education: From Supra-National Strategies to Institutional Realizations

Emma Dafouz

Having served for several years as policy advisor for curricular internationalization in one of Spain's biggest and best-known universities, I am more than pleased to find a book that finally answers the questions to some of my recurrent problems – a book that addresses the concept of quality in internationalized multilingual universities from an applied linguistic perspective.

Although interest in quality and quality assurance in internationalized higher education institutions (HEIs) has ranked highly in recent research studies in Europe, USA and China (Yemini & Sagie, 2016), such interest has often sidelined the multifaceted roles of language(s) in these growing multilingual scenarios. With the exception of studies concerned with English language proficiency levels, which have proliferated in the last years as a result of English-medium education (e.g. Dearden, 2014; Lei & Hu, 2014), other quality issues regarding language(s) are rather scarce. Similarly, supranational reports and policy recommendations aligning these two aspects, while hugely interesting, have often not reached a wider audience or managed to provide concrete and tangible examples that illustrate quality assurance processes in particular HEIs.

To fill this gap, here is the book that enables us to recognize that quality in multilingual HEIs may be approached from very different and complementary perspectives. As the literature has pointed out (see Adams, 1993), quality has multiple meanings: it is dynamic, because it changes over time; it may be assessed by quantitative and/or qualitative measures; and it should always be seen within a certain context. In this regard, this volume offers all three perspectives. Firstly, it describes how different processes (whether formal or informal) may be used to assess the quality of an institution, and how such quality assurance processes may change over time depending on a myriad of factors (e.g. political, ideological, pedagogical, sociocultural, etc.). Secondly, it examines diverse measures, from quality indicators to a key indicator matrix, developed in very diverse settings to assist university leadership and curriculum planners in the design and assessment of quality measures. And, thirdly, it explores different teacher professional development programmes, based in linguistically and geographically diverse contexts, to make us see that quality should also be addressed from a qualitative and classroom-level angle. In other words, the book widens the traditional focus on the construction of quality in HEIs by combining diverse ways in which language issues may be addressed in multilingual universities, from the micro-, to the meso- and macro-level perspective. Most importantly, in my view, this is done without losing sight of the local realities and practices on which to build internationalized multilingual universities and, therefore, viewing quality as fitness for purpose (Harvey & Green, 1993).

Having undertaken university responsibilities where language matters, internationalization and quality issues were tightly interconnected, I envisage that Fernando Rubio-Alcalá's and Do Coyle's edited volume will make a critical and valuable contribution to the interplay of all three angles. Moreover, this work will inspire individual institutions to assess and enhance the quality of their international dimension and include specifically the role of language(s) in such quality assurance processes, placing at the centre their own stated aims and objectives. I am confident that it will stimulate reflection and conceptual growth among researchers working in this field and, concurrently, it will encourage planned action for a wide range of practitioners, from teacher professional developers to curriculum planners and content and language experts. While all these stakeholders play different but decisive roles in the implementation of quality assurance processes in internationalized multilingual HEIs, their voices and actions are not always visible. This publication, therefore, stands out by providing us with detailed descriptions of how such agents are engaged in the complex construction of quality, and by reminding us that, after all, quality is everybody's business.

References

Adams, D. (1993) Defining educational quality. *Educational Planning* 9 (3), 3–18.
Dearden, J. (2014) *English as a Medium of Instruction – a Growing Global Phenomenon*. London: British Council.

Harvey, L. and Green, D. (1993) Defining quality. *Assessment & Evaluation in Higher Education* 18 (1), 9–34.

Hu, G. and Lei, J. (2014) English-medium instruction in Chinese higher education: A case study. *Higher Education* 67, 551–567

Yemini, M. and Sagie, N. (2016) Research on internationalization in higher education – exploratory analysis. *Perspectives: Policy and Practice in Higher Education* 20 (2–3), 90–98. doi:10.1080/13603108.2015.1062057

Introduction

Fernando D. Rubio-Alcalá and Do Coyle

Globalization is a worldwide phenomenon which affects all domains of human endeavours. In the academic sphere, globalization has emphasized the need for institutions to internationalize, resulting in the implementation of a wide range of policies and strategies to attract international incoming students and also to encourage local ones to study abroad. Thus, the influence of globalization on language learning has been particularly significant, and a stronger need to manage and communicate information for very different purposes has arisen. Accredited language proficiency has become a requirement in most recruitment processes. Some universities consider it an indicator of students' eventual successful employability. In addition, pressure to increase the number of language accredited teachers, it is believed, will significantly improve an institution's international profile. Consequently, language policy has become a major issue in higher education.

In this panorama, one of the main actions promoted by stakeholders is the development of multilingual programmes, which are proliferating across nations. Accordingly, research studies are being conducted to investigate the effectiveness of such programmes, and an influx of literature is emerging that discusses the nature of language policy and its resulting influence. Despite the plethora of academic commitment and initiatives, there is a paucity of literature dealing specifically with the quality of the programmes, let alone those that can help programme managers to design, launch and evaluate new programmes.

One of the major challenges in presenting this volume lies in finding shared definitions of fundamental key concepts associated with multilingual programmes in higher education. In essence, while there are generally accepted key principles associated with internationalization, multilingual programmes, English-medium instruction (EMI) and so on, local and national contextual variables determine not only how these concepts are interpreted and understood but how they are enacted and become realities for students. It is not surprising that complex terms, including Englishization, internationalization, multilingual programmes (e.g. EMI, ICLHE) and quality, permeate the chapters. De Wit and Hunter (2015) define internationalization as

> The *intentional process* of integrating an international, intercultural or global dimension into the purpose, functions and delivery of

post-secondary education in order to enhance the quality of education and research for all students and staff to make *a meaningful contribution to society*. (de Wit & Hunter, 2015: 29, authors' emphasis)

Yet Brandenburg *et al.* (2019) also warn that 'labels' tend to focus on only one or two 'priorities' (e.g. curriculum and mobility) and ignore increasingly urgent imperatives such as cross-border and borderless education, the impact of globalization and so on. It is also well documented that the majority of multilingual programmes in higher education use the medium of English, and hence student *multilingual* experiences tend to be contained within EMI or similar study contexts. The EMI phenomenon is defined by Dearden (2014: 2) as 'the use of English to teach academic subjects (other than English) in countries or jurisdictions in which the majority of the population's first language is not English'. Notwithstanding the importance of EMI programmes in Anglophone countries, Dearden points out that while definitions usefully differentiate between teaching *in* and teaching *through* English – as in the case of content and language integrated learning (CLIL) – the use of EMI as an 'umbrella' term embraces many different interpretations which require detailing according to individual contexts. Similarly, CLIL has been referred to as an 'umbrella' term, especially in the secondary sector for learning a language (not necessarily English) and a curriculum subject simultaneously. While definitions such as these are deliberately open to contextual variations which are well documented and argued, the more recent move towards integrating content and language in higher education (ICLHE) has promoted debate embracing pedagogic, social and moral implications of teaching and learning in higher education *through* a second (other, additional, foreign, heritage, community) language. ICLHE opens up multilingual programmes in higher education not only to funded 'visiting students' (e.g. through the European Erasmus scheme) but to migrant and ethnic communities, instigating an education which 'explicitly aims to benefit the wider community, at home or abroad, through international or intercultural education, research service and engagement' (Benneworth, 2019).

In line with such definitions, perhaps the most crucial issue with regard to multilingual programmes is to explore the quality and inclusivity of learning experiences that these offer to such a diverse range of students. These are indisputable in general terms for higher education anywhere. However, each of these tenets requires careful unravelling in order for higher education institutions across the globe to grow, to action, to evidence and to celebrate their own visible pathways for multilingual experiences which are underpinned by values that are socially just, culturally responsive, inclusive, critically aware and future-oriented in our dynamic and rapidly changing world.

It is for this reason that each author will invite the reader to engage with definitions and interpretations of phenomena across contexts, studies and reflections in order to make sense of the specificities while applying these to a broader canvas. This is line with Hult's (2010) call to apply a much wider analytical lens to uncover the exigencies of quality multilingual programmes and the responsibilities of those who design and develop them. This volume, therefore, has been written to respond to that call and fill gaps that exist in the definitions, descriptions and actions leading to the quality assurance of multilingual programmes in higher education. Recognized scholars come to the fore to share their expertise in identifying key elements that contribute to quality multilingual programmes. The rationale of individual contributions is grounded in pertinent literature, and each chapter raises issues for urgent consideration. Language policy is first addressed as one of the cornerstones of multilingual programmes. Initially, decisions need to be made identifying specific actions leading to discussion and definitions of quality indicators. When these indicators are organized according to shared basic principles, grouped in matrices or lists, they offer programme coordinators guidance to manage and evaluate quality programmes. Finally, the implications of developing such programmes in terms of professional development for teachers in higher education are highlighted, including affective pressures inherent in multilingual teaching.

A Foreword by Emma Dafouz opens the volume. She welcomes the ways in which the authors approach issues of quality from very different and complementary perspectives – adopting, for example, temporal, evaluative and developmental positioning.

Patrick Studer starts by raising the dilemma of how internationalization can serve as a means for global communication and understanding or, in terms of unintended consequences, how it might promote barriers to diversity. This tension is emphasized using the construct of efficiency versus identity. English as the lingua franca is particularly addressed and the role it plays in multilingual settings is analysed. Studer presents a comprehensive review of the literature to account for the potential ideological impact current policy making has on perceptions of multilingualism in higher education. He points out that university quality rankings define multilingualism only as a means of measuring teaching 'excellence' and eventual student employment rates. They omit reference to indicators focusing on cultural and linguistic diversity. The hegemony of English in internationalization can be counterbalanced by its potential capacity to be perceived as a functional tool, i.e. as the medium of communication. In sum, he concludes that the ideologies underlying internationalization lead to a very limited perception of multilingualism.

The second chapter is devoted to language policy and its impact on quality outcomes. Inmaculada Fortanet-Gómez analyses the ambiguous term 'quality' in terms of four basic key areas: digital communication, travel and/or study, geographical contexts and migration. Consideration is given to different attitudes towards the foreign language according to individual or societal needs. When quality is described as a 'distinguishable attribute of multilinguals', this leads to an analysis of determinant features such as competence in languages, cognitive organization, age and context of acquisition, social and cultural capital and ways in which individuals identify with each language. Fortanet provides a full account of how those aspects interplay in a specific multilingual setting. However, when quality is considered to indicate a degree of excellence or superiority, this impacts on the need to achieve high-level outcomes in terms of language, content and literacy standards. Furthermore, she suggests a range of factors that influence optimal achievement in multilingual education, focusing on contextual, pedagogical and individual factors. In sum, Fortanet analyses the relationship of quality and multilingual education from diverse angles and uses her experience as a programme leader and researcher to offer practical ways and tangible actions to further develop multilingualism.

Finardi, Moore and Guimarães address further tensions that may exist in language policy between 'external' internationalization and internationalization at home. From a wider perspective, they advocate a balance between the impact of globalization and glocalization which takes into account embracing global horizons while maintaining local identity and values. The role of English as the language of instruction is again discussed. Many higher education institutions are encouraged to adopt English as a medium of instruction (EMI) without addressing the underlying 'hidden' conflicts implicit in language policies leading to 'Anglicization' or 'Englishization'. The potential of EMI contexts to develop interculturality or integration within and across programmes remains unexplored and unrealized. To make such undercurrents more visible, the authors present a study analysing the tensions embodied in language policy from the perspective of two higher education institutions located in two contrasting locations – one in the global North (Spain) and the other in the global South (Brazil). The differences between both institutions emphasize that initial contextual considerations and decisions about language policies are of paramount importance, especially those that focus on the roles of first and other language instruction in multilingual programmes. Without clarification which embraces diversity and provides means of enabling more effective communication among international speakers, a coherent action plan will not be operationalized and underlying issues of study in first and other language will remain 'hidden'.

Båge and Valcke claim that if higher education institutions want to make a meaningful contribution to society, internationalization and their multilingual programmes should go beyond current proposals and should instead be the means to promote sustainable development. From this perspective, quality is realized by including global engagement, intercultural competencies and social justice (i.e. attention to diversity and inclusion) in curricula. To ground and exemplify their rationale, the authors describe the transition of a multilingual programme (which they prefer to call

'English-medium education') conducted at the Karolinska Institute, Sweden, into a programme built on sustainable development goals (SDGs). As a result, an action plan was passed leading to the internationalization of the curriculum, so that the 'international classrooms' could address cultural, linguistic and didactic challenges rooted in creative and interactive methodological approaches rather than in more 'traditional' teacher-led 'knowledge transfer'. The authors emphasize the need for constructive alignment between intended learning outcomes, teaching and learning approaches, and assessment and feedback. In sum, Båge and Valcke suggest that when students engage in quality education, they will be equipped with confidence and competence to enable them to work with people they do not know, to be able to communicate effectively both orally and in writing, to find creative solutions to complex challenges and to act upon informed fact-based opinions accordingly and responsibly.

Once the initial principles and paradigms for the quality of language policy plans have been presented and analysed, the volume continues with the analysis of contributory dimensions that support the design of university language policies aimed at enhancing the internationalization process. Víctor Pavón asserts that in order to assure the quality of the courses offered in a language other than the official language, attention needs to be paid to the following: organization; models of instruction; problems associated with benchmarking; language proficiency entry levels; and teacher professional development. Thus, he recommends that both top-down and bottom-up strategies are essential for designing effective multilingual programmes. Additionally, a clear definition of the programme objectives clarifies the nature of models of instruction that are pertinent for success. Moreover, Pavón argues that the most essential component in ensuring quality in multilingual programmes is dependent on human resources including highly qualified and appropriately experienced staff, with a minimum of C1 accredited levels of proficiency (according to the *Common European Framework of Reference for Languages*). Minimum entry levels for students enrolling in these programmes should also be 'benchmarked' to prevent language becoming a barrier or a burden for both lecturers and students during the lessons. Addressing the realities of classroom learning emphasizes lecturers' involvement in professional development, to minimize potential feelings of discomfort or resentment. This matter is further developed in Maria Ellison's chapter.

David Marsh and Wendy Díaz Pérez propose a *key indicator matrix* to establish multilingual programmes. Four operational parameters embrace the matrix, namely governance, management, praxis and outcomes. Governance includes, for example, language policy (with clear objectives and expected outcomes), aligned or in conjunction with the university international strategy plan and incentives for lecturers and students. Management comprises the development of staff language competences, the coordinated work of content and language teachers (see Lasagabaster's chapter), the provision of resources and support and a professional development programme. Praxis refers to how methodologies are applied so that scaffolding and other techniques are implemented. They also propose that performance, when measured by outcomes, should be compared to those of first language groups. These parameters are articulated into a set of indicators which stakeholders and programme managers can use to ensure effective and successful results. The authors describe the journey over a decade of work, in which needs analyses were first made in 2010 leading to the implementation after 2013 of the multilingual programme at the University of Guadalajara, México. They emphasize that universities are complex organizations and the implementation of multilingual programmes must address the culture of organizational structures. Thus, to limit potential barriers, parameters need to be considered from multiple perspectives. Furthermore, the matrix serves as a tool to evidence clearly defined elements of quality assurance, so that managers and key stakeholders are informed of the processes and subsequent development and/or changes can be assured.

The next chapter also deals with explicit indicators to measure the quality of multilingual programmes. Ávila-López, Rubio-Cuenca and López-Lechuga report on the roadmap and results of the AGCEPESA project (Analysis and Quality Assurance of Plurilingual Studies in Higher Education in Andalusia), led by Fernando D. Rubio-Alcalá. The main goal was to develop a quality assurance tool for plurilingual education programmes. In order to make external validity explicit, the tool was designed from the discussions and conclusions of more than 25 experts, who met in four different symposia. Additionally, a systematic review of the literature was carried out to identify evidence-based practice studies (see Rubio-Alcalá *et al.*, 2019) leading to the construction of the Inventory for Plurilingual Programmes in Higher Education (IPPHE; see Rubio-Alcalá *et al.*, 2018). The tool consists of 30 quality indicators organized into the following parameters: organizational aspects; curriculum; language level and methodology; teachers' and students' incentives; and quality assurance (evaluation plan, sustainability and impact). The authors expand on each indicator and give a rationale for their inclusion in the tool. The IPPHE has been designed to guide higher education programme managers and other stakeholders in evaluating bilingual and plurilingual programmes and to make clear the necessary steps involved in designing robust and effective evidence-based quality measures.

The last two chapters are devoted to analysing specific factors that may raise the quality of multilingual programmes. First, David Lasagabaster addresses *team teaching*, focusing on collaboration between language and content teachers in these programmes. He starts by raising a key question: Are language objectives included in course syllabi? This is of paramount importance in contexts where student proficiency levels are lower than desired and which therefore require teachers to make adaptations to teaching styles, e.g. by exploring ways of scaffolding language to make learning accessible. Lasagabaster identifies the most problematic linguistic issues for teachers and students, and then moves on to study their perceptions about how team teaching could be implemented in these contexts. Results indicate that both teachers and students hold positive attitudes towards team teaching. They also show some concerns, such as a possible reduction of content if compared to non-EMI classes. Results also reveal that lecturers denote a strong sense of commitment to the EMI courses, but their motivation could be compromised if supportive actions are not put into place. Team teaching is then proposed as a key factor for professional development, with a focus on supporting content teachers with the management and performance of linguistic items. The author finally points out the difficulties that may arise during collaborative work, evidenced by how language and content teachers are informed by different epistemologies which impact on their modus operandi. Lasagabaster reiterates the urgent need to train content teachers so that they become language aware in terms of being language facilitators and making language accessible rather than focusing on grammar.

Maria Ellison explores the affective dimension of multilingual teaching. She describes 'performance' as a complex affective challenge, which may threaten belief, self-esteem, position and identity. She points out that negative emotions can dominate positive ones, and that causes are divided into three categories: lecturer language, the international classroom and self-image. She reports that many lecturers are concerned with their own language-level proficiency and their limited repertoire of discourse strategies in the classroom. Their self-perception tends to be low as a result of student evaluations which can lead to a reduction in confidence. Other tensions within the 'international classroom' emerge related to cultural diversity, including misunderstandings between local and international students. The third category, self-image, is also challenged as the EMI lessons may prevent lecturers from behaving 'naturally' – such as being extrovert, anecdotal or humorous. As a result, Ellison pinpoints the urgent need for professional development and training to address the role of affect in multilingual learning and teaching. She suggests that reflection and reflective practice are key to enabling teachers to become agentic and self-confident. Ellison then provides a range of approaches to encourage reflective practice, making the case that self-analysis facilitates a crucial deconstruction of professional identity. She emphasizes the need for reflective practices to include some form of written or spoken reflection which may be individual or collective, public or private. She recommends the use of reflective journals as a means to articulate issues visually and heighten awareness, as well as the development of critical/collegial partnerships for interaction with other peers to support broader perspectives and to enrich thinking. She also advocates the judicious and collaborative use of structured observation by a field expert. Finally, she suggests the importance of engaging in action research by lecturers with their students to deepen a shared understanding of the underlying affective intricacies of the EMI classroom.

In sum, this volume aims to address the paucity of existing literature that focuses on the quality and the evaluation of multilingual programmes in higher education. Contributors have analysed the roles played by language policies in different contexts. They have also explored ways in which practice is guided by theories and policies – and vice versa. In addition, examples of practical tools have been included to enable programme developers and stakeholders to engage in the guided design and planning of effective bilingual programmes. Finally, perhaps the most consistent message across the chapters lies in the critical need to develop multi-dimensional support for both teachers and students in order to encourage them together to embrace complexity as both a challenge and a benefit in co-constructing quality learning environments.

We hope the volume makes a significant contribution to the field, and leads to discussion and reflection, experimentation, orientation and critical analysis. We also hope this will inspire the use and adaptation of innovative tools to raise the quality of each and every one of the myriad of multilingual programmes – present and future – to be the very best they can be. This is our challenge.

References

Benneworth, P. (ed.) (2019) *Universities and Regional Economic Development: Engaging with the Periphery*. Abingdon: Routledge.

Brandenburg, U., de Wit, H., Jones, E. and Leask, B. (2019) Defining internationalisation in HE for society. *University World News: The Global Window on Higher Education*, 29 June. See https://www.universityworldnews.com/post.php?story=20190626135618704.

Dearden, J. (2014) *English as a Medium of Instruction – a Growing Global Phenomenon*. London: British Council.

de Wit, H. and Hunter, F. (2015) The future of internationalization of higher education in Europe. *International Higher Education* 83, 2–3. doi:10.6017/ihe.2015.83.9073

Hult, F. (2010) Analysis of language policy discourses across the scales of space and time. *International Journal of Sociology of Language* 202, 7–24.

Rubio-Alcalá, F.D., Arco, J.L., Ávila, F.J., et al. (2018) Quality Assurance Inventory for Plurilingual Programs in Higher Education (QAIBPHE). Unpublished presentation at the International Conference on Quality of Plurilingual Programs in Higher Education, Huelva, Spain.

Rubio-Alcalá, F.D., Arco-Tirado, J.L., Fernández-Martín, F.D., López-Lechuga, R., Barrios, E. and Pavón-Vázquez, V. (2019) A systematic review on evidences supporting quality indicators of bilingual, plurilingual and multilingual programs in higher education. *Educational Research Review* 27, 191–204. doi:10.1016/j.edurev.2019.03.003

1 Internationalization, Quality and Multilingualism in Higher Education: A Troublesome Relationship

Patrick Studer

Introduction

Internationalization is a policy area of significant relevance and interest to higher education institutions (HEIs) which is aimed at enhancing higher education quality in an increasingly interconnected world. In their internationalization efforts, HEIs chiefly rely on national and supranational initiatives issued by policy agencies. In Europe, the European Union (EU) and particularly its legislative branch, the European Commission (EC), constitutes a powerful policy trendsetter in Europe. Over the course of the past few decades, the EU has developed an ambitious agenda and launched numerous initiatives to advance internationalization in higher education. This is not surprising, given the high cultural and linguistic diversity inside the EU and in Europe as a continent. In proposing ways for HEIs to develop relationships 'across nations', EU policy makers cannot avoid touching on a sensitive theme at the heart of the union, its internal diversity.

Internationalization policies are, first and foremost, argumentative texts that assert facts and propose actions in specific areas of concern. In the case of the EU they constitute a myriad and complex mesh of documents that are embedded in rules of procedure. In this chapter, I will take a critical look at the EU's internationalization policy as laid down in key green and white papers (Communication and Working Documents) and resolutions (Conclusions, Decisions, Opinions, Recommendations). Offering an in-depth, critical reading of key internationalization policy documents issued by the EU, the chapter analyses the potential ideological impact current policy making has on the perception of multilingualism and, in particular, the English language, in higher education. The chapter rests on the assumption that the ideologies underlying internationalization permit a very limited perception of multilingualism, and one that is detrimental to the English language.

Referring to recent critical discourse-analytic studies at the interface of English-medium instruction, higher education quality and internationalization, this chapter opens by situating the theoretical perspective informing the critical reading of policy documents of the EU. The chapter then continues by reviewing the explanatory potential of the concept of efficiency and identity in language planning and as a driver of quality in internationalization. In a third step, the chapter discusses examples taken from key policy documents in the area of internationalization that highlight policy tensions and contradictions from a European perspective. The chapter focuses on two recent planning episodes of the EC which have shaped the current policy agenda and which point towards the period following Europe 2020. I have labelled these episodes 'Higher education in the world' and 'Strengthening European identity through education and culture'. The chapter concludes by critically discussing the implications of current policy making in internationalization on the perception of quality relating to multilingualism in higher education.

Ideological Conceptualizations of Language

In previous studies, I looked at how language policy planning unfolded at the micro-interactive level. I particularly focused on how, in language-planning settings, policy actors developed stance and positions with regard to what they believed about language and about the policy actions that should be taken. I argued in these studies that language planning in spontaneous speech followed certain positioning cycles that could be related to specific cultural, or ideological, conceptualizations of languages (Studer, 2013a, 2014; Studer *et al.*, 2010). I further noticed in Studer (2012, 2013a) that such conceptualizations tended to be contradictory, creating tensions in actors that needed to be resolved communicatively by reducing complexity and minimizing one of the two poles of the contradiction.

These previous studies were embedded in the assumption that consciousness is a fundamentally ideological phenomenon and must therefore be interpreted sociologically. According to this assumption, we do not 'adopt' ideologies consciously but, instead, we wade through the 'ideological mist' of our own consciousness. This critical approach to exploring our own communicative actions is, of course, not new and has been expressed in works on the philosophy of language and critical discourse analysis. Valentin Voloshinov (1986: 12) is arguably the most radical exponent of this school of thought, claiming that '(t)he individual consciousness is a social-ideological fact'. It is assumptions like these that also underlie the critical discourse-analytic paradigm and its purpose of uprooting, or 'subverting', the taken-for-granted: 'Subversive argumentation does not take the form of external critique in the sense of "what you believe is wrong"; it is more like "I show you what you actually believe"' (Schleichert, 2005: 115–116, my translation).

In what follows I am adopting a methodological translation of this critical sociological perspective, which I outlined in detail in Studer (2013a: 194–198). Drawing on literature in social psychology and social representations theory, I proposed four levels of analysis that can be fruitfully combined when exploring ideology in language planning (Studer, 2013a: 198). These layers of analysis offer different vantage-points of looking at ideology in language, progressing in four steps:

(a) Searching for textual evidence, that is, evaluative common-sense expressions or concepts, and their objectification in the form of arguments.
(b) Identifying social actors against whom these expressions and concepts may be directed (ideological contradiction).
(c) Defining the potential pragmatic effect of such communicative behaviour on social actors (linguistic action).
(d) Describing the formal ideological theories underlying communicative behaviour.

While this approach is evidence based, it remains interpretative in essence, based on a qualitative analysis of language in use. This interpretative and qualitative focus on the study of language policy and planning echoes Fischer's (2003: 60; 69) perception of public policy as an 'intellectual construct' which is 'discursively constructed' and which cannot simply be researched but 'has to be interpreted'. Public policy is complex and so is the discursive process in which it is embedded.

Policy, and the planning process leading up to policy outcomes, is an expression of ideology per se and by definition: '(P)ublic policy is the broad framework of ideas and values within which decisions are taken and action, or inaction, is pursued by governments in relation to some issue or problem' (Brooks, 1989: 16). Considine's (1994: 3–4) critical understanding of policy as action in support of 'a preferred value' by stakeholders agrees with the definition of ideology as communicative practice aimed at 'concealing the legitimacy of the "other side" (…) and thus at achieving hegemony in a debated belief system' (Studer, 2013a: 194, based on Billig, 1982). This view of policy as a process and product of ongoing debate marks a clear turn away from 'objectivist and instrumental notions of judgment and action' towards a perception of policy as 'a process of deliberation which weighs beliefs, principles, and actions under conditions of multiple frames for the interpretation and evaluation of the world' (Dryzek, 1993: 214, referring to Bernstein, 1983). Since the argumentative turn in the mid-1990s, studies have focused on the deliberative character of policy planning, with actors drawing from frames as sources of arguments (e.g. Fischer, 2003; Fischer & Gottweis, 2012; Hajer & Wagenaar, 2003) and, more recently, on the ambiguity and dynamics of frames (e.g. ambiguity in Dekker, 2017; framing in van Hulst & Yanow, 2014). However, while policy planning is fundamentally ideological, Dryzek (1993, referring to Paris & Reynolds, 1983) argues that ideologies are not automatically equal:

> They vary in their internal coherence, their ability to provide cogent warrants for policy claims, and their congruence with empirical reality. In other words, some ideologies are more 'rational' than others. Thus the goal of policy inquiry is not to test hypotheses or to develop policy evaluations or prescriptions but, rather, to enhance the rationality of particular ideologies. (Dryzek, 1993: 226, referring to Paris & Reynolds, 1983)

Citing Kemp (1985) and Habermas' ideal speech, Dryzek (1993: 228) continues by arguing that policy-planning deliberations can be qualified in terms of how free they are from 'deception, self-deception, domination, strategizing, and any exclusion of participants or arguments'. Habermas' ideal speech situation, obviously, is no natural state of mind; it requires a constant, proactive effort on the part of actors engaging in dialogue to free themselves from falling into ideological traps.

Ideology, so far, has been introduced as something inherent in consciousness and particularly evident in policy and planning, requiring an analytic focus on policy actors' claims about truth and social facts, as well as on actors' efforts towards disambiguating their own ideological entanglements. Shohamy (2006) adds another perspective from where policy planning, and in particular language policy planning, can be seen as manipulative action in itself which interferes with the natural growth and development of language, a 'living organism'. In this view, language as an organism is appropriated by language planners and stripped of its creative and untamed powers. Similarly, speakers of languages exposed to policies are limited in their freedom to express and define themselves through and with language; language policy affects their fundamental linguistic human rights. This radical view of language policy planning reflects a fundamental conflict and dilemma, which merits further attention in the following section.

Efficiency or Identity: A Perpetual Dilemma in Language Policy Planning

Following the argumentation presented above, I would like to explore a little further a fundamental contradiction in language planning that seems to inform and underlie the types of policy texts of concern in the present study. By this I refer to the inherent contradiction in policy discourses between language for efficient communication and language as an asset to enhance diversity.

The contradiction between language for efficient communication and language for identity is, of course, not a phenomenon specific to language planning; it is inherent in our understanding of communication. Suffice it, in this chapter, to refer to Bühler's (1934/1990) organon model, which has entered into numerous other communication models over the past decades. In Bühler, the orientation to the 'thing', the semantic substance of a message, is in constant tension with speakers' orientation to one another; in fact, efficiency in communication can only be achieved at the expense of the relationship two speakers in contact are building. The same distinction is emphasized in Watzlawick *et al.*'s (1967) famous opposition pair of digital and analogue communication.

Swiss sociolinguist Georg Bossong (1994) discussed this tension specifically in the context of language planning, referring to the diglossic situation in Catalonia. At the time, Bossong found that elements of regional identity, expressed through Catalan, clashed with the efficiency attributed to the standard variety of Castellano. This led to the warning in his conclusion that the language needs of this region must not be ignored, as indifference to the region may otherwise lead to unrest. Bossong's conclusion not only foreshadowed what was to come 25 years later when political tension did strike Catalonia, but also touched on other themes underlying the European project that have been expressed in European language-policy efforts – the idea of linguistic diversity as a concept advocating linguistic human rights, and the distinction between a 'language of the heart' and a language for functional use.

Multilingualism as an asset for businesses has been emphasized in EU language policy for quite some time (cf. the ELAN study, Hagen *et al.*, 2006). The perspective underlying this perception of multilingualism, obviously, is strongly utilitarian; language serves as a bridge, a facilitating tool, for efficient communication between business enterprises. The idea of multilingualism expressed in these policy documents as a superordinate functional variety echoes Bossong's description of a standard variety which conflicts with language used for personal and individual expression. The new framework strategy for multilingualism (COM 2005 596), which was written around the time when the first Commissioner for Multilingualism was appointed in Europe, adopted an efficiency-heavy argumentation of multilingualism. However, with respect to the predominance of English in higher education, the document announced that further action was needed to study the potential adverse effects that English-medium instruction may have in non-English speaking countries:

Higher education institutions could play a more active role in promoting multilingualism amongst students and staff, but also in the wider local community. It needs to be recognised that the trend in non-English-speaking countries towards teaching through the medium of English, instead of through the national or regional language, may have unforeseen consequences for the vitality of those languages. The Commission intends to study this phenomenon in more detail shortly. (COM 2005 596: 6)

The contradiction between efficiency and identity was subsequently addressed in the often-cited Maalouf report (Maalouf et al., 2008), in which a group of intellectuals around Amin Maalouf argued for the differentiation between learning an 'international language' and learning an 'adoptive language', a language of the heart (cf. 2009/C 77/25; COM 2008 566 final; speech of Orban, 2008).

While it is always useful to speak more than one language, the proposal to 'adopt' a second language in addition to English, from a policy perspective, serves a different, more fundamental goal, which is to promote and celebrate linguistic diversity. Thus, it can be interpreted as a contribution to securing basic linguistic human rights and preserving national and regional varieties. In fact, the promotion and celebration of linguistic diversity has been a key element and highly sensitive point of the European project, which is carefully laid out in various EU foundation documents and also enshrined in the UN and UNESCO Declaration and Conventions (cf. Studer et al., 2008: 25–35). Diversity, in the EU, is strongly perceived as an alternative vision to that of a 'melting pot' (Studer, 2012: 123), focusing on basic linguistic human rights connected to diatopic identity, emphasizing subsidiarity as a fundamental cornerstone of the EU. This policy focus, however, appears to be in fundamental disagreement with the idea of internationality facilitated by the use of a global lingua franca. At the same time, it paints a traditional picture of language communities living in autochthonous regions. Language policy in the EU, it seems, remains a 'puzzle to the mind' (Studer, 2012: 125), with inherent contradictions deriving from tendencies towards unification, principles of subsidiarity and the language-learning needs of citizens.

The contradiction in EU language policy highlighted in this section reflects a fundamental political tension inherent in the European concept of diversity. Borrás-Alomar et al. (1994: 28), in the same year as Bossong, critically assess the idea of a Europe of the regions, in which '(r)egions become (...) one of the centres of a bipolar territorial organization in which the concentration of powers in a supranational body like the European Community, as a requisite to achieve greater efficiency, finds its ideal corollary in a regional articulation of the territory'. Diatopic identity, in this depiction, is complemented by a supranational structure that offers inter-regional identity. A consequence of this thinking would ultimately lead to the abandonment of the nation-state idea. While this seemed, at the time, a legitimate aim to pursue, the authors concluded that Europe was not ready for this idea. Similar to Bossong's call for attention to the region, the authors' assessment of Europe in the 1990s embodied an implicit warning, anticipating the more serious test of the European project we are currently experiencing 25 years later: 'The 1990s so far have heralded a revival of nationalism, even racism in Europe – a development which is very much at odds with the rationalism and supranationalism that the European Community stands for' (Borrás-Alomar *et al.*, 1994: 22).

Efficiency as a Driver of Quality in Internationalization

If we want to outline the interconnections between the internationalization of higher education (IoHE) and multilingualism, we need to understand, first of all, the rationales driving internationalization and the argumentative positions and contradictions they represent. It does not take much reading to realize that the tension between efficiency and identity also extends to the concept of internationalization, and to the role of language therein. Internationalization, by definition, embodies an outward, or outgoing, perspective that is meant to reach beyond regional or national contexts. Indeed, it is hardly surprising to recognize that IoHE can be perceived as a threat to national integrity and as a trend towards linguistic and cultural homogenization (Knight & de Wit, 1999: 18) which, precisely, the EU has so explicitly sought to avoid (cf. The new framework strategy for multilingualism, COM 2005 596). In other words, internationalization, even in its most neutral conceptualization, is not only not politically neutral but a potential threat to the very core idea of diversity the EU stands for.

This threat to diversity is most clearly visible in interpretations of internationalization that emphasize its economic focus, expressed through concepts such as employability and the marketization of higher education. This conceptualization of internationalization, which has recently come under criticism by researchers and policy makers (cf., for example, Akdag & Swanson, 2018: 67–69), foregrounds two priorities for action: the professional outlook of graduates in a globalized or internationalized work environment and the entrepreneurial structures of academia itself (Robson *et al.*, 2018: 24). In both priorities, economic considerations directly interfere with the understanding of internationalization driving academic excellence through building international scientific communities. In fact, economic benefit – be it the students' or the university's – may well come at the *expense* of academic excellence, as it highlights science that is applicable to industry and the selection of students based on financial interests.

Internationalization can, however, be seen as a driver of higher education quality (Wihlborg & Robson, 2018: 10, with reference to de Wit & Hunter, 2015; generally in Knight & De Wit, 1999; van der Wende *et al.*,

1999) in two interrelated ways that are expressive of two fundamentally different visions of HEIs. In the first vision, internationalization in HEIs contributes to preparing students for successful work life after they graduate; in the second vision, internationalization contributes to offering students the best academic environment available for their studies. While both visions are intended to ultimately benefit the students, they place significantly different accents on this process. Internationalization as a quality driver has been present particularly with respect to HEIs' pursuit of excellence in teaching and research. In this context, 'hard' parameters have been established that are measured and integrated in university ranking systems (THE, ARWU, QS). These parameters, which count little towards the overall quality of a HEI, are based on a limited set of indicators that emphasize the international mix of faculty and students through mobility and employment as well as international research cooperation (Studer, 2018: 1–5). HEIs broadly adopt these parameters in their mission statements and strategies.

Language appears in two ways in this economic context. Firstly, language is perceived as an instrument, a tool, facilitating efficient internationalization; it is essentially conceptualized in opposition to Shohamy's (2006) perception of language as a living organism. The effect of this efficiency-based view of language use, and language learning, is that language is perceived as a thing in the service of something else, much like a hammer is used for driving a nail into the wall. The effect, one can imagine, is that people are either assumed to be 'equipped' with the necessary tools for the job when they participate in international activities or, if they are not, they are expected to equip themselves with those tools so they fulfil the basic criteria. The tools, i.e. the 'hammer', have standardized sizes and shapes that are believed to work best for the job they have to fulfil, so people assume they have to follow certain language competence standards to learn the basics for communication in an internationalized environment. Secondly, and as a direct result of the first, some languages appear as tools with greater use and value than others, leading to the hegemony of languages of internationalization, in particular English, to the neglect of others (Wihlborg & Robson, 2018: 9). This has been well documented in studies dealing with elite multilingualism (e.g. Barakos & Selleck, 2019; cf. also Garcia, 2015, with respect to language education policies). Internationalization, as much as the languages involved in it, is tied to HEIs that 'sell perceived superiority of knowledge and experience to international others' (Akdağ & Swanson, 2018: 73). Thus, internationalization, especially when considered through the lens of efficiency, figures in a vision of HEI quality that is intended to enhance interconnectedness and exchange in the name of academic excellence. This vision, however, comes at the expense of cultural and linguistic diversity.

When conceptualized from the perspective of identity, on the other hand, the threat of internationalization to cultural and linguistic diversity appears much softer but also less relevant to HEIs' position in international quality rankings. In this second meaning, internationalization can be understood as a process in the service of intercultural learning and (global) citizenship (Knight & de Wit, 1999: 20). The rationale underlying policy efforts from an identity perspective resembles in structure and principle the idea of learning international and adoptive languages: internationalization can be seen as a driver of an international, a 'global' mindset (Jones & Killick, 2013) that facilitates a broad sensitivity to, and competence to interact with, the cultural 'other', at home or abroad, touching on themes such as social diversification, inclusion and tolerance. This international mindset can be understood as the *cultural lingua franca* one can learn in order to function in intercultural contexts. While this cultural lingua franca can be learned by all students, mobile students can, moreover, choose to 'adopt' a host culture with which they engage in depth through mobility programmes.

Student mobility has formed an integral element of internationalization since its beginnings. The internationalization of non-mobile students, on the other hand, is a much newer phenomenon which has only received greater attention in recent years, within the paradigms of comprehensive internationalization (Hudzik, 2011), internationalization of the curriculum (Leask, 2015) and internationalization at home (Beelen & Jones, 2015). Although the EU has identified the internationalization of non-mobile students as a key pillar of its internationalization strategy 2020, internationalization at home, especially with respect to its focus on culturally sensitive pedagogies and its social and values-based approach (Robson *et al.*, 2018), is markedly absent from university ranking systems. The internationalization of curricula, in particular, has been identified as running the risk of being a symbolic commitment rather than a transformative one (Turner & Robson, 2008) and of being concerned with policy making rather than with the impact of policies on actors (Green & Whitsed, 2015: 5). With respect to language policies, Schiffman (2003, 2007) has maintained the risk of policy failure if their impact on actors is not taken into appropriate consideration.

Representations of Language in Current Internationalization Policy

I will now focus the above discussion more specifically on recent policy-planning 'episodes' (Studer *et al.*, 2010: 257) to illustrate further the effect the tension between efficiency and identity has on the representation of language in the context of internationalization. For this purpose, I will review selected text excerpts from key policy documents of the EU. In particular, I will look at key green and white papers (Communication and Working Documents) and resolutions (Conclusions, Decisions, Recommendations) that constitute policy steps in the Rules of Procedure of the Commission (C(2000) 3614). I will also make reference to commissioned and third-party studies that directly inform or underline the argumentation in these policy documents. I will focus on two relevant planning episodes, which I have labelled 'European Higher Education in the World' (2010–2013) and 'Strengthening European Identity through Education and Culture' (2017–2018).

It has already been maintained that the opposition between efficiency and identity constitutes a fundamental contradiction and inherent tension in language and internationalization policy planning. I have also maintained that efficiency can be understood as a driver of quality in higher education which, at the same time, entails a utilitarian perspective of multilingualism that presents a potential threat to diversity. This interpretation is consistent with my analysis of the EU's multilingualism policy, which has oscillated between promoting linguistic diversity and language skills for the participation in a dynamic economy (on the inherent contradiction, cf. Studer, 2012; on multilingualism policy related to business, cf. Studer, 2013b: 189–193; on the development of multilingual policy in the EU, cf. Studer *et al.*, 2008: 48–67). I have argued in Studer (2012: 118) that the two poles of the multilingualism policy continuum are mutually exclusive. If one pole is strengthened, the other pole is simultaneously weakened, resulting in language-planning cycles that reflect a check and balance mechanism in policy making.

Language, we may therefore assume, shows up in internationalization policy particularly as an instrument of power in situations of social conflict (Haugen, 1980: 151; Nelde's law in Nelde, 1990). Languages, in this context, can be interpreted as symbols and objects of status allocation in a struggle between 'elites' and 'counterelites' (Cooper, 1989: 120). Cooper further notes that language status planning is fundamentally reactive and occurs in response to a change already underway in communities:

> Although status planning can, in principle, be devoted to maintaining the functional allocation of a community's languages, maintenance typically becomes a goal only after change is under way. ... Efforts to *maintain* an allocation, in other words, are really efforts to *return* to an earlier, more desirable state of affairs. Whether efforts are directed to returning to an old allocation or to forwarding a new one, status planning typically works for change. (Cooper, 1989: 120)

Cooper, in his description, emphasizes factors driving status planning that project very different visions of a state-to-be: one that is founded on a progressive future; the other on a romanticized picture of how it once was. This dichotomy, of course, is not exclusive to language planning but has been described as driving change in other contexts (e.g. education in general, cf. Studer & Perrin, 2017). Ager (2001) embeds this interplay between old and new in a policy cycle that is initiated when policy actions result in inequalities, which can then be revised and adapted. Let me illustrate this interplay with the example of language planning in internationalization policy.

Higher Education in the World (2010–2013)

The first planning episode, called 'European higher education in the world' (2010–2013), revolves around the publication of a policy document under that name (COM 2013 499) which summarizes the EU's higher education strategy until 2020. This document, in turn, makes reference to other, previously published policy documents. I will review some key passages from these documents, starting with a Conclusion of the European Council in 2010. The first thing that strikes the critical reader when looking out for ideological framing comments concerning language in this conclusion is the explicit reference to language (and intercultural) competences being in service of advancing employability and enriching human capital:

> Such (learning) mobility provides a means of *enriching human capital and strengthening employability through* the acquisition and exchange of knowledge, the development of linguistic and intercultural competences, and the promotion of interpersonal contacts. (2010/C 135/04: 12, emphasis added)

This framing comment, which follows the ideological thread laid out in the Lisbon strategy (cf. Studer, 2013b, for details), is interesting not only for what it says but, more importantly, for what it takes for granted. I have argued elsewhere (Studer, 2012: 117–118) that the term multilingualism can be 'interpreted as a short form of Europeanness – a young, urban, open and geographically mobile society'. References to language in internationalization policy underline this interpretation by emphasizing the perception of employability and capital relying on skills needed for cross-border business interaction. Moreover, we can derive from this comment a reference to a young, urban and geographically mobile *English-speaking* society, since cross-border business is best carried out in international languages of wider communication. By extension, this picture of a young, urban, mobile and English-speaking elite is in conflict with its counterelite, the non-mobile, less flexible, regionally focused (and probably older) population that depend and insist on their native languages at work. The quote also opens up a vision of a modern society against a picture of what once was, and what now is undesirable in an international workspace. One wonders how comments like these are read by promoters of regional minority languages such as Romansh or Basque or Plattdeutsch. The policy document from which this quote is taken does not provide further details about what the promotion of language skills means in terms of language learning and teaching in higher education, but we can infer from the above lines a focus on the interface between English, intercultural communication and communication in professional contexts (Studer, 2013b: 192).

The 2011 Communication document entitled 'Supporting growth and jobs' specifies the skill set as a 'right mix of skills', such as 'transversal competences, e-skills for the digital era, creativity and flexibility and a solid understanding of their chosen field' (COM 2011 567: 2). While equally vague in tone, this document echoes earlier policy documents such as the 2006 European Reference Framework of Key Competences which lists eight learning competences that should be promoted beyond academic knowledge. Two abilities on this list concern language education specifically (communication in the mother tongue and communication in foreign languages). This is echoed more broadly in the 2018 Council Recommendations on Key Competences for Lifelong Learning, calling on member states to promote lifelong learning by 'increasing the level of language competences and supporting learners to learn different languages relevant to their working and living situation' (COM 2018 24: 17). The authors of the 2011 Communication document connect this skill set to international mobility, which is presented as a key driver of quality of higher education in Europe (COM 2011 567: 3).

The 2012 Communication document 'Rethinking education' further develops the theme, adding a sense of shortcoming and urgency which indicates a language awareness in Haugen's (1980: 151) sense: '… European education and training systems continue to fall short in providing the right skills for employability' and call on Member States to 'bring the learning experience closer to the reality of the working environment', emphasizing that the 'most pressing challenges for Member States are to address the needs of the economy and … youth unemployment' (COM 2012 669: 2).

'Rethinking education' differentiates between transversal skills and language learning. It refers to the transversal skills as the ability 'to think critically, take initiative, problem solve and work collaboratively…' (COM 2012 669: 3). Languages, not specifically for HEIs, are considered a 'factor of competitiveness' to increase employability and mobility, while 'poor language skills are a major obstacle to free movement of workers'. The UK and France are singled out as negative examples falling short on delivering on the mother-tongue-plus-two policy advocated by the Barcelona European Council in 2002, as only small percentages of pupils reach the level of independent users of one foreign language by the end of their lower secondary education. The conclusions in this Communication document are derived from an accompanying working paper (SWD 2012 372) entitled 'Language competence for employability, mobility and growth', which outlines a post-English vision:

> English is becoming de facto the first foreign language. It is the most taught foreign language, both in Europe and globally, and it plays a key role in daily life – but: **it is proficiency *in more than one* foreign language that will make a decisive difference in the future.** This calls for language policies and strategies inspired by a clear vision of the value of language

skills for mobility and employability. (SWD 2012 372: 2, emphasis in original)

This working paper, which is much more specific concerning the problems caused by a predominance of the English language in business, relies in its argumentation on multiple sources, including the Report of the Business Forum for Multilingualism (Davignon *et al.*, 2008). The Davignon report (2008) was written in the spirit of other studies such as ELAN and PIMLICO which, similarly, inspired the EU's multilingualism policy (Studer, 2013b). The working paper, when discussing the role of English, makes further reference to the OMC thematic working group which issued a publication 'Languages for Jobs. Providing multilingual communication skills for the labour market' (OMC Group, 2012). In it, the authors make their case for the economic usefulness of other languages in addition to English. Arguing that 'language skills are always a means to an end' (OMC Group, 2012: 13), they add a new argumentative thread: they strip English of its status as a foreign language, thus eliminating its cultural specificity, its 'organic life' (Shohamy, 2006) and otherness to language learners. Nuance, cultural specificity and aesthetics, by implication, are reserved for native speakers of English and, implicitly, for learners of 'real' foreign languages.

> In large parts of Europe and beyond, English is already considered **more as a basic skill than a foreign language**. Speaking like a native speaker is becoming less relevant as English becomes a component of basic education in many countries. Against that background, the need to maintain the advantage by moving beyond English will be felt more acutely. (OMC Group, 2012: 15, emphasis added)

The above policy documents form the argumentative backdrop to the 2013 European strategy 'European higher education in the world', which is to 'contribute to the objectives of the Europe 2020 strategy' (COM 2013 499). In this document, the main argumentative lines established in previous policy analyses are embedded in a call for a comprehensive internationalization strategy focusing on three key areas (mobility, internationalization at home and digital learning, and institutional collaboration). The importance of language skills is particularly highlighted in relation to internationalization at home. It is unsurprising that, in this policy document, proficiency in English is referred to as a 'de facto part of any internationalisation strategy for learners, teachers and institutions' (COM 2013 499: 6), and that more attention should be paid to the promotion of multilingualism and, particularly, local languages:

> Increase the opportunities offered to students, researchers and staff to develop their language skills, particularly local language tuition for individuals following courses in English, to maximise the benefits of European linguistic diversity. (COM 2013 499: 7)

Strengthening European Identity through Education and Culture (2016–2019)

The second planning episode I am going to look at in some more detail is named after a Communication document entitled 'Strengthening European identity through education and culture' (COM 2017 673). I will begin my discussion with 'Strengthening European identity' and, as in the previous section, make cross-references to other relevant policy documents that are either cited directly or that may have informed its underlying argumentation. 'Strengthening European identity through education and culture' is relevant to the present discussion as it underlines the tone of other recent policy documents stressing renewed efforts in established policy topics. While this Communication document does not specifically deal with higher education, it makes reference to two critical documents, entitled 'Vision of European Education Area' (COM 2016 381) and 'A renewed agenda for higher education' (COM 2017 247), and results in two joint Council Recommendations: 'On a comprehensive approach to the teaching and learning of languages' (2019/C 189/03) and 'On promoting common values, inclusive education, and the European dimension of teaching' (2018/C 195/01).

While in 'Strengthening European identity' emphasis is placed on language learning in vocational education and upper secondary schools, it renews the dilemma multilingualism presents to the EU, which has been emphasized in the analysis of the first planning episode ('European higher education in the world'). The document, although not making explicit reference to English, specifically highlights the problem multilingualism is perceived to be causing. Renewing the call for comprehensive curricula that facilitate the development of key competences (COM 2017 673: 4), multilingualism is described as 'one of the greatest assets in terms of cultural diversity in Europe and, at the same time, one of the most substantial challenges' (COM 2017 673: 7). Analysis of this line is complex as it allows multiple readings. In the context of the present discussion, it makes sense to read in the word 'multilingualism' a reference to (societal) multilingualism which contributes to cultural diversity in Europe. Looking at the sentence from this perspective, multilingualism can be perceived as a uniquely European asset as Europe is defined through its culturally and linguistically diverse members. This interpretation also reflects the EU's motto 'Unity in Diversity', emphasizing Europe as an entity that strives to unite all members in their uniqueness. In a similar sense, individual multilingualism, or plurilingualism, can be considered an asset since it expresses the very idea of European citizens using different languages as a bridge to other cultures. The reference to multilingualism being 'one of the most substantial challenges', on the other hand, can mean various things. Firstly, it may contain a reference to the challenge multilingual competence poses to the individual, and the infrastructural problems connected to offering foreign language learning opportunities in compulsory and higher education. Secondly, it also contains a reference to the challenge to promote linguistic diversity when it comes to language use in the internationalized economy, and the type of language education that should be offered to pupils and students. If both pupils and students are to be prepared for work in an international context, then some languages, English being at the forefront of them, are simply valued more than others, which has implications for infrastructural decisions stakeholders should be taking. In its conclusion, 'Strengthening European identity' renews the EU's commitment to an old idea, which is presented as a vision for 2025, 'where, in addition to one's mother tongue, speaking two other languages has become the norm'.

The dilemmas set out above also run through other policy documents. The most important council recommendation concerning languages which resulted from 'Strengthening European identity', entitled 'On a comprehensive approach to the teaching and learning of languages' (2019/C 189/03), is entirely devoted to setting out an agenda for the promotion of multilingualism in schools and vocational education across Member States. In its preamble it reiterates the well-known assumptions concerning multilingualism, highlighting its relevance as a key competence at the heart of the vision of a European Education Area. While the ideas expressed in this recommendation are not new, the reader notices the attempt at describing multilingual competence as simultaneously serving identarian *and* utilitarian functions. In other words, it seems that the authors of the recommendation tried to reconcile the ideological contradiction mentioned above by packing both functions into one argument. It comes as little surprise, though, that the claim of such a broad argument is finally mitigated using epistemic modality expressing possibility rather than assertion:

> Multilingual competence is one of the key competences that *could foster* employability, personal fulfilment, active citizenship, intercultural understanding and social inclusion; it is defined as 'the ability to use different languages appropriately and effectively for communication'. (2019/C 189/03, Paragraph 13, emphasis added)

In its recommendations, however, the document falls back into a post-English, pro-diversity argumentation, which is already visible in the first planning episode analysed above: 'Schools could offer a wider range of languages in addition to the main global languages of communication' (2019/C 189/03, Annex: Paragraph 1). The way this sentence is phrased, one is likely to read an emphasis on the 'wider range of language', implying that the 'main global languages of communication' are not enough. The reader may also notice again the use of the epistemic modal 'could' instead of 'should', which renders the recommendation vague and less binding. It may seem surprising that this council recommendation, like

'Strengthening European identity', does not emphasize language learning in higher education. Referring to the accompanying staff working document (SWD 2018 174), the recommendation states that '(w)hile challenges exist in all education sectors, they are particularly acute in vocational education and training where less emphasis is put on language learning' (SWD 2018 174: Paragraph 6). The fact that language in higher education, in this case, does not play a bigger role, however, may also have other reasons. University entrants may already have a higher level of language competence than other school leavers (SWD 2018 174: 12) but, following my argumentation so far, we may also assume that HEIs are governed by economic principles of language use. This becomes clearer when we look at the third policy document relevant to this discussion.

While at pre-university and vocational levels the dilemma between identity and efficiency in language is still visible, in 'A renewed agenda for higher education' (COM 2017 247) a utilitarian perspective of language is again foregrounded, echoing the claims made during the first planning episode studied, 'Higher education in the world'. Contrary to the first planning episode, however, language here is markedly absent as an explicit factor in the argumentation (and also in backing documents such as, for example, SWD 2016 195). The document opens by stating a 'mismatch between the skills Europe needs and the skills it has' (COM 2017 247: 3). While not directly addressing languages, the document subsumes language skills under 'transversal skills and key competences' students 'need to acquire' that 'will allow them to thrive' (COM 2017 247: 5). Those skills and key competences, in the context of the document, are in the service of study programmes that 'prepare students for jobs where shortages exist or are emerging' (COM 2017 247: 5). The document further stresses that study programmes should be more tailored to professional needs, and higher education should allow students 'to acquire skills and experiences through activities based around real-world problems, include work-based learning and, where possible, offer international mobility' (COM 2017 247: 5). This economic line of argumentation is further developed in connection with the innovation theme ('Innovation is the most important driver of economic growth', COM 2017 247: 7) and other themes referring to HEIs as 'entrepreneurial actors' and emphasizing excellence through international cooperation and mobility (COM 2017 247: 8). Higher education is also called on to become more 'effective and efficient' (COM 2017 247: 9) by integrating incentive and reward structures.

Discussion and Conclusion

In this chapter, I have presented a critical reading of policy activities and documents at the interface of linguistic diversity, internationalization and quality in higher education. In doing so, I had to tackle a topic that touches on 'the heart' of the EU, its linguistic diversity. I have tried to highlight fundamental issues embodied in the political concept of linguistic diversity in order to facilitate a critical discussion of how they might be reflected in, and shape, policy activities in the area of internationalization in higher education. My assumption was that the three themes – linguistic diversity, internationalization and quality – were intertwined, and that they were so in an intricately complex way. I was proved right.

The discourses that 'govern' language policy in the EU are deeply contradictory, and languages of the EU hold different values in different contexts, even if this contradicts the basic principle of diversity. But complexity, in this chapter, also showed in another way. If we were to assess the quality of policy making in the fields touched upon in this chapter in terms of how 'free from deception' they might be, we might be disappointed. While I do not believe that there is active deception involved on the part of the policy makers, this chapter has been a constant struggle on my part not to fall into the ideological traps of well-formulated and polished policy texts. In this struggle, I have read all texts with respect to their argumentative force in relation to language. Language, therefore, was relevant in my analysis both in its absence and presence in policy texts: its presence indicated a 'social conflict' in which language would become an instrument of power to tip the balance towards one side; its absence signalled the promotion of a reality that might render the political interpretation of language controversial.

Throughout the chapter, we have seen that language is traditionally incorporated into policy activities in order to advocate the fundamental principle of linguistic diversity and linguistic human rights as a measure to preserve regional identity. This is seen in the 'mother-tongue-plus-two' principle and the idea of an adoptive language in addition to an international language of wider communication. In policy texts relating to internationalization in higher education, however, multilingualism appears more consistently in connection with its function of facilitating international communication, stressing efficiency as its key asset. Projecting a young, international, urban picture of an internationalized community, these texts seem to suggest a policy focus on the learning of international languages of wider communication, notably English. In particular, the texts studied in the context of 'European higher education in the world' explicitly address the issue of a predominance, a hegemony of English which should be overcome. To this end, the texts outline a post-English scenario, where English becomes a basic skill, not a foreign language to learn. Emphasis is subsequently placed on highlighting the importance of competence in other languages than English. While still arguing within the remit of a utilitarian perspective of language serving the economy, the argumentation shifts from communicative efficiency ('getting the job done') to communicative quality ('getting the job done in an excellent way'):

The special status of English should not lead to disregard the importance of other languages. The Report of the Business Forum for Multilingualism points out that 'it is other languages that will make the difference between mainstream and excellence and provide a competitive edge'. (SWD 2012 372: 22)

My review of key policy documents above, particularly of 'European higher education in the world', shows that language enters higher education policy as an argumentative resource used to steer the discussion in the direction that is consistent with the EU's perception of linguistic diversity. At the same time, we notice that linguistic diversity cannot be achieved when foregrounding economic objectives. While the tone in 'European higher education in the world' seems more assertive, more recent policy documents adopt a vaguer tone. Multilingualism is acknowledged as both an asset and a challenge for education, and its intended effect is portrayed as a possibility rather than a fact. When turning to policy documents that specifically deal with higher education, it strikes me that language is largely absent from the policy agenda and is subsumed under skills and competences, which constitute abilities that were defined from an economic perspective. Multilingualism, in this context, is not introduced as an 'instrument of power' to shift the agenda to one side but rather seems to have been omitted so as not to have to address the controversial potential it might raise.

Let me put these findings into a broader perspective by revisiting, briefly, the 'New framework strategy for multilingualism' (COM 2005 596: 6), which I quoted above and which stated in 2005 that the predominance of English may have 'unforeseen consequences for the vitality of those (other) languages'. Fifteen years on, we find that language, in its political interpretation, has become (or still is) an argumentative resource that is inherently contradictory and does not seem to be doing a good job of clarifying its role in higher education policy. Clearly, this sentiment is shared by others. While not specifically cross-referenced in any of the abovementioned policy documents, other studies were commissioned by the EU in the period following 2014 which focus on internationalization in higher education. One such study, carried out by de Wit *et al.* (2015), deserves mention in this context, not only because of its impact on European education policy but also because the authors take a position against an 'efficient' interpretation of multilingualism in internationalization that focuses on English-medium instruction (EMI, ETP). English is repeatedly referred to in this study in connection with its (pre-)dominance in IoHE. EMI, when primarily introduced to attract foreign students, is seen to raise quality concerns (de Wit *et al.*, 2015: 48). The authors comment on internationalization in various nations but seem to be particularly critical when nations focus heavily on teaching through English. This is seen in the authors' comments on Finland ('establishing English-taught courses and programmes has taken precedence over internationalising the curriculum', de Wit *et al.*, 2015: 91) or Italy where the internationalization of the curriculum is 'understood principally as teaching in English or developing joint/double degrees', and where universities do not fare well in rankings (de Wit *et al.*, 2015: 124). A similar assessment can be found for Romania, Norway or the Netherlands. They conclude:

> There is a need, in an environment of increased dominance of English as the language of communication in research and education, to stimulate bilingual and multilingual learning at the primary and secondary education level as a basis for a language policy based on diversity in European higher education. (de Wit *et al.*, 2015: 285)

In these lines, we hear a similar post-English sentiment as expressed in various policy documents, and an intention to counterbalance the hegemony of English in internationalization. While this argumentation seems to make perfect sense from a European perspective, I still wonder whether this approach does justice to reality. English is de facto the language of internationalization, and by stripping it of its status as a language and relegating it to a basic skill, do we not ignore the larger potential of English as an 'organism' that offers vast possibilities to communicate, beyond efficient communication between speakers of different languages? Why is it about which languages we use in internationalization rather than about how we use these languages in interaction with cultural others? By 'how' I do not mean 'how well' in terms of a proficiency level, but 'how creatively', 'how uniquely' we succeed in communicating to the other who we are. This can be done in any language we choose, so why not start with English? I would propose lifting English out of its functional corner and putting it back in the place where it belongs, right next to all the other adoptive languages we may choose in life.

References

Ager, D. (2001) *Motivation in Language Planning and Language Policy*. Clevedon: Multilingual Matters.

Akdağ, E.G. and Swanson, D.M. (2018) Ethics, power, internationalisation and the postcolonial: A Foucauldian discourse analysis of policy documents in two Scottish universities. *European Journal of Higher Education* 8 (1), 67–82.

Barakos, E. and Selleck, C. (2019) Elite multilingualism: Discourses, practices, and debates. *Journal of Multilingual and Multicultural Development* 40 (5), 361–374.

Beelen, J. and Jones, E. (2015) Redefining internationalization at home. In A. Curaj, L. Matei, R. Pricopie, J. Salmi and P. Scott (eds) *The European Higher Education Area* (pp. 59–72). Cham: Springer.

Bernstein, R.J. (1983) *Beyond Objectivism and Relativism*. Philadelphia, PA: University of Pennsylvania Press.

Billig, M. (1982) *Ideology and Social Psychology: Extremism, Moderation, and Contradiction*. New York: St Martin's.

Borrás-Alomar, S., Christiansen, T. and Rodríguez-Pose, A. (1994) Towards a 'Europe of the regions'? Visions and reality from a critical perspective. *Regional Politics and Policy* 4 (2), 1–27.
Bossong, G. (1994) Sprache und regionale Identität. In G. Bossong, M. Erbe, P. Frankenberg, C. Grivel and W. Lilli (eds) *Westeuropäische Regionen und ihre Identität* (pp. 46–61). Mannheim: Palatium Verlag.
Brooks, S. (1989) *Public Policy in Canada*. Toronto: McClelland & Stewart.
Bühler, K. (1934/1990) *Theory of Language: The Representational Function of Language (Sprachtheorie)* (trans. D. Fraser Goodwin). Amsterdam: John Benjamins.
Considine, M. (1994) *Public Policy: A Critical Approach*. London: Macmillan.
Cooper, R.L. (1989) *Language Planning and Social Change*. Cambridge: Cambridge University Press.
Dekker, R. (2017) Frame ambiguity in policy controversies: Critical frame analysis of migrant integration policies in Antwerp and Rotterdam. *Critical Policy Studies* 11 (2), 127–145.
de Wit, H. and Hunter, F. (2015) The future of internationalization of higher education in Europe. *International Higher Education* 83, 2–3. doi:10.6017/ihe.2015.83.9073
de Wit, H., Hunter, F., Howard, L. and Egron-Polak, E. (2015) *Internationalisation of Higher Education*. Brussels: European Union.
Dryzek, J.S. (1993) Policy analysis and planning: From science to argument. In F. Fischer and J. Forester (eds) *The Argumentative Turn in Policy Analysis and Planning* (pp. 213–232). Durham, NC: Duke University Press.
Fischer, F. (2003a) *Reframing Public Policy: Discursive Politics and Deliberative Practices*. Oxford: Oxford University Press.
Fischer, F. and Forester, J. (eds) (1993) *The Argumentative Turn in Policy Analysis and Planning*. Durham, NC: Duke University Press.
Fischer, F. and Gottweis, H. (eds) (2012) *The Argumentative Turn Revisited: Public Policy as Communicative Practice*. Durham, NC: Duke University Press.
Garcia, N. (2015) Tensions between cultural and utilitarian dimensions of language: A comparative analysis of 'multilingual' education policies in France and Germany. *Current Issues in Language Planning* 16 (1–2), 43–59.
Green, W. and Whitsed, C. (2015) *Critical Perspectives on Internationalising the Curriculum in Disciplines: Reflective Narrative Accounts from Business, Education and Health*. Rotterdam: Sense.
Hagen, S., Foreman-Peck, J., Davila-Philippon, S. and Nordgren, B. (2006) *ELAN: Effects on the European Economy of Shortages of Foreign Language Skills in Enterprise*. London: CILT.
Hajer, M.A. and Wagenaar, H. (eds) (2003) *Deliberative Policy Analysis*. Cambridge: Cambridge University Press.
Haugen, E. (1980) Language problems and language planning: The Scandinavian model. In P.H. Nelde (ed.) *Sprachkontakt und Sprachkonflikt* (pp. 151–157). Wiesbaden: Steiner.
Hudzik, J.K. (2011) *Comprehensive Internationalization: From Concept to Action*. Washington, DC: NAFSA, Association of International Educators.
Jones, E. and Killick, D. (2013) Graduate attributes and the internationalized curriculum: Embedding a global outlook in disciplinary learning outcomes. *Journal of Studies in International Education* 17 (2), 165–182.
Kemp, R. (1985) Planning, public hearings, and the politics of discourse. In J. Forester (ed.) *Critical Theory and Public Life* (pp. 177–201). Cambridge, MA: MIT Press.
Knight, J. and de Wit, H. (1999) *Quality and Internationalisation in Higher Education*. Paris: OECD.
Leask, B. (2015) *Internationalizing the Curriculum*. London: Routledge.
Nelde, P.H. (1990) *Language Attitudes and Language Conflict*. Bonn: Dümmler.
Paris, D.C. and Reynolds, J.F. (1983) *The Logic of Policy Inquiry*. New York: Longman.
Robson, S., Almeida, J. and Schartner, A. (2018) Internationalization at home: Time for review and development? *European Journal of Higher Education* 8 (1), 19–35.

Schiffman, H.F. (2003) Tongue-tied in Singapore: A language policy for Tamil? *Journal of Language, Identity & Education* 2 (2), 105–125.
Schiffman, H.F. (2007) Tamil language policy in Singapore: The role of implementation. In V. Vasih, S. Gopinathan and Y. Liu (eds) *Language, Capital and Culture* (pp. 209–226). Rotterdam: Sense.
Schleichert, H. (2005) *Wie man mit Fundamentalisten diskutiert, ohne den Verstand zu verlieren. Anleitung zum subversiven Denken*. Munich: Beck.
Shohamy, E. (2006) *Language Policy: Hidden Agendas and New Approaches*. London: Routledge.
Studer, P. (2012) Conceptual contradiction and discourses on multilingualism. In P. Studer and I. Werlen (eds) *Linguistic Diversity in Europe: Trends and Discourses* (pp. 115–135). Berlin and New York: de Gruyter Mouton.
Studer, P. (2013a) Managing language ideologies in informal language planning episodes. In B. Erzsebet, P. Studer and J. Nekvapil (eds) *Ideological Conceptualizations of Language: Discourses of Linguistic Diversity* (pp. 193–216). Frankfurt: Peter Lang.
Studer, P. (2013b) Linguistics applied to business contexts: An interview with Patrick Studer. *Revista Virtual de Estudos da Linguagem – ReVEL* 11 (21), 187–198.
Studer, P. (2014) Language planners' cultural positioning strategies in joint negotiation of meaning. In J. Conacher and B. Geraghty (eds) *Intercultural Contact, Language Learning and Migration* (pp. 61–81). London: Bloomsbury Academic.
Studer, P. (2018) Introduction. In P. Studer (ed.) *Internationalizing Curricula in Higher Education: Quality and Language of Instruction. Bulletin suisse de linguistique appliquée VALS-ASLA* 107, 1–5.
Studer, P. and Denis, P. (2017) Discours et professionnalisation: Entre défi conceptuel et place de la recherche en formation des enseignants. *Actes de la recherche de la HEP-BEJUNE* 11, 139–157.
Studer, P., Kreiselmaier, F. and Flubacher, M. (2008) *Language Policy-planning in a Multilingual European Context*. Bern: Institut für Sprachwissenschaft.
Studer, P., Kreiselmaier, F. and Flubacher, M. (2010) Language planning of the European Union: A micro-level perspective. *European Journal of Language Policy* 2 (2), 251–270.
Turner, Y. and Robson, S. (2008) *Internationalizing the University: An Introduction for University Teachers and Managers*. London: Continuum Press.
van der Wende, M., Beerkens, E. and Teichler, U. (1999) Internationalisation as a cause for innovation in higher education. In B. Jongbloed, P. Maassen and G. Neave (eds) *From the Eye of the Storm* (pp. 65–93). Dordrecht: Springer.
van Hulst, M. and Yanow, D. (2016) From policy 'frames' to 'framing': Theorizing a more dynamic, political approach. *American Review of Public Administration* 46 (1), 92–112.
Voloshinov, V.N. (1986) *Marxism and the Philosophy of Language* (trans. L. Matejka and I.R. Titunik). Cambridge, MA: Harvard University Press.
Watzlawick, P., Beavin-Bavelas, J. and Jackson, D. (1967) Some tentative axioms of communication. In *Pragmatics of Human Communication – A Study of Interactional Patterns, Pathologies and Paradoxes*. New York: W.W. Norton.
Wihlborg, M. and Robson, S. (2018) Internationalisation of higher education: Drivers, rationales, priorities, values and impacts. *European Journal of Higher Education* 8 (1), 8–18.

Cited reports and policy documents (in chronological order)

Communication documents

COM 2005 596: A new framework strategy for multilingualism. Brussels, 22 November 2005.
COM 2008 566: Multilingualism: An asset for Europe and a shared commitment. Brussels, 18 September 2008.

COM 2011 567: Supporting growth and jobs – an agenda for the modernisation of Europe's higher education systems. Brussels, 20 September 2011.
COM 2012 669: Rethinking education: Investing in skills for better socio-economic outcomes. Brussels, 20 November 2012.
COM 2013 499: European higher education in the world. Brussels, 11 July 2013.
COM 2016 381: Working together to strengthen human capital, employability and competitiveness. Brussels, 10 June 2016.
COM 2017 247: On a renewed EU agenda for higher education. Brussels, 30 May 2017.
COM 2017 673: Strengthening European identity through education and culture. Brussels, 14 November 2017.

Conclusions, opinion and recommendation documents

2009/C 77/25: Opinion of the European Economic and Social Committee on 'multilingualism'. Brussels, 31 March 2009.
2010/C 135/04: Council conclusions of 11 May 2010 on the internationalisation of higher education. Brussels, 26 May 2010.
COM 2018 24: Council recommendation on key competences for lifelong learning. Brussels, 17 January 2018.
2018/C 195/01: Council recommendation on promoting common values, inclusive education, and the European dimension of teaching. Brussels, 22 May 2018.
2019/C 189/03: Council recommendation on a comprehensive approach to the teaching and learning of languages. Brussels, 22 May 2019.

Staff working documents

SWD 2012 372: Language competences for employability, mobility and growth. Brussels, 20 November 2012.
SWD 2016 195: Commission staff working document accompanying the document 'A new skills agenda for Europe: Working together to strengthen human capital, employability and competitiveness', 10 June 2016.
SWD 2018 174: Commission staff working document accompanying the document 'Proposal for a council recommendation on a comprehensive approach to the teaching and learning of languages'. Brussels, 22 May 2018.

Speeches

Orban, L. (2008) The contribution of multilingualism/language learning to intercultural dialogue. Oslo, 6 June.

Reports

Davignon, E.V., Albrink, W., Dyremose, H., et al. (2008) *Languages Mean Business. Companies Work Better with Languages. Recommendations from the Business Forum for Multilingualism Established by the European Commission*. Brussels: European Commission.
Maalouf, A., Limbach, J., Pralong, S., et al. (2008) *A Rewarding Challenge. How the Multiplicity of Languages Could Strengthen Europe. Proposals from the Group of Intellectuals for Intercultural Dialogue Set up at the Initiative of the European Commission*. Luxembourg: Office for Official Publications of the European Communities.
OMC Group 'Languages for Jobs' (2012) *Languages for Jobs. Providing Multilingual Communication Skills for the Labour Market. Report from the Thematic Working Group 'Languages for Jobs', European Strategic Framework for Education and Training*. Brussels: European Commission.

2 Building a Language Policy for Quality Multilingualism in Higher Education: From Theory to Practice

Inmaculada Fortanet-Gómez

Introduction

In recent years, there have been a great number of studies on multilingualism and multilingual education (Aronin & Hufeisen, 2010; Bhatia & Ritchie, 2012; Singleton & Aronin, 2019, to name just a few), some of which have dealt with language policies (Cenoz & Gorter, 2019; Fortanet-Gómez, 2013; Hornberger, 2002; Menken & García, 2010). However, although the term 'quality' is mentioned in most of these publications, it is not the focus of the research. *Merriam-Webster's Collegiate Dictionary* (Merriam-Webster, 1999) provides eight definitions of quality, of which three are pertinent to this study:

- quality is a peculiar and essential character or the nature of something (*her ethereal quality*);
- a distinguishing attribute or characteristic (*possesses many fine qualities*); or
- a degree of excellence (*the quality of competing air service*); or superiority in kind (*merchandise of quality*).

In the following sections, I present several perspectives of multilingualism as developed by a growing number of researchers in order to ascertain the quality of both individual and societal multilingualism within the institution and also of the society surrounding it. Then, I analyse the three groups of factors conditioning multilingual education: the situational factors, the pedagogical factors and the individual factors as well as their practical application to the context I know the best, Universitat Jaume I (UJI). In the final part of the chapter, I explain the multilingual plan for quality learning in a multilingual context designed for this university.

Quality as the peculiar and essential character or the nature of something

What is the quality of multilingualism? In a previous work (Fortanet-Gómez, 2013: 3), I defined multilingualism as 'the social and the individual situation in which two or more languages are known and used by speakers'. The *Common European Framework of Reference for Languages* (Council of Europe, 2001, 2018: 28) 'distinguishes between multilingualism (the coexistence of different languages at the social or individual level) and plurilingualism (the dynamic and developing linguistic repertoire of an individual user/learner)'. This document points out differences there might be between the users' resources in one language and in the other language/s they know. In this sense, multilingualism affects the society and plurilingualism refers to the condition of individuals.

What do we associate the term 'multilingualism' with? I shall present four current key areas: digital communication, travel and/or study, geographical contexts and migration.

A range of languages, especially English, are needed today in order to use emergent technologies, digital media and social networks. These technologies can be related to work, but also to leisure. For example, nowadays digital materials and the use of technologies are expanding in education (European Commission, 2017). Moreover, in the labour market the ability to deal with electronic commerce, including instruction manuals, insurance and commerce documents, is often associated with particular jobs. However, many people buy only for their own consumption, expanding this work skill into leisure. Other extended uses of technology are the international video games in which the participants in a game come from different countries or watching films and series in their original versions. In all these situations, the use of other languages is often assumed.

Another extended use of foreign languages, again mainly English, is for travel. Low-cost companies have made travelling accessible to the general public. Although some travellers are tourists who have limited contact with the local communities and even choose to communicate mostly with speakers of their home language, there are other travellers who aim to learn about the people they encounter in those countries. Sometimes it is the nature of the visit that involves interaction with local communities, such as when there are cultural, social or humanitarian aims involved. In other cases, the reason for travelling to another country is related to work or to studies, where the nature of the language required will demand a more advanced or deeper understanding. Most often, English will be the language used as a lingua franca for communication between local people and visitors when it is the only language they share.

The third most common condition for multilingualism is related to the place where speakers live. It is usual to find multilinguals in areas near national borders, as well as in areas where there is a local and a state language, that is, where different local languages coexist within a state. This has been present throughout history, and there is a great variation in the way it is dealt with by governments and society. Whereas in some regions the local language is reinforced by means of teaching and the support of the media using it, in other regions the use of the local language is restricted to colloquial spoken interaction with family and friends. Finally, immigration is a growing reality on a global scale. Immigration may be due to several reasons, among them studies and work; however, unlike in the case of travellers, immigrants intend to remain in the destination country for a long time.

These different circumstances provide a wide scope on the perceptions people have about the quality or nature of multilingualism. For example, in terms of freedom of choice, for Erasmus exchange students going to Germany for a semester, learning German is an aim and it is done willingly. Students will need to acquire and use a high level of spoken and written academic discourse. However, if they just travel there to visit a friend or for sightseeing, using English or maybe even Spanish will be enough, and they will not need a high proficiency in the language. On the other hand, people who have to immigrate for work reasons may not have chosen to learn the language of the country where they will have to live and work. For them it is an obligation and their priority will be to learn the oral language for daily use as efficiently as possible, as well as those skills they will need to accomplish their work tasks. Freedom of choice may mark people's attitude towards a particular language. Interestingly, all these situations of multilingualism may coincide in time and in place and even in the same multilingual people, who may have this condition due to several of the circumstances described above.

Quality as the essential character of multilingualism may also differ according to whether we take the perspective of society or of the individual. Societal multilingualism refers to a society in which a significant group of individuals share the knowledge of two or more languages, whereas in individual multilingualism an individual has knowledge of at least two languages (Baetens Beardsmore, 1982). Examples can be found everywhere, such as at UJI, a multilingual university with the historical local language Valencian (a variety of Catalan), Spanish (the state language) and English (the lingua franca of the academy). Evidence of societal multilingualism can be found in the university landscape, such as in the emergency signs on the walls of the corridors between the classrooms (see Figure 2.1). The language use is shown by the insertion of the three languages in the sign. However, the choice of the size, the colour and the

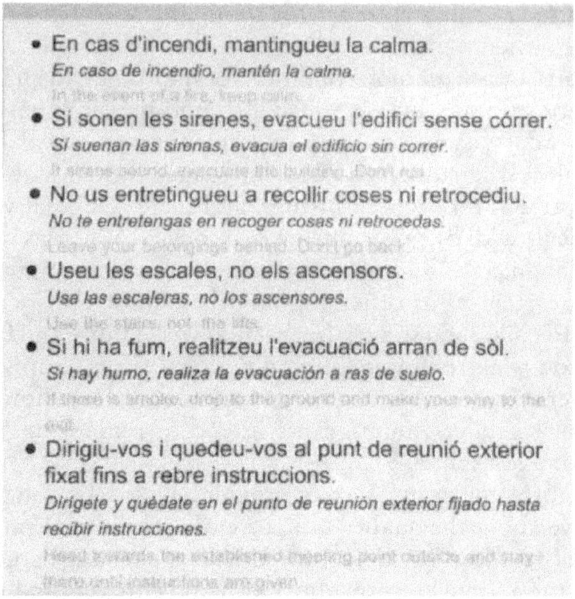

- En cas d'incendi, mantingueu la calma.
  En caso de incendio, mantén la calma.
  In the event of a fire, keep calm.

- Si sonen les sirenes, evacueu l'edifici sense córrer.
  Si suenan las sirenas, evacua el edificio sin correr.
  If sirens sound, evacuate the building. Don't run.

- No us entretingueu a recollir coses ni retrocediu.
  No te entretengas en recoger cosas ni retrocedas.
  Leave your belongings behind. Don't go back.

- Useu les escales, no els ascensors.
  Usa las escaleras, no los ascensores.
  Use the stairs, not the lifts.

- Si hi ha fum, realitzeu l'evacuació arran de sòl.
  Si hay humo, realiza la evacuación a ras de suelo.
  If there is smoke, drop to the ground and make your way to the exit.

- Dirigiu-vos i quedeu-vos al punt de reunió exterior fixat fins a rebre instruccions.
  Dirígete y quédate en el punto de reunión exterior fijado hasta recibir instrucciones.
  Head towards the established meeting point outside and stay there until instructions are given.

Figure 2.1 Emergency sign in three languages

font of the text in the three languages marks their social status and the language policy of the university. Valencian is the priority language, followed by Spanish. In contrast, for those who can only understand English, it may be difficult to read what they have to do, as due to its status, the instructions in this language are written in a small font and a low-contrast colour.

Regarding individual multilingualism, this refers to individuals who have access to more than one linguistic code as a means of social communication (Hamers & Blanc, 2000). Individual multilingualism can be analysed according to several dimensions. One of these dimensions is the competence the person has in the languages he or she knows and uses, which does not need to be the same for all languages (Grosjean, 2010). Also important is the cognitive organization of these languages, which is often related to the time and context of acquisition. So, depending on how individuals learned the languages they know – simultaneously, i.e. they learn two or more codes for the same realities, or successively, i.e. more languages are added in the course of life – the way these languages are assimilated in their brain will differ. These different experiences may lead to compound, coordinate and subordinate multilinguals (de Groot, 2011).

Multilinguals have the ability to use their condition in different ways. In Europe, following the Council of Europe's (2007) terminology, I will refer to plurilingualism, since the individual does not 'keep languages and cultures in strictly separated mental compartments, but rather builds up a communicative competence to which all knowledge and experience of language contributes and in which languages interrelate and interact' (Council of Europe, 2007: 4). Canagarajah (2009) remarks that for the plurilingual individual the relevant matter is not the proficiency, or the advance in this proficiency, in each of the languages he or she knows, but the integrated competence of all languages, which can be used for different purposes. Herdina and Jessner (2002) deal with this competence of plurilinguals, which they call the multilingual factor (M-factor) for the skills they develop: language learning skills, language management skills and language maintenance skills. On the other hand, García (2009), Thibault (2017) and Lin (2018) focus on the multilingual individual's ability to communicate using a whole repertoire of languages, which they call 'translanguaging', that is, 'multiple discursive practices in which bilinguals engage in order to make sense of their bilingual [multilingual] worlds' (García, 2009: 45). Lin (2018) goes a step further and argues that it is not only words that multilingual individuals choose from the several languages they know, but they get into a flow of meaning-making in which there is an ensemble of agents and receivers, translanguaging and trans-semiotizing, that is, the coordination of verbal discourse in several languages, registers and genres, as well as gestures, facial expressions, sounds, visual images, etc. Along the same lines, there are many different approaches to the research on multilingualism which have become more holistic in recent years, so that multilingualism is not seen as an addition of languages but as a global feature (Cenoz, 2013; Mazak & Carroll, 2017; van der Walt, 2013).

Quality as a distinguishable attribute of multilinguals

According to Hamers and Blanc (2000), there are six dimensions that seem especially relevant in order to ascertain the quality of multilinguals: their competence in languages, cognitive organization, age and context of acquisition, social status, cultural status and how they identify culturally with each language.

In order to ascertain the qualities of the students at UJI, I distributed a questionnaire to my own students[1] about their personal features, regarding competence of languages, age and context of acquisition, sociocultural status and cultural identity. All the students asked were multilingual. These were not easy questions for them to answer. In general, two groups could be distinguished:

- local students
- international students

Local students, born in Spain, had either Spanish or Valencian as their first or mother tongue, and their cultural identity was associated with one or both of these two languages, which they used regularly. They learned their second language, Valencian or Spanish, when they started school, and acquired English later on also at school, especially in secondary education. Some students also learned a second foreign language, such as French, in this period. Although English as well as the second foreign language were important to them, their competence in these languages was much lower than in Valencian and Spanish.

Regarding international students, many were born in other countries, where some of them also spent their school years. They were mostly European (especially Romanian, as there was a strong immigration movement from this country some years ago), but also from other parts of the world, such as Africa. Their mother tongue was that of their original country or region in that country (one student was born in Romania near the border and spoke Hungarian as her L1). Some of them had lived in other countries before coming to Spain, where they also learned the language. They acquired Spanish and Valencian at primary or secondary school when they arrived in Spain. Most of them also learned English at school.

These are the characteristics, the quality or peculiar character of multilingual students, as all students interviewed were multilingual. However, when asked about their competence in the use of the languages they know, there were differences depending on languages. For example, in a previous study conducted at UJI (Fortanet-Gómez, 2013), where Spanish, Valencian and English are languages of instruction, most of the 889 students who answered the survey (a normalized sample of the total population) declared that they knew at least three languages: Valencian, Spanish and English. However, undergraduate students reported feeling more confident when reading academic materials or understanding a lecture in their discipline in Spanish, rather than in Valencian or English. The main differences were found in speaking, since many students could speak Valencian fluently as well as Spanish but found difficulties when speaking English. In contrast, graduate students found fewer difficulties with the English language. They could read and understand materials, attend lectures and speak with some fluency, as English was often considered the main language of science in their discipline. Moreover, it must be noted that the number of international students is much higher in graduate than in undergraduate studies at UJI, so the profile of the average student is different (Fortanet-Gómez, 2013).

Quality of today's multilingual education

So far I have dealt with the quality or essential nature of multilinguals, who have sometimes reached this status because they have learned several languages at home, but mainly because they have learned them at school, that is, by means of multilingual education. Genesee (2004: 564) defines multilingual education as '[e]ducation that aims to promote bilingual [or multilingual] competence by using both [or all] languages as media of instruction for significant proportions of the academic curriculum'. Multilingual public education is always a response to a language policy of a state or a bilingual region. What are the reasons to implement multilingual education? These reasons differ, depending on whether the languages used as mediums of instruction are local or foreign languages. Local languages are introduced in the classrooms mainly due to movements in defence of local and regional languages and to protect languages in danger of extinction. Instruction in foreign languages responds to the globalization of knowledge and to the need to reinforce language learning courses (Fortanet-Gómez, 2013). Some international organizations have supported the idea of multilingual education; that is, when leaving secondary school, children should be able to operate in at least three languages 'which should represent the normal range of practical linguistic skills in the twenty-first century' (UNESCO, 2003: 32).

Quality as degree of excellence or superiority in kind of multilingual education

The third meaning of quality I will discuss in this chapter is that of excellence. The question is: How can excellence be achieved in multilingual education? Three main types of achievements can be measured in multilingual education: language achievements, content achievements and literacy achievements (Fortanet-Gómez, 2013).

Language achievements

Language achievements are those that have been most commonly analysed. For many people, reaching a higher command of the language of instruction should prevail, especially if the aim of the programme is to improve the language competence of students. However, researchers have reported peculiarities in language achievements through multilingual education. For example, most students following multilingual programmes attain more functional proficiency in the use of the additional language than those who just follow language courses (Genesee & Lindholm-Leary, 2013). This is due to the applied use of the language of instruction to the academic context. These students also seem to acquire more comprehension skills (reading and listening) in the target languages than production skills (writing and speaking) and vocabulary (Aguilar & Muñoz, 2013; Heras & Lasagabaster, 2015). In the case of local languages, balanced multilingualism can be achieved in geographical multilingualism and with minority languages when these are used as mediums of instruction and usually also as languages of socialization outside the classroom (Cots *et al.*, 2012). In Europe, the Council of Europe (2007) established an aim to achieve plurilingual competence for the whole population, something difficult to attain in the short term.

Literacy achievements

Literacy is a term mainly used for the early acquisition of languages, although it can be applied to any level of competence. It refers to reading and writing for different purposes (from completing a manual task following instructions to studying at university) or in different genres (reading literature for leisure, writing a research article, etc.). Literacy is related to underlying cognitive processes and conveys different levels of proficiency (Bialystock, 2001). There has been very little research on the literacy achievements of multilingual education as compared to monolingual education. Some of these studies have addressed the development of multilingual literacy skills in schoolchildren (O'Brien *et al.*, 2014) or in programmes for immigrants in which multilingual education is only aimed at the majority language (or certain skills in that language) (Bialystock, 2001). Immigrants need command of the dominant language in the area where they want to live and work, and the skills they need are usually speaking and sometimes writing for very specific purposes. Another focus of interest regarding literacy has been plurilingual competence or the M-Factor described above: students learn to identify and use the suitable register and the right genres in each of the languages they learn (Coste *et al.*, 2009; Moore & Gajo, 2009). Moreover, other researchers have shown interest in multimodal and multilingual competence (Kyppö & Natri, 2016; de Saint Georges, 2013) or translanguaging and trans-semiotizing (Lin, 2018).

Content achievements

Regarding content or subject knowledge, it has usually been expected that students should obtain the same results as in monolingual standard programmes (Genesee, 2013). However, there are several researchers who maintain that content needs to be adapted to multilingual education and internationalization for a coherent multilingual international education, although this is not usually done and the international component is still not considered in content assessment (Halbach, 2012). In any case, content achievements need to take account of additional factors, which may bias the results obtained. These factors may include: motivation, which tends to be higher in multilingual groups; the background of students, e.g. students with different command of the foreign language producing dissimilar content achievements; and overall performance, since some multilingual groups are only offered to selected gifted students. In addition, there is the component of international students, who may already know about the content of the subject or, on the contrary, may lack some previous essential knowledge (Doiz *et al.*, 2013).

Approaches to Multilingual Education

Multilingual education has been present at universities for many centuries. However, it was during the last decades of the 20th century and in the 21st century that it has emerged as a generalized tendency. There have been several approaches to multilingual education, some of them associated to particular contexts. *Language across the curriculum* (Martin, 1976) aimed at the improvement of the English language for native students in the UK, although there were several later developments stemming from this that were addressed at foreign languages (Silva & Brice, 2004). *Content-based instruction* (Grabe & Stoller, 1997) started in the United States in order to overcome the difficulties immigrant children had in following mainstream classes. It was complemented by sheltered groups and adjunct language instruction. *Immersion programmes* started in Canada with the aim of changing the reality of being a bilingual country with two monolingual areas (Lambert & Tucker, 1972; Lyster, 2007). Nowadays, this is the approach most often followed to introduce local and regional languages in mainstream education. Some subjects are taught in the state language while others are taught in the regional or local language. Both languages are also used in the social context. The aim is to get an equal competence and use in both (Vila i Moreno, 2009). The approach of *languages for specific purposes* (LSP) or *English for specific purposes* (ESP) focuses on the teaching and learning of languages for particular functions, jobs, professions or studies, and has been found in universities and professional training programmes since the 1980s. As Swales (2000) points out, there are many differences between LSP/ ESP and second language acquisition (SLA). The main difference is linked to the fact that the former are devoted to the preparation of adults for professional and academic contexts, whereas the latter is 'focused on grammar and its acquisition by young and often beginner learners' (Swales, 2000: 61). *English as a medium of instruction* (EMI) is the approach followed in most higher education institutions worldwide, especially when not all of the students have the same mother tongue or L1 and need a lingua franca to communicate (Palfreyman & van der Walt, 2017; Zhang, 2018). On the other hand, *content and language integrated learning* (CLIL) or *integrating content and language in higher education* (ICLHE) is the approach most often followed in the training of university lecturers who teach in English (or other languages) in today's universities, especially in Europe (see definition in the Introduction to this book). The idea behind this approach is to teach both content and language at the same time. However, the line separating CLIL and EMI is very fine. There are many content teachers who claim that they are not language teachers and not interested in teaching language and, therefore, would better support EMI as the approach followed in their teaching (Fortanet-Gómez, 2012).

Factors Conditioning Multilingual Education

Multilingual education takes place in certain contexts and conditions which cannot be ignored when designing suitable plans (Fortanet-Gómez,

2013). There are several factors that condition multilingual education. These factors can be grouped into three types:

- situational factors;
- pedagogical factors;
- individual factors.

Situational factors

Situational factors refer to the geographical and social setting of the educational institution. Several variables can be analysed, such as the area's population diversity, language policies, opportunity for language use, status of languages, linguistic characteristics, attitudes, economy, religion, culture and ideologies. For example, to define a multilingual plan for my university, Universitat Jaume I, I had to consider that the local population, from which 95% of the students come, is formed of people who may have Spanish or Valencian as their L1, as well as of a percentage of immigrants who have other L1s and who present a very wide range of linguistic circumstances. The status of and attitudes towards the several languages they know can be varied, as well as their religions, culture and ideologies. UJI is a public university and, in principle, it should be accessible to everyone. Policies are also very relevant, since they mark the constraints for the institutional language plan. In almost every context there are supranational, national and local policies. In Spain, at a national level we have the recommendations for a multilingual policy issued by the Conference of Rectors (Bazo Martínez & González Álvarez, 2017) and the Strategy for the Internationalisation of Universities (MECD, 2016). In contrast, at a regional level there is no policy addressed at universities, but there is a law which regulates plurilingual pre-university education (Generalitat Valenciana, 2018). This law sheds some light on how well prepared students will be when reaching university regarding multilingual education and their command of the three languages they will face as languages of tuition. However, this kind of policy varies from one region in Spain to another, so it will not affect students coming to study at UJI who have undergone their primary and secondary education in other state regions.

When designing a language plan, it is also very important to analyse the relationships between the stakeholders. There are two main types of stakeholder: those external and those internal to the education centre. Internally, it is essential that the main participants, teachers and students agree on the value of multilingual education, since it will entail effort for all of them while also adding value. The support of the administration is also very important, since they may facilitate many of the changes multilingual communication will bring about, such as internationalization, more interest in language learning, etc. Finally, the fourth and maybe the most important internal stakeholders are the decision makers, that is, the authorities at university level: deans, executive councils, the university assembly and the management team. At this level it is also useful to have a project coordinator who can deal with all stakeholders and organize the several actions.

The stakeholders in the second group are external: society in general, policy makers and decision makers, and the future employers of graduate students. Especially important are families as part of the society; even though their voices are not so clearly heard at universities as they are in primary and secondary school, families still have a strong influence on university students. Languages are linked to culture and identity and, therefore, they are a highly sensitive matter and the influence of social media can be critical. In many universities there is a social council representing the society. Their role is also important and their opinion very relevant, since they may be devoted promoters or ferocious critics of the language plan in front of the rest of the society.

Even though policy makers, often senior administrative officers, and decision makers, politicians, do not pay much attention to the specific policies and plans of universities, it is useful to seek their support by agreeing on recommendations that align with language policies such as the aforementioned Strategy for the Internationalisation of Universities (MECD, 2016). Finally, it is also relevant to get the support of graduate students' employers. Most university students aim to finish their studies and obtain secure employment related to their expertise. If language requirements are aligned with those that the university relate to future employability, this will increase the motivation of students. Figure 2.2 summarizes the stakeholders and their relationships.

Pedagogical factors

The second group of factors conditioning a multilingual plan has two main components. On the one hand, there is the language component and, on the other, the learning/teaching component.

The language component

There are at least three main functions of language in multilingual education: language as target product, language as medium of instruction and language as medium of communication. It is important to look at these functions separately but also in combination.

When considering language as a target product, the first and main questions are: Which languages? Why? Then other additional questions should be asked such as: Should the university provide language courses for students? In regular mainstream curricula? Compulsory or optional? Should they be general or specific for professional or academic purposes (LSP/LAP)? In the case of English, native language as a model or a lingua franca?

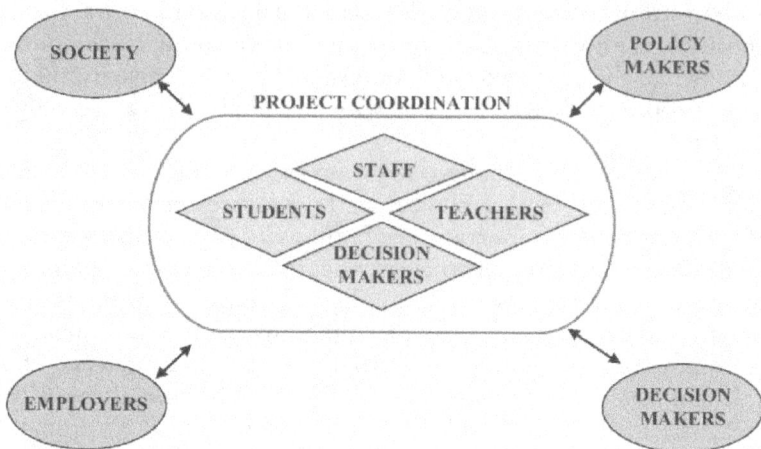

Figure 2.2 Stakeholders' relationships in a multilingual education programme in higher education
Source: Fortanet-Gómez (2013).

With regard to language as a medium of instruction, the most relevant aspects deal with the competence of teachers and students in the language, which may condition the selection of studies with a second or third language of instruction. This is the main concern for teachers, who not only have to become more proficient in a second language but have to be confident of its use as a language of instruction. Specific teacher training courses may support teachers in becoming more confident and competent users. Other important questions should be asked, such as: Which studies should be taught in a different language? In which language? The whole course? In two languages? Should the whole university or centre follow the same model? These may be controversial questions which might provoke debate, but after thorough discussion, decisions need to be made as a starting point to establish a language policy involving multilingual education.

The third function is that of language as a medium of communication. It is very important to decide and clarify the use of languages in the language policy. Which should be the language of communication within the university? And in the classroom? For example, at UJI the use of languages for institutional communication in emails was regulated, as well as the protocols for answering an institutional phone call or assisting the general public face to face, giving a preference to the Valencian language and then adapting the language of communication to the needs of the interlocutor and the situation.

It is also important to consider the relationship between all these functions. Languages learned exclusively in the classroom in specific courses or as languages of instruction will be more related to cognitive academic language proficiency (CALP; Cummins, 2000), while those spoken socially will provide the students with basic interpersonal communication skills (BICS).

The learning/teaching component

Although there is no single established method for multilingual education, some pedagogies seem to achieve good results in a number of universities around the world. In general, researchers nowadays support the use of more than one language in the classroom, that is, multilingual practices or translanguaging (Lin, 2018), in order to improve language learning in context, as well as to emphasize key points, reiterate the meaning, provide a clue about something difficult to understand, or just to enhance student and teacher personal interaction in Chinese universities (Chen *et al.*, 2020) or to promote higher-order thinking skills in Indonesia (Khair *et al.*, 2020). Students need to practise the language, not only to read and understand but also to produce the language, and teachers need to be able to supervise the correct and understandable use of the language produced. However, the focus of the integration of content and language in higher education is to reach the objectives of a given syllabus.

Another pedagogical component especially useful in ICLHE contexts is scaffolding, that is, some specific assistance in order to solve a problem that the student cannot solve without that assistance. However, scaffolding in ICLHE may need special training, as noted by Nashaat (2015), who found a gap in university teachers' scaffolding practices. Today it is usual to find a combination of teachers' and technological scaffolding (Pea, 2004), so the human assistance may be supported by multimodal and digital materials, electronic presentations, videos or virtual classrooms. Notwithstanding, successful introduction of teaching in an additional language may need different kinds of scaffolding, like that needed when students have to migrate from CLIL in secondary education to EMI in higher education (Lopriore, 2017) or from just having EFL classes to EMI programmes (Arnbjörnsdóttir, 2017).

According to Stoller (2002), project work is a good way to coordinate the learning of languages and the learning of content, as well as participative methodologies such as those requiring team or group work in class, experiential learning, collaborative learning (Laal & Ghodsi, 2012) or computer online international learning (Robin & Guth, 2015).

Individual factors

Individual factors comprise the third group of factors that condition multilingual education. Profiling members of the university (i.e. students, university teachers and administration staff) is critical to achieving an understanding of the ways in which the policy may be operationalized as well as any potential barriers.

In the next subsections I will describe the characteristics of the members of my university, UJI. These may be similar to those at some other universities, especially small public universities in peripheral areas of Spain, although they may differ substantially from other institutions. This profiling was made by means of a survey of 889 students, 78 lecturers and 36 members of the administrative staff – a statistically significant sample of the general cohort (Fortanet-Gómez, 2013).

Who are today's university students?

As a general rule, undergraduate students at UJI range between 18 and 22 years of age, whereas most master's students are between 21 and 23, although there may be some older students. The majority of undergraduate students come from secondary high school and only a small group come from professional training courses.

There are local and national students, but also a considerable number of immigrant students. Local students are usually bilingual, as they learn Valencian or Spanish (depending on which is their L1) as a second language at school. Many of the immigrant students have undertaken their previous studies in Spain and are second-generation immigrants. However, they keep up their original family heritage language. Most students have never had any experience of CLIL. The number of international students, that is, those who register for the whole degree course, is very scarce in bachelor's courses but is gradually increasing in master's courses. There are also some exchange students, especially in some subjects in bachelor's degrees. Exchange students are temporary or visiting students; they register and pay their fees at their university of origin and spend one semester or one complete academic year at a foreign university, the university of destination, where they take some subjects under the same conditions as mainstream students and get recognition for that in their curriculum at home. In sum, the linguistic background of students participating in bilingual programmes is rather varied.

International exchange grants are available for students in all majors, but only about 20% take up this opportunity. The main stated reasons are that they cannot afford to go abroad or that they want to focus on their studies and do not wish to be distracted. However, it is also noted that there are few students with proficiency in a foreign language, and most have only learned some English. That may also be the reason why, in general, they are not very eager to go abroad or to interact with 'non-Spanish', so very often there is a need for the teacher's assistance in order to integrate the foreign students in the class. Logically, subjects taught in English have a higher number of foreign students and tend not to be the most popular among local students.

Although, as said above, there may be variations at different universities, this composition is very similar to the scenarios described by other researchers for European multilingual higher education (Smit, 2010; Smit & Dafouz, 2013).

The qualities of a university teacher

It is controversial to try to define the characteristics of a good or excellent university lecturer, given the variety of lecturing styles and of the preferences of students. First of all, it needs to be pointed out that Spanish and most European higher education systems prioritize research over teaching. University teachers are obliged to be researchers, and this function is the one that gets most recognition in terms of career trajectory. Regarding languages, in many fields it is essential to know English as most research studies are published in this language (Fortanet-Gómez, 2013). Teaching thus remains in second place and lecturers often devote less time to it than to research. While studies (e.g. Kreber, 2009) have identified features of excellent university teaching, this is contextually embedded. Yet some factors are clearly linked to good teaching at any age: good relationships with students; good knowledge of the subject matter; adequate design, selection and presentation of materials; and collaborative relationships with colleagues.

In multilingual education these aspects become even more relevant. Teachers need to have a good command of the languages of instruction and they have to adapt not only to the background knowledge of their audience in relation to the subject matter but also to their language skills. Very often, innovative teaching techniques, especially those related to technologies, lead to better achievements, as they make subjects that integrate content and language learning more attractive to the students.

The role of administrative staff

Although they do not receive much attention, the involvement of administrative staff is essential for the success of a language policy, as they act in support of teaching and research. The staff in language centres and in international relations offices usually have a good knowledge of international languages as this is necessary for their daily work, but it is good that most or all staff know several languages and are involved in multilingualism and internationalization (Fortanet-Gómez, 2013).

There are strategic administrative positions in which some specific skills in foreign languages are essential, such as those that involve assisting students or people in general, like telephone services or reception desks as well as information offices and the library.

The Multilingual Language Policy and Plan at Universitat Jaume I

After considering all the aspects presented above, I decided that in order to define a language policy for my university, UJI, I needed to ask internal stakeholders about their opinions of and expectations for multilingual education, and I designed an online survey for this purpose. Asking university members would not only provide me with their points of view but would also get them involved in the future plan, as they could feel part of the process of creation.

In the online survey there was participation by 6% of the population, that is, of all students, lecturers and staff – significant according to statistical rules. The number of respondents was 889 students, 78 lecturers and 36 administrative staff. The questions dealt with the actual characteristics of the community members and asked about their opinions and expectations regarding the knowledge and use of languages, mainly the three priority languages for UJI: Valencian, Spanish and English (to learn more about this survey, see Fortanet-Gómez, 2013).

The results of the survey indicated a clear need for a language policy, including teacher training and recognition of the effort required to learn languages and to use them as mediums of instruction (or language of communication in the workplace for the administrative staff). In general, there was a predisposition by students and staff to introduce multilingual practices at the university. With regard to English, most university members declared they had a low command of this language. Moreover, two main drawbacks were identified. There were a few people with extreme positions: those who perceived English as a threat to the wider use of Valencian, and those who regarded Valencian as a minority language which could have a negative influence on the university's prestige. On the other hand, budget assignation was one of the main concerns, as the country's economic situation was unfavourable at the time which affected the university's public funding.

Objectives of the multilingual language plan at UJI

After several meetings and much debate, the governing bodies of the university decided that UJI should have its own language policy which had to be presented in a multilingual plan to be implemented over several years. This plan should include three languages: Valencian, as the priority language of the institution; Spanish, the state official language; and English, as the international lingua franca. The objectives of the plan were structured around two axes:

(1) people, with the general aim that all members of the university community should be more plurilingual in teaching and learning, research and administration settings; and
(2) the institution, with the aim of spreading the culture of a multilingual teaching and research institution, which should be reflected in the institutional information and by guaranteeing language quality in all academic, administrative and institutional activities.

The plan had 15 specific objectives (10 related to the people and five related to the institution), which had to be reached by means of 50 actions and 57 indicators of success. While some objectives dealt with just one of the languages, mainly Valencian or English, as these needed special support compared to Spanish, the majority language, some other objectives were related to the use of all languages.

Axis 1: People
(1) Increase the use of Valencian and make Valencian the language of communication between people in all university activities.
(2) Guarantee the plurilingualism of all students and staff in at least the three priority languages.
(3) Guarantee the principle of linguistic security; that is, all activities must necessarily be carried out in the language in which they were publicly announced.
(4) Improve the academic community's language skills and guarantee the possibility of taking courses and attaining language certificates.
(5) Improve the linguistic quality of academic texts.
(6) Increase the number of subjects taught in English and in Valencian.
(7) Increase the use of Valencian in research knowledge transfer and social science dissemination.
(8) Encourage mobility between universities in the Catalan-speaking regions to strengthen innovation and the exchange of experiences among the staff that use Valencian at work.
(9) Promote the language integration of people from other cultural and linguistic areas.
(10) Increase the range of cultural activities in Valencian.

These objectives should lead university members (students, teaching and administrative staff) to qualify as good or excellent plurilinguals.

Axis 2: The institution
(11) Use Valencian as the regular and priority language in the development of administrative, academic and institutional activities.
(12) Increase the number of courses in Valencian (up to 25%) and in English (up to 10%).
(13) Make active multilingualism a value of the university and of all of its members, so that all members are aware of this value and participate and propose initiatives to promote it.
(14) Report on the advantages of multilingualism and raise awareness in the university community towards the use of Valencian in the development of administrative, academic and institutional activities.
(15) Guarantee the quality of the several languages used in the institutional documents.

These objectives should make the university more multilingual, as several languages coexist at all levels, and multilingualism should contribute to the quality or excellence of all university activities: teaching and learning, research and management.

Some outstanding actions and outcomes

The plan was approved in 2011 and implemented at UJI over the following seven years. Some of the actions developed were especially effective.

In order to attain the objective of increasing the number of people with a certified level of English, more language courses and certification exams with a reduced fee were organized by the university language service, so that in two years more than 1000 university members achieved a language certificate.

It was important for the university to guarantee the use of several languages in the institutional online tools and texts, and therefore to have a clear policy for the internal use of languages. In order to reach this objective, the language service published a Manual for Language Use so that everyone could check the languages to be used in each situation. For example, when sending an email message to all the students at the university, versions in Valencian, Spanish and sometimes English, depending on the topic of the message, had to be included.

The plan made multilingual teaching a priority for the university. That meant that all lecturers should be ready to teach in any of the three languages. In order to achieve this objective it was considered necessary that all new tenured teachers should have at least a B2 level in English. After two years, 23 teachers in all areas achieved a certificate at this level, and in order to assist them a Guide for Multilingual Teaching was published.

All in all, after the seven years in which the multilingual plan was in force, 80% of the actions were accomplished. Languages were the focus of many meetings of the various committees at the university and, after much debate, UJI achieved the culture and image of a multilingual university. Language matters were considered in a transversal way; that is, all university members were involved in the language plan. The use of languages for internal communication was clearly defined and many more university members became multilingual after taking courses and getting their certification. There were more courses taught in English in all academic fields, with more teacher training and support, and teaching in English was recognized by the institution with a reduction of the lecturers' teaching load to give them more time to prepare their classes. Multilingualism was considered a key element in the improved quality of the university, among its members and also by external stakeholders, which should lead to the attraction of more and better students and a higher position in university rankings.

Conclusion

Quality has been defined as the nature or distinguishing characteristic of something, as well as a degree of excellence or superiority in kind. When planning a language policy for a particular higher education institution, it is essential to define the quality of both individual and societal multilingualism in context. In addition, at least three kinds of achievements should be central to the process of teaching and learning content and language in an integrated way: language achievements, literacy achievements and content achievements. Furthermore, three groups of factors conditioning multilingual education need to be given special consideration: situational factors, pedagogical factors and individual factors.

There is no one model for all. Language policies have to be adapted to the context – the time, place and circumstances in which they have to be implemented – and they have to be materialized in language plans. Even so, there are some recommendations that may be valid for language policies and plans in most contexts. In order to guarantee success, all stakeholders (or as many as possible) must be in agreement with the objectives of the plan. Although there will always be several opinions, it is better to have meetings with as many involved groups and individuals as possible so that they feel part of the plan. Even external stakeholders are important: people responsible for previous educational levels, students' families, media and employers, as languages are always socially and politically sensitive.

Institutions should ascertain whether they can devote some of their budget to recognizing the efforts made to comply with the actions in order to reach the objectives of the plan, as with no budget or a much reduced one it is very difficult to get teachers, students and academic staff to put in the extra effort required. There should be short-, mid- and long-term objectives, and their accomplishment should have a strict and detailed follow-up. The timing of objectives may be changed over time if they cannot be accomplished as expected. A strict periodic follow-up can help to redefine the plan when needed. And, finally, there is a need for a system to control quality as degree of excellence regarding the language use, the achievements of students regarding language, literacy and content, the improvement in education programmes and the internationalization of the institution, which are very often the ultimate aims for a language policy. Quality is, therefore, essential and a key word in all policies.

With regard to the future, my view is that multilingualism will continue to evolve, not only at Universitat Jaume I and in the society it serves, but also in the world. I believe that in the future all individuals will be multilingual: there will be little space for monolingualism and individualism as every individual will be a part of an extensive and complex network of digital and personal relationships, requiring the social and professional command of several languages.

Note

(1) It was distributed to about 50 students taking a course in academic English in their second year of the bachelor's degree in English studies at Universitat Jaume I, in May 2018.

References

Aguilar, M. and Muñoz, C. (2013) The effect of proficiency on CLIL benefits in engineering students in Spain. *International Journal of Applied Linguistics* 24 (1), 1–18.

Arnbjörnsdóttir, B. (2017) Transitioning EAL students from EFL classes to EMI programs at the University of Iceland. Paper presented at the ICLHE 2017 Conference, Copenhagen.

Aronin, L. and Hufeisen, B. (eds) (2010) *The Exploration of Multilingualism: Development of Research on L3, Multilingualism and Multiple Language Acquisition*. Amsterdam: John Benjamins.

Baetens Beardsmore, H. (1982) *Bilingualism: Basic Principles*. Clevedon: Multilingual Matters.

Bazo Martínez, P. and González Álvarez, D. (coord.) (2017) *Documento Marco de Política Lingüística para la Internacionalización del Sistema Universitario Español*. Madrid: CRUE-IC. See https://is.muni.cz/do/rect/metodika/VaV/vyzkum/hr4mu/CRUE_DMPL_14.10.16_EN.pdf.

Bhatia, T.K. and Ritchie, W.C. (eds) (2012) *The Handbook of Bilingualism and Multilingualism*. Chichester: Blackwell.

Bialystok, H. (2001) *Bilingualism in Development: Language, Literacy and Cognition*. Cambridge: Cambridge University Press.

Canagarajah, A.S. (2009) The plurilingual tradition and the English language in South Asia. In L. Lim and E.-L. Low (eds) *Multilingual, Globalizing Asia: Implications for Policy and Education* (pp. 5–22). AILA Review 22. Amsterdam: John Benjamins.

Cenoz, J. (2013) Defining multilingualism. *Annual Review of Applied Linguistics* 33, 3–18.

Cenoz, J. and Gorter, D. (2019) Educational policy and multilingualism. In D. Singleton and L. Aronin (eds) *Twelve Lectures on Multilingualism* (pp. 101–132). Bristol: Multilingual Matters.

Chen, H., Han, J. and Wright, D. (2020) An investigation of lecturers' teaching through English as a medium of instruction: A case of higher education in China. *Sustainability* 12 (10), 4046.

Coste, D., Moore, D. and Zarate, G. (2009) *Plurilingual and Pluricultural Competence: Studies Towards a Common European Framework of Reference for Language Learning and Teaching*. Strasbourg: Council of Europe. See https://rm.coe.int/168069d29b (accessed 15 June 2020).

Cots, J.M., Lasagabaster, D. and Garrett, P. (2012) Multilingual policies and practices of universities in three bilingual regions in Europe. *International Journal of the Sociology of Language* 216, 7–32.

Council of Europe (2001) *Common European Framework of Reference for Languages*. See https://www.coe.int/en/web/common-european-framework-reference-languages (accessed 15 June 2020).

Council of Europe (2007) *From Linguistic Diversity to Plurilingual Education: Guide for the Development of Language Education Policies in Europe*. Strasbourg: Council of Europe. See https://rm.coe.int/16806a892c (accessed 17 June 2020).

Council of Europe (2018) *Common European Framework of Reference for Languages: Companion Volume with New Descriptors*. Strasbourg: Council of Europe. See https://rm.coe.int/cefr-companion-volume-with-new-descriptors-2018/1680787989.

Cummins, J. (2000) *Language, Power and Pedagogy: Bilingual Children in the Crossfire*. Clevedon: Multilingual Matters.

de Groot, A.M.B. (2011) *Language and Cognition in Bilinguals and Multilinguals: An Introduction*. New York: Psychology Press.
de Saint Georges, I. (2013) Multilingualism, multimodality and the future of education research. In I. de Saint-Georges and J.-J. Weber (eds) *Multilingualism and Multimodality: Current Challenges for Educational Studies* (pp. 1–8). Rotterdam: Sense. See http://orbilu.uni.lu/bitstream/10993/9135/1/1d.%20Introduction%20 08022013.pdf (accessed 15 June 2020).
Doiz, A., Lasagabaster, D. and Sierra, J.M. (2013) *English-Medium Instruction at Universities: Global Challenges*. Bristol: Multilingual Matters.
European Commission (2017) *Digital Competence Framework for Educators (DigCompEdu)*. See https://ec.europa.eu/jrc/en/digcompedu (accessed 15 June 2020).
Fortanet-Gómez, I. (2012) Academics' beliefs about language use and proficiency in Spanish multilingual higher education. *AILA Review* 25, 48–63.
Fortanet-Gómez, I. (2013) *CLIL in Higher Education: Towards a Multilingual Language Policy*. Bristol: Multilingual Matters.
García, O. (2009) *Bilingual Education in the 21st century: A Global Perspective*. Oxford: Wiley/Blackwell.
Generalitat Valenciana (2018) *LEY 4/2018, de 21 de febrero, de la Generalitat, por la que se regula y promueve el plurilingüismo en el sistema educativo valenciano* [2018/1773]. See https://www.dogv.gva.es/datos/2018/02/22/pdf/2018_1773.pdf.
Genesee, F. (2004) Bilingualism for majority language students. In T.K. Bhatia and W.C. Ritchie (eds) *The Handbook of Bilingualism* (pp. 547–576). Oxford: Blackwell.
Genesee, F. (2013) Insights into bilingual education from research on immersion programs in Canada. In C. Abello-Contesse, P.M. Chandler, M.D. López-Jiménez and R. Chacón-Beltrán (eds) *Bilingual and Multilingual Education in the 21st century: Building on Experience* (pp. 24–41). Bristol: Multilingual Matters.
Genesee, F. and Lindholm-Leary, K. (2013) Two case studies of content-based language education. *Journal of Immersion and Content-Based Language Education* 1 (1), 3–33.
Grabe, W. and Stoller, F.L. (1997) Content-based instruction: Research foundations. In M.A. Snow and D.M. Brinton (eds) *The Content-based Classroom: Perspectives on Integrating Language and Content* (pp. 5–21). New York: Longman.
Grosjean, F. (2010) *Bilingual: Life and Reality*. Cambridge, MA: Harvard University Press.
Halbach, A.M. (2012) Teaching (in) the foreign language in a CLIL context: Towards a new approach. In R. Breeze, C. Llamas Saíz, C. Martínez Pasamar and C. Tabernero Sala (eds) *Integration of Theory and Practice in CLIL* (pp. 1–14). Amsterdam: Rodopi.
Hamers, J.F. and Blanc, M.H.A. (eds) (2000) *Bilinguality and Bilingualism*. Cambridge: Cambridge University Press.
Heras, A. and Lasagabaster, D. (2015) The impact of CLIL on affective factors and vocabulary learning. *Language Teaching Research* 19 (1), 70–88.
Herdina, P. and Jessner, U. (2002) *A Dynamic Model of Multilingualism*. Clevedon: Multilingual Matters.
Hornberger, N.H. (2002) Multilingual language policies and the continua of biliteracy: An ecological approach. *Language Policy* 1 (1), 27–51.
Khair, A.U., Rosmayanti, V. and Firman, A. (2020) Translanguaging pedagogy in promoting higher order thinking skills (HOTS) in Indonesian higher education. *Asian EFL Journal* 27 (2), 259–287.
Kreber, C. (2009) The modern research university and its disciplines: The interplay between contextual and context-transcendent influences on teaching. In C. Kreber (ed.) *The University and its Disciplines: Teaching and Learning Within and Beyond Disciplinary Boundaries* (pp. 3–18). New York: Routledge.
Kyppö, A. and Natri, T. (2016) Promoting multilingual communicative competence through multimodal academic learning situations. Paper presented at the 23rd EUROCALL Conference, Limassol, 24–27 August. See https://eric.ed.gov/?id=ED572151 (accessed 15 June 2020).

Laal, M. and Ghodsi, S.M. (2012) Benefits of collaborative learning. *Procedia – Social and Behavioral Sciences* 31, 486–490.

Lambert, W.E. and Tucker, G.R. (1972) *Bilingual Education of Children: The St. Lambert Experiment*. Rowley, MA: Newbury House.

Lin, A.M.Y. (2018) Theories of trans/languaging and trans-semiotizing: Implications for content-based education classrooms. *International Journal of Bilingual Education and Bilingualism* 22 (1), 5–16. doi:10.1080/13670050.2018.1515175

Lopriore, L. (2017) Scaffolding continuity in language education. From CLIL to EMI: A way and ways. Paper presented at the ICLHE 2017 Conference, Copenhagen.

Lyster, R. (2007) *Learning and Teaching Languages Through Content: A Counterbalanced Approach*. Amsterdam: Rodopi.

Martin, N. (1976) Language across the curriculum: A paradox and its potential for change. *Educational Review* 28 (3), 206–219.

Mazak, C. and Carroll, K. (2017) *Translanguaging in Higher Education: Beyond Monolingual Ideologies*. Bristol: Multilingual Matters.

MECD (Ministerio de Educación, Cultura y Deporte) (2016) *Estrategia para la internacionalización de las universidades españolas 2015–2020*. See https://sede.educacion.gob.es/publiventa/descarga.action?f_codigo_agc=18182&request_locale=en (accessed 15 June 2020).

Menken, K. and García, O. (eds) (2010) *Negotiating Language Education Policies: Educators as Policymakers*. New York: Routledge.

Merriam-Webster (1999) *Merriam-Webster's Collegiate Dictionary* (10th edn). Springfield, MA: Merriam-Webster. See https://www.merriam-webster.com (accessed 15 June 2020).

Moore, D. and Gajo, L. (2009) Introduction: French voices on plurilingualism and pluriculturalism. Theory, significance and perspectives. *International Journal of Multilingualism* 6 (2), 137–153.

Nashaat, N. (2015) Investigating scaffolding in ICL classes in higher education. Paper presented at the ICLHE 2015 Conference, Brussels.

O'Brien, B.A., Yin, B., Li, L., Zhang, D., Chin, C.F., Zhao, S. and Vaish, V. (2014) *Bilingualism, Literacy and Reading Achievement*. NIE Working Paper Series No. 4. Singapore: National Institute of Education. See https://www.nie.edu.sg/docs/default-source/nie-working-papers/niewp4_for-web_v2.pdf?sfvrsn=2 (accessed 15 June 2020).

Palfreyman, D.M. and van der Walt, C. (2017) *Academic Biliteracies: Multilingual Repertoires in Higher Education*. Bristol: Multilingual Matters.

Pea, R.D. (2004) The social and technological dimensions of scaffolding and related theoretical concepts for learning, education and human activity. *Journal of Learning Sciences* 13 (3), 423–451.

Robin, J. and Guth, S. (2015) Collaborative online international learning. An emerging format for internationalizing curricula. In A.S. Moore and S. Simon (eds) *Globally Networked Teaching in the Humanities: Theories and Practices* (pp. 15–27). New York: Routledge.

Silva, T. and Brice, C. (2004) Research in teaching writing. *Annual Review of Applied Linguistics* 24, 70–106.

Singleton, D. and Aronin, L. (eds) (2019) *Twelve Lectures on Multilingualism*. Bristol: Multilingual Matters.

Smit, U. (2010) *English as a Lingua Franca in Higher Education: A Longitudinal Study of Classroom Discourse*. Amsterdam: Mouton de Gruyter.

Smit, U. and Dafouz, E. (eds) (2013) *Integrating Content and Language in Higher Education: An Introduction to English Medium Policies, Conceptual Issues and Research Practices across Europe*. AILA Review 25, 1–12. Amsterdam: John Benjamins.

Stoller, F.L. (2002) Project work: A means to promote language and content. In J.C. Richards and W.A. Renandya (eds) *Methodology in Language Teaching: An Anthology of Current Practice* (pp. 107–119). Cambridge: Cambridge University Press.
Swales, J. (2000) Languages for specific purposes. *Annual Review of Applied Linguistics* 20, 59–76.
Thibault, P.J. (2017) The reflexivity of human languaging and Nigel Love's two orders of language. *Language Sciences* 61, 74–85.
UNESCO (2003) *Education in a Multilingual World*. Paris: UNESCO.
van der Walt, C. (2013) *Multilingual Higher Education: Beyond English Medium Orientations*. Bristol: Multilingual Matters.
Vila i Moreno, F.J. (2009) Language in education policies in the Catalan language area. In J. Cenoz and D. Gorter (eds) *Multilingualism and Minority Languages. AILA Review* 21, 31–48.
Zhang, Z. (2018) English-medium instruction policies in China: Internationalisation of higher education. *Journal of Multilingual and Multicultural Development* 39, 542–555.

3 Glocalization and Internationalization in University Language Policy Making

Kyria Finardi, Pat Moore and Felipe Guimarães

Introduction

The conceptual link between globalization and internationalization is so close that it is hard to know whether internationalization is an agent of globalization or a result but, as Wächter (2000: 9) reminds us, they differ in implementation. While globalization is reactive, 'relatively uncontrolled' (unbridled, some might say) internationalization (in theory at least) is proactive, moulded by 'conscious action'. In other words, it is planned. In this chapter we address the planning question from a language policy perspective.

Globalization has led to an increase in the flows of people, information and goods, and greater contact between people from diverse linguistic and cultural backgrounds in diverse linguistic and cultural foregrounds. This naturally creates a tension between local and global and a need for a counterbalance. This can be described as the need to *glocalize*, that is, to react to global forces while maintaining local identity and values.

One of the first authors to discuss glocalization was Robertson (1995). The term 'glocal' derived from an agricultural principle (in Japan) to adapt farming techniques to local conditions. It was also adopted in Japanese business, when using a global outlook adapted to local conditions – it became a marketing buzzword at the beginning of the 1990s. Within the world of business, glocalization is related to the 'tailoring and advertising of goods and services on a near-global basis to increasingly differentiated local and particular markets' (Robertson, 1995: 28). This concept has been used in other contexts/fields to describe the tensions between local assertions in contrast to globalizing trends, situations in which, as Robertson (1995: 29) noted, 'the very idea of locality is sometimes cast as a form of opposition or resistance to the hegemonically global'.

If globalization is in diametric opposition to glocalization, in the case of internationalization in higher education there is increased discussion about what is known as internationalization at home (IaH). An early (and oft-cited) definition of the concept of internationalization in higher education was proposed by Knight (1993) as 'The process of integrating an international dimension into the research, teaching and services function of higher education' but, as Wächter (2000: 5) notes, the definition is rather superficial. In Europe one of the principle drivers of internationalization was the original Erasmus programme (1987–2013) which focused primarily on student mobility and secondarily on teacher/researcher mobility. The Erasmus goal was that 10% of European students should engage in mobility but concern for the other 90%, coupled with charges of elitism, has led to a reassessment of the notion, and in a major European study published in 2015 de Wit *et al.* proposed an extended definition:

> The **intentional** process of integrating an international, intercultural, or global dimension into the purpose, functions and delivery of post-secondary education, **in order to enhance the quality of education and research for all students and staff, and to make a meaningful contribution to society.** (European Parliament, 2015: 29, emphasis in original)

This revised initiative is in favour of local enrichment – internationalization at home – to offset the emphasis on mobility, such as: a focus on interculturality; internationalization of the curriculum; and the recruitment of international staff and/or bilingual education explicitly fostering L2 acquisition (for further discussion, see Balaji, 2018; Crowther *et al.*, 2000; Dafouz & Smit, 2014; Patel & Lynch, 2013; Salimi & Safarzadeh, 2018; Wächter, 2000).

Since globalization (and, consequently, internationalization) increases the contacts between people from different linguistic and cultural backgrounds, language policies are called for to deal with conflicts that might arise from such contacts. Indeed, according to Grin (2003), conflict is bound to occur in contexts where more than one language coexists, giving rise to a need for some kind of intervention in the form of language policies to determine, for example, which languages should be used when, for what purpose and by whom.

Regarding the use of languages in institutional changes as well as in the internationalization process, Hughes (2008) observes that Anglophone countries (mainly Australia, the UK and the United States) have dominated the internationalization of higher education, in particular with regard to student mobility. The spread of English as the lingua franca of academia is well documented and universities wishing to internationalize are encouraged to adopt English-medium instruction (EMI).

Supporters of the use of English in higher education institutions (HEIs) claim that it can 'facilitate social mobility, higher earnings, and integration into the dominant culture' (Ricento, 2006: 8). Nevertheless, this view faces fierce criticism from those who call for a more multilingual approach to internationalization in HEIs, based on the imperative to distinguish internationalization from Anglicization (e.g. Dafouz et al., 2016; de Wit, 2011; Grin, 2018). Many non-Anglophone countries (apart from those in Northern Europe, perhaps) struggle to offer courses in English as a strategy to attract more international students, such as in the case of Brazil (British Council & Faubai, 2018).

This study looks at the tensions embodied in language policy from the perspective of two HEIs located in two different epistemological locations, one in the global North (Spain) and the other in the global South[1] (Brazil).

Review of the Literature

Language policy

Before a definition of language policy is offered, a caveat must be made: Spolsky (2004: 7) warned that 'a simple cause-and-effect approach using only language-related data is unlikely to produce useful accounts of language policy, embedded as it is in a "real world" of contextual variables'. The consideration of these variables is important in relation to an ecology of languages, since the dynamic forces in everyday activity are far more powerful than motivated policies. Indeed, a myriad of variables and changes in society arguably affect language use and choice more than official language policies.

Rajagopalan (2013: 21) defines language policy as discussions about languages intended to create actions of public interest related to the languages that are relevant for the population of a given nation, state or even larger transnational environment. Despite interventions in the form of language policy, conflicts are bound to exist, since language policy is about choice, be it the choice of an accent or expression or of a specific language. It may be the choice of an individual, a group of individuals or a body with authority over a defined group of individuals. It may be found in the language practices of an individual or group or in the beliefs about language of an individual or group. Language policy emerges in the struggles between ideologies and practices, where overt and covert mechanisms are used to manipulate and control the use of languages (Shohamy, 2006). Thus, language policies should be observed beyond declared policy statements, because languages have been used, according to Shohamy (2006: xvii), to create, impose and perpetuate 'collective identities, homogenous and hegemonic ideologies, unified standards and categories of inclusion and exclusion'.

In the realm of language policy it is common to see tensions between globalization and glocalization, in exchanges between people defending homogeneity for the sake of a 'national identity' and people who demand the recognition of cultural and linguistic diversity within a single nation. From this perspective, the de facto language policy of a community is more likely to be found in its practices than in its policies. Unless the language policy is consistent with the language practices and beliefs of a given community, and with the other contextual forces that are in play, it may have negligible effects. Research in the context of bilingual education, for example, frequently finds teachers subverting the supposed norms of classroom interaction, with first language use in contexts that are idealized as English-only (see Dearden, 2014, on EMI; or Moore & Nikula, 2016, on CLIL).

Considering that language policies are related to 'economic, political, and social structures and processes' (Ricento, 2006: xi), one can examine the effects of ideologies about language by observing language practices and behaviours. These policies reflect power relations among various social groups as well as political and economic interests, in a world where the notion of nation-state with a single language is constantly being discussed and deconstructed. This is why language policies need to be discussed, so that individuals can define what is meaningful and worthwhile regarding (different) language(s) use. Following Spolsky (2004), we distinguish between three aspects of language policy, namely practices, beliefs and planning. Although we focus mostly on the third component at the institutional level, we will attempt to inform the discussion with the practices and beliefs prevalent in the two communities when possible.

Regarding the development of language policies, it is important to bear in mind that 'language policy for any independent nation state will reveal the complex interplay of four interdependent but often conflicting factors: the actual sociolinguistic situation; a set of beliefs [...]; the recent pull of English as a global language; and the even more recent pressure for attention to the rights of linguistic minorities' (Spolsky, 2004: 133).

As such and as previously mentioned, in this study we will attempt to analyse the language policies at Pablo de Olavide University, Spain (UPO) and the Federal University of Espírito Santo, Brazil (UFES), taking into account these four factors and their impact in terms of the tensions with regard to glocalization in these two contexts.

Many authors would agree that any account of multilingualism today should include an analysis of the role of English (e.g. Finardi & Csillagh, 2016; Jenkins, 2015). In the case of UPO in Spain, given the predominance of its use as a lingua franca in Europe, we might expect English to be promoted. The scenario is somewhat different in Brazil, where English does not have the status of a lingua franca (Finardi, 2014, 2016). Regarding the ideologies affecting language policies in Brazil, much was inherited from Portugal, a country with an ideological monolingual national policy. It is possible to observe a trace of this policy in the creation of the community of Portuguese-speaking countries (Angola, Brazil, Cape Verde, Guinea-Bissau, Mozambique and São Tomé e Príncipe) formed in 1999 to guarantee the diffusion of Portuguese. Language policy in Brazil and in Latin America has been assimilationist in the sense that colonial languages were imposed on speakers of other languages. Generalizing the linguistic panorama in Brazil, Spolsky (2004: 148) claims that 'in practice (it is) multilingual in various degrees, but in ideology by-and-large monolingual'.

Language policies and quality in higher education

The notion of quality, frequently collocated with terms like 'control', 'assurance' and 'assessment', emerged in the private sector during the late 1970s and early 1980s. While 'quality' seems self-evident, since researchers (in higher education) began to explore the concept, a variety of interpretations have been proffered, including: 'fitness for purpose' (e.g. Woodhouse, 1999: 29); relevance (e.g. Meneghel *et al.*, 2018) and/or 'stakeholder priorities' (e.g. Gvaramadze, 2008: 445) (see Green, 1994, for an overview; Fortanet-Gómez, this volume).

Given the multifarious nature of the notion, it would be very easy for individual institutions to claim quality. This has led to an increase in activities external to HEIs known as external quality reviews (EQR), developed by various agencies at national, regional and sectoral levels. Such agencies hold HEIs accountable for the resources they receive by providing independent assessment/accreditation of quality, thus assisting institutions to improve their quality.

Growing international cooperation in higher education has created peer pressure for institutions to develop strong quality assurance (QA). The Trends 2015 report on learning and teaching in European universities notes that since the Bologna Process was launched, 22 countries have established national QAs for education, with half of these being set up since 2005 (European Commission, 2010). Eleven countries in the European Higher Education Area (EHEA) do not have established QAs, and those that do have recently broadened their mission to include additional dimensions such as the social dimension, lifelong learning and internationalization. Considering the legally binding power of QA, it is seen by HEIs as a powerful driver for institutional change.

In Europe, a document on quality was jointly produced in 2015 by the European Association for Quality Assurance in Higher Education (ENQA), the European Students' Union (ESU), the European University Association (EUA) and the European Association of Institutions in Higher Education (EURASHE). The declared goal of the document, *Standards and Guidelines for Quality Assurance in the European Higher Education Area* (ESG), is to contribute to the common understanding of QA for learning/teaching, across borders and among various stakeholders.

Engagement with processes for QA (particularly external) allows European HEIs to demonstrate quality and increase transparency, helping to build mutual trust and recognition of qualifications and programmes (e.g. EURASHE, 2015). Therefore, the ESG focus on quality related to learning/teaching in HEIs includes the learning environment and links to research/innovation. Moreover, ESG applies to all HEIs in the EHEA, regardless of the mode of study or place of delivery.

Wächter *et al.* (2015) provide a useful overview of the intricacies of quality management in HEIs from an international perspective and include case studies of both Spain (Annex, pp. 46–53) and Brazil (Annex, pp. 61–66). In Spain, a national body, ANECA (National Agency for Quality Assessment and Accreditation), works in tandem with regional agencies to oversee the question from three main perspectives: in the first instance, all degree programmes must be officially approved (accreditation); institutions are monitored and audited regularly; and lecturers and researchers have to go through evaluation processes in order to obtain tenure. In Brazil, different bodies are responsible for undergraduate and postgraduate programmes, SINAES (the National Higher Education Assessment System) and CAPES (Coordination for the Development of Higher Education Personnel), respectively. See below for further discussion.

Specifically relating to quality and internationalization, Knight and de Wit (1999) developed a project called the 'Internationalisation Quality Review Process' (IQRP) in order to: (a) increase awareness of the need for quality assessment/assurance in the internationalization of HEIs; (b) develop a process in which HEIs can use a set of guidelines to assess/enhance the quality of the internationalization process; and (c) strengthen the contribution of internationalization for the quality of HEIs.

In a similar vein, but with a research-based focus, Rubio-Alcala *et al.* (2019) conducted a systematic review designed to validate the strength of evidence supporting quality indicators in plurilingual practices in higher education. What they found, however, was a paucity of research that could meet the standards of unbiased reporting. They argue that there is a need to attend to the quality standards of the research itself and ensure that it is not biased at the outset.

Hughes (2008: 111) warns that 'institutions without a robust language policy, adequate preparatory training and ongoing support may, [therefore,] damage more than the quality of teaching'. Elsewhere he suggests: 'Excellent non-English-speaking institutions cannot compete to train "global citizens" and this works to exclude their educational and national values […] for promoting international understanding' (Hughes, 2008: 123). In other words, some institutions may be abandoning local/national values in favour of English as an international academic language, leaving international understanding (and multilingualism) behind. That is why the discussion around language policies in the context of internationalization of higher education and the tensions to glocalize afforded by them is so important, especially in non-Anglophone countries.

Language policies for higher education in Brazil

The study of language policies in Brazil is very challenging because there is no convergence between policies proposed for the various stages of education (primary, secondary and tertiary). In higher education, Finardi and Archanjo (2018) suggest that language policies can be analysed in internationalization programmes and actions. In the case of Brazil, these authors investigated language policies embodied in the internationalization initiatives *Science without Borders* (SwB), *English without Borders* (EwB) and *Languages without Borders* (LwB). These programmes will be discussed below.

Language policies for internationalization in Brazil

In higher education, until recently there was no explicit policy for foreign languages. However, that has changed dramatically over the last decade, due to the increasing internationalization of Brazilian institutions with public investment in mobility programmes such as Science without Borders in 2011–2015. SwB was funded by the Brazilian Ministry of Education (MEC) and the Ministry of Science, Technology and Innovation (MCTI), with an investment of around 10 billion BRL (around €2 billion), and sent more than 100,000 students abroad. Finardi and Archanjo (2018) suggest that two of the most important legacies of SwB are: (1) the inclusion of internationalization in the institutional plans of Brazilian universities; and (2) the creation of the LwB programme.

In 2012, the English without Borders programme was created in order to improve the English language proficiency of SwB applicants. EwB offered free online courses, face-to-face classes and a proficiency test (TOEFL ITP) for university students and SwB candidates. In 2014, EwB was expanded and renamed 'Languages without Borders' to include eight languages: English, German, French, Spanish, Italian, Japanese, Chinese and Portuguese as a foreign language (PFL), becoming a major internationalization programme and language policy driver in Brazil. Although SwB was discontinued in 2015, LwB was still going strong and was funded by the Brazilian government, at the time of writing, having recently induced the creation of language policies for internationalization in its member institutions. Indeed, the language policy at UFES was promulgated to meet the requirements of the LwB call and, were it not for this programme, perhaps UFES would not have an official language policy today.

It is important to note how LwB represents an implicit language policy and how it is 'glocalized' in the context of UFES. The Brazilian Coordination for the Development of Higher Education Personnel

(CAPES) financed part of the LwB activities. As previously mentioned, of the three actions offered by the programme (face-to-face and online language courses and language proficiency tests), only the actions related to English are financed by CAPES. The offer of other actions in other languages is left to each member institution to decide (and finance).

In the Brazilian context of higher education, we should also acknowledge the role of Faubai, the Brazilian Association for International Education, which promotes annual events to discuss internationalization and related topics such as the role of foreign languages. Faubai has a Language Policy for Internationalization working group which has produced a guide for institutional language policies for internationalization.[2] Another action by the Faubai working group was a survey carried out with the support of the British Council (BC), to find out the number of courses delivered in foreign languages in Brazilian HEIs. This led to the publication of the Brazilian 2018–2019 EMI Guide with the offer of EMI courses in Brazil. A comparison of the two versions of the EMI Brazilian survey that produced the EMI Brazilian guide carried out by the British Council and Faubai in 2016 and in 2018 showed a steep increase in the EMI offered in Brazil, as reported in Martinez (2016) and Gimenez et al. (2018).

In 2017, CAPES launched a public call for funding postgraduate programmes, called CAPES-PrInt, for the internationalization of Brazilian HEIs, which required a strategic plan to develop proficiency in foreign languages (especially English) within the academic community. Numerous HEIs submitted proposals for funding but only 25 universities were selected (among them, UFES). The CAPES-PrInt call was inductive, requiring candidate institutions to formalize internationalization and language policies. This reflected the requirements of the LwB programme one year earlier, specifically for language policies.

Considering that UFES recently approved its internationalization plan and language policy resolution, we can claim that both the LwB and the CAPES-PrInt call had a strong influence on these documents. Moreover, if we analyse the role of what are considered 'priority countries' for academic mobility[3] and English in these programmes and documents, it is possible to see a globalization trend that recognizes the hegemonic force (and internationalization potential) of the global North and English.

CAPES' language policy is so explicitly in favour of English as an academic lingua franca that any researcher aiming to apply for funds at CAPES has to deliver the proposal in Portuguese/English only. Another trace of an inductive language policy that we can see embodied in the CAPES PrInt call is that Portugal is not on the list of 'priority' countries for Brazilian academics. Perhaps this is a washback effect of the SwB program which, as noted above, received much criticism on account of sending many Brazilians to Portugal simply because of lack of proficiency in foreign languages.

Taken together, the analysis of national policies embodied in Brazilian programmes such as LwB and the CAPES-PrInt call shows at least three tendencies: (1) a globalizing tendency by locating English as an international language; (2) an inductive nature by affecting (and sometimes dictating) institutional language and internationalization policies; and (3) a glocalizing nature, evident in the resistance to the previous two actions and efforts made by some of these institutions (UFES included), to guarantee the rights of minority languages such as Brazilian sign language (LIBRAS), indigenous languages and other foreign languages. This will become evident in the analysis of language policies at UFES below.

Language policies for internationalization in Spain

The cornerstone of rules and regulations regarding language use in Spain rests on the Spanish Constitution of 1978. In Article 3, it is stated that Castilian is the official language of the State and that all Spaniards must know and have the right to use it. That said, Spain is far from being a monolingual nation. Basque, Galician and Catalan are recognized as co-official languages and there is a wealth of other regional languages such as Valencian, Aragonese or Asturiano which feature in regional legislation. The multiple languages of Spain are considered a wealth and cultural heritage, to be respected and protected.

Regarding the scenario in HEIs, two points need to be made. Firstly, it should be acknowledged that Spain is very pro-European (Lorenzo & Moore, 2009) and tends to adhere to European goals. Secondly, as noted previously, responsibility for education is divided between national and regional ministries and so there is variation. That said, national legislation does factor other languages into the equation. For example, the *Real Decree 412/2014* (https://www.boe.es/buscar/act.php?id=BOE-A-2014-6008) states that, for students who obtained a degree abroad, Spanish universities can use admission procedures in English or in other foreign languages. Indeed, the *Real Decree 99/2011* (https://www.boe.es/buscar/act.php?id=BOE-A-2011-2541), which indicates the rules for higher education at the doctoral level, states in Article 15.1.b that part of the doctoral thesis (at least the abstract and conclusions) must be written and presented in one of the common languages of that specific field of knowledge, which may be different from the official languages in Spain. These regulations (among others) indicate that the Spanish government is concerned with the use of multiple languages in Spanish higher education.

In 2014 the Spanish Ministry of Education, Culture and Sport (MECD) published the *Strategy for the Internationalization of Spanish Universities* (2015–2020) with the declared intention to 'increase Spain's attractiveness and competitiveness within a framework of worldwide competition for talent (students, professors, researchers, professionals, entrepreneurs)' (MECD, 2014: 4). Under the heading of 'Internationalisation

Factors', the document presents a SWOT (strengths, weaknesses, opportunities, threats) analysis of the following areas:

(a) Entry and exit mobility. Talent canvassing.
(b) Recognition of qualifications and study periods.
(c) Accreditation of programmes and teaching staff.
(d) Research. International doctorate programmes.
(e) Transference of knowledge and innovation.
(f) Employability.

The document concludes that the successful internationalization of the Spanish system rests on two main pillars: 'quality and the Spanish language' (MECD, 2014: 23). Recognizing that Spanish is both a widely spoken L1 and an increasingly sought after L2, the document favours dual/bilingual education over (monolingual, i.e. English-only) L2 education:

> Spanish universities, unlike those in other countries, can and must show their commitment to *bilingual qualifications in Spanish and English*, offered to their students, providing tuition in two of the languages that create the most professional opportunities. (MECD, 2014: 23, emphasis added)

In doing so, alongside promoting Spanish as an international language, it is also advocating glocalization and IaH, 'to ensure that the benefits of internationalization also reach the majority of the students who do not study abroad' (MECD, 2014: 24). As noted above, any new degree programme must first be approved by ANECA. When the notion of bilingual degrees was first mooted, the lack of an accreditation process for bilingual degrees presented an initial stumbling block. However, the situation appears to have been resolved since new bilingual degrees are now receiving approval.

More recently, the body known as CRUE (*Conferencia de Rectores de Universidades Españolas*) published a document entitled *Linguistic Policy for the Internationalisation of the Spanish University System* (2017), which has been officially adopted by all public Spanish universities. This document clearly endorses the European Directorate General's report into the Internationalisation of Higher Education (de Wit *et al.*, 2015), as is illustrated by its insistence on the tertiary system comprising three bodies of stakeholders – students, faculty members and administrators – bringing everyone into the discussion. The CRUE document focuses on three key areas of language policy to promote internationalization – certification, training and incentives – addressing each from the perspective of each of three university collectives.

With regard to certification, Spanish university entrance exams (*selectividad*) always include a foreign language (English, French, German or Italian), and since the academic year 2009–2010 undergraduate students have been obliged to certify a minimum B1 level in a foreign language in order to obtain their degree. This has been contentious because not all degree programmes include foreign language teaching and thus some students have been obliged to 'top-up' their university education through parallel (self-funded) study.

Most (if not all) public universities in Spain host language centres where the university community can study and certify competence in foreign languages. They provide a good example of the tensions inherent in internationalization/glocalization. Until recently, most of this certification was dominated by the 'big' European providers (Cambridge, Trinity, Goethe and Alliance Française). However, 2014 saw the establishment of ACLES (*Asociación de Centros de Lenguas en la Enseñanza Superior*), with which many public university language centres have affiliated, resulting in the collaborative development and implantation of a system of 'home-grown' language certification. ACLES is now a member of CERCLES (European Confederation of Language Centres in Higher Education), which means that ACLES certification is increasingly recognized outside Spain. This process arguably presents us with a good example of IaH.

Regarding teacher certification, CRUE proposes a minimum C1 level in the language of instruction for faculty members involved in bilingual courses. This appears to be becoming a standard requirement, albeit one that might benefit from research (Dearden, 2014: 7). In the case of administrative staff, the document adopts a pragmatic stance, and suggests that a sliding scale of B1–C1 be applied in the case of promotions and recruitment, depending on the person's responsibilities.

For students, the idea of training (development) revolves largely around preparation for academic and professional mobility in multilingual, multicultural, social and professional environments. It is noteworthy that the document promotes the development of communicative skills in both the L1 and L2, thus adhering to the MECD's prioritizing of Spanish while emphasizing the bilingual nature of the endeavour. That said, there is terminological fuzziness. In tertiary-level bilingual education, a distinction is sometimes made between teaching *in* another language, EMI (in the case of English), and teaching *through* another language, variously known as ICLHE or CLIL. EMI, in theory at least, implies courses provided in English to students who already have sufficient competence in the language, whereas with ICLHE the assumption would be that students will be developing language skills in tandem with content skills/knowledge.

When addressing training for faculty members the document refers to both teaching 'in' and 'through' foreign languages without seeming to make a distinction, although it does reflect on some of the implications of bilingual instruction:

> not merely the changing of the lingua franca, but also the manner in which the classes are managed, prepared and taught, with specific training given to the use of materials and a redefinition of the assessment model. (CRUE, 2017: 5)

From the perspective of incentives, we find a predictable range of measures designed to increase the linguistic and intercultural capacities of the Spanish system (subsidies, funding, preferential treatment for those involved in bilingual programmes, etc.). But it is also worth pointing out that this section (unlike the other two) explicitly mentions an incentive for incoming international students – a need for 'the necessary linguistic support in the official language(s) of the autonomous community, with courses and timetables adapted to their needs' (CRUE, 2017: 6).

Language Policies at the Federal University of Espírito Santo and Pablo de Olavide University

As stated at the outset of this chapter, the aim of this study is to explore the question of tensions between internationalization and glocalization in bilingual tertiary programmes at a macro-level through the analysis and discussion of the recently published language policies of two public universities located in the geopolitical North (Spain) and South (Brazil). The research design is contrastive, and the method of analysis is qualitative. The language policies of the two institutions (UPO and UFES) will be analysed individually first, and then contrasted, wherever possible, with the beliefs and practices of the academic community.

Language policies at UFES

UFES recently approved a language policy for internationalization[4] as one of the requirements for being a member institution of the LwB programme. UFES language policy was hotly debated in the university community. It required a series of negotiations between the central administration and the language and education departments, which strongly opposed the policy because of its 'internationalization' nature – threatening, according to their view, local identities and languages.

Those who defended this view (of threat) suggested that the policy should include a role for LIBRAS (Brazilian sign language), indigenous languages and other foreign languages in the text. In the end, the will of the central administration prevailed (not before a long political negotiation) and mentions of these languages were removed from the document. The resolution approved by the UFES board does not make any reference to LIBRAS or any indigenous or minority language, thus making it implicit that UFES is aligned with national programmes such as the SwB and EwB and with financing institutions like CAPES regarding their views on the role of English as the most important (and sometimes only) language for internationalization.

With regard to Spolsky's (2004) second component of language policy (practice), we can find some evidence in the language requirements of postgraduate programmes at UFES. Most programmes have an entrance examination test and public call which requires candidates to prove proficiency in one additional language (for master's courses) or in two additional languages (for doctoral courses). The use of the term 'additional' language as opposed to 'foreign' language was intentional here because some postgraduate programmes consider, for example, LIBRAS a first language and so deaf candidates can show proof of Portuguese (as an additional language) to enter, just as foreigners can show proof of Portuguese.

The fact that most postgraduate programmes do not require proof of specific levels of proficiency in English indicates resistance to national organizations and programmes like Faubai, CAPES and the EwB programme, which assign a distinctive role to English in comparison to other foreign languages. Concerning glocalization trends, it is possible to say that the UFES language policy document resists the notion that English is the only 'internationalization' language, as is evident in the mention of foreign languages (rather than English only) in the document and in the requirements of most postgraduate programmes at UFES.

Language policy at UPO

Although it is the youngest public university in Spain, only created in 1997, UPO regularly features in Spanish HEI internationalization rankings. In the 2016 CRUE report *La Universidad Española en Cifras*, it was ranked first in Andalucía and second nationally. Admittedly, this is partly due to mobility. Spain (and Andalucía) is a particularly popular destination among European Erasmus students, so incoming figures are high. The UPO campus also includes the *Centro Universitario Internacional* (CUI), which receives many North American students coming for Spanish language and culture courses. One should note that UPO already offers various practical activities, double degrees and degrees in English.

UPO published its first explicit language policy in 2018. In the introduction, it acknowledges the influence of both the CRUE document discussed above and a regional document, the *Plan Estratégico de Desarrollo de las Lenguas en Andalucía, Horizonte 2020* (PEDLA), published in 2017.[5] In doing so it signals a merging of international and local concerns. While the CRUE document is focused on internationalization, PEDLA is decidedly local and is largely concerned with pre-university education. It is worth noting that Andalucia's bilingual education project is a reference in Europe with over 1000 schools now offering bilingual primary and secondary education. While English dominates, other languages – notably French and German – are also involved. It could be argued, therefore, that students who have experienced bilingual education prior to university should be given the opportunity to continue.

In contrast to UFES, UPO's language policy is not designed solely to promote internationalization. The declared priorities are: to promote the teaching of Spanish (both as L1 and L2); to improve stakeholder linguistic competences (both in L1 and L2s); and to increase the provision of courses and programmes in foreign languages (for example, the university has recently introduced three new double honours degrees in international relations with translating/interpreting in English, French and German). There are also initiatives expressly aimed at IaH, such as the organization of declaredly multilingual social events on campus.

Regarding Spanish, one of the stated goals of the policy is to increase contact between diverse 'groups' in the Spanish foreign language community. As well as the work of the CUI, the document highlights the master's in Spanish as a foreign language (SFL), which is one of the longest running and most popular master's courses on offer at the university. A recent outreach initiative has also seen the organization of free Spanish courses for refugees and immigrants. It is noteworthy that the document goes beyond SFL and encompasses Spanish as an L1. The creation of a new post at the university, *Defensor(a) de español*, something along the lines of an ombudsperson for Spanish, seeks to ensure the 'correct' use of the language, coupled with a proposal to organize support for academic writing in Spanish for the whole university community.

Discussion

In this section we will compare and contrast pertinent aspects of the two language policies:

(1) *Impetus for policy making*
Both universities have drafted language policies in a top-down manner and in response to national policy (LwB in Brazil, and the MECD and CRUE documents in Spain) rather than as local initiatives. This alone might give rise to tensions between national and local. We can observe this in the question of official languages on campus: since both universities are located in officially monolingual regions, we might expect decisions regarding the official language of the institution to be relatively tension free. However, as noted above in the Brazilian context – and spurred by the university staff, some of whom are involved in projects with local Guarani-speaking communities, for example – the question is fairly contentious.

(2) *Stakeholders*
The Brazilian document focuses primarily on staff (both academic and administrative) and less on students, whereas the Spanish document, in line with national guidelines, factors the student body into the equation. Green (1994), noting the expansion of the HEI sector and increasing competition between universities to attract students, identified a trend in Europe for universities to conceive of students as clients (who need to be satisfied). In Brazil we could argue that this is

less relevant because public universities, which are free, are relatively few and far between. Private universities, which account for around 80% of the market in Brazil (Wächter *et al.*, 2015: 165), may need to be more concerned with 'customer satisfaction'; public universities know that the satisfaction lies in successfully obtaining a place.

(3) *Languages of instruction*
   (a) Local languages for native speakers. Potentially one of the most striking differences between the two documents relates to their concern for L1 teaching. UPO's language policy includes measures to support and improve Spanish, even for Spanish L1 speakers; UFES' policy makes no mention of national students. That said, UFES policy is declaredly a policy *for internationalization*.
   (b) Local languages for non-native speakers. UFES does factor in support for Portuguese as a foreign language with the provision of courses for foreigners, but UPO arguably provides more opportunities. This is potentially a pragmatic response to local conditions since UPO hosts many more overseas students than UFES. If UFES' overseas student body were to grow, perhaps new measures would be introduced.
   (c) Other languages. Both universities are promoting courses taught in/through other/additional languages and both lean towards 'mostly English'. That said, UPO's policy includes more measures designed explicitly to further the goal, such as propaedeutic courses for first year students who need additional support to access bilingual streams, and an internal internship programme for (language) students to participate as classroom assistants in courses taught through other languages.

(4) *Teaching in/through other languages*
   (a) The question of *in* or *through* other languages parallels the distinction between EMI and ICLHE (as discussed above). There is clear potential for tension here. A preference for EMI might well be evidenced by a requirement for students enrolling in bilingual streams to provide evidence of a priori linguistic competence. A preference for ICLHE would underline a commitment to language development in tandem with content. Actually, neither university comes out clearly in favour of one or the other stance, suggesting that this may be perceived as a decision for teachers rather than administrators.
   (b) Teacher development. Both universities are planning teacher development focusing on both methodological and linguistic questions. Perhaps the implementation of these programmes will contribute to a greater understanding of the in/through question and more fine-tuning of pedagogical strategies, etc. This remains

to be seen. Research has found that university content teachers in declaredly bilingual scenarios have problems with considering themselves responsible for language development (see, for example, Rubio-Cuenca & Moore, 2018).
(c) Incentivization. UPO is in the process of implementing a rewards scheme for teachers who teach in bilingual streams. For example, they receive a (small) reduction in their teaching load and extra merit in teacher evaluation programmes. Thus far, UFES has not envisaged this kind of incentivization. In the long term they might find it necessary to do so, particularly considering the (small) number of teaching staff who are proficient in a foreign language and the implicit workload.

Conclusion

In this chapter we briefly review questions of internationalization and glocalization/internationalization at home and we discuss some of the intricacies of (language) policy making. We then present the two contexts that provide data for the discussion – Brazil and the Federal University of Espírito Santo (UFES) and Spain and Pablo de Olavide University (UPO). Both are mid-sized public institutions located in the capitals of their respective regions and both have recently published language policies. We have outlined the main similarities and differences between the two documents. What emerges is the importance of context as a driving force. While both universities have been prompted to officialize language policy by top-down (national) policies, both have incorporated local concerns.

From the perspective of quality, both universities envisage the establishment of language policy commissions to monitor the implementation (and potential need for modification) of their policies, yet in both scenarios these are still 'work in progress'. We can therefore observe a concern with quality even in the absence of mechanisms to control, assure or assess it. We might consider this 'emerging quality'.

Concern for quality can also be seen, even if in an emergent state, in the plans for stakeholders, although UPO seems to be ahead of UFES in this respect. Regarding languages for instruction, and perhaps given the status of Spanish and Portuguese (as both L1 and L2) and English (as a lingua franca), the analysis shows that UPO is more aligned with quality concerning the local languages for native speakers, the local languages for non-native speakers and other languages. Finally, in terms of the offer of courses and activities in or through other languages, we can see that once more UPO is more advanced in as much as it provides teacher support and incentives for those willing to teach in/through other languages, while UFES is yet to develop these measures.

Notes

(1) Santos and Meneses (2014) define the global North as a geopolitical rather than a geographical concept, composed of hegemonic countries, whereas the global South is represented as the group of countries of the periphery, regardless of whether they are in the geographical north or not.
(2) http://faubai.org.br/pt-br/wp-content/uploads/2019/01/Documento-do-GT-de-Pol%C3%ADticas-Lingu%C3%ADsticas-da-FAUBAI.pdf
(3) Priority countries are defined in UFES' institutional meetings for strategic planning, being the choice of countries heavily influenced by national guidelines, such as the ones from CAPES.
(4) See http://www.daocs.ufes.br/sites/daocs.ufes.br/files/field/anexo/ilovepdf_merged_0.pdf#overlay-context=resolu%25C3%25A7%25C3%25B5es-de-2018-cepe (accessed 24 August 2018).
(5) https://www.juntadeandalucia.es/export/drupaljda/plan_estrategico.pdf

References

Balaji, S. (2018) Glocalization as globalization: Evolution and transformation of a sociological concept. *International Journal of Multidisciplinary Education Research* 7 (10), 84–96.
British Council and Faubai (2018) *Guide to English as a Medium of Instruction in Brazilian Higher Education Institutions 2018–2019*. São Paulo: British Council.
Council of Europe (2007) *From Linguistic Diversity to Plurilingual Education: Guide for the Development of Language Education Policies in Europe*. Strasbourg: Council of Europe. See https://rm.coe.int/16806a892c (accessed 17 June 2020).
Crowther, P., Joris, M., Otten, M., Nilsson, B., Teekens, H. and Wächter, B. (2000) *Internationalisation at Home: A Position Paper*. Amsterdam: EAIE.
CRUE (Conferencia de Rectores de Universidades Españolas) (2016) *La Universidad Española en Cifras*. See https://www.crue.org/wp-content/uploads/2020/02/UEC_Digital_WEB.pdf (accessed 12 March 2019).
CRUE (Conferencia de Rectores de Universidades Españolas) (2017) *Linguistic Policy for the Internationalisation of the Spanish University System* (English version). See https://www.crue.org/wp-content/uploads/2020/02/Politica_Executive-summary_Version-Final-Reducido.pdf (accessed 12 March 2019).
CRUE (Conferencia de Rectores de Universidades Españolas) (2018) *Código de Universidades*. Madrid: Agencia Estatal Boletín Oficial del Estado.
Dafouz, E. and Smit, U. (2014) Towards a dynamic conceptual framework for English-medium education in multilingual university settings. *Applied Linguistics* 37 (3), 397–415.
Dafouz, E., Hüttner, J. and Smit, U. (2016) University teachers' beliefs of language and content integration in English-medium education in multilingual university settings. In T. Nikula, E. Dafouz, P. Moore and U. Smit (eds) *Conceptualising Integration in CLIL and Multilingual Education* (pp. 123–143). Bristol: Multilingual Matters.
Dearden, J. (2014) *English as a Medium of Instruction, a Growing Global Phenomenon*. Oxford: British Council.
de Wit, H. (2011) Globalisation and internationalization of higher education. *Revista de Universidad y Sociedad del Conocimiento* 8 (2), 241–248.
de Wit, H., Hunter, F., Howard, L. and Egron-Polak, E. (2015) *Internationalisation of Higher Education*. Brussels: European Parliament.
EURASHE (2015) *Standards and Guidelines for Quality Assurance in the European Higher Education Area*. Brussels: European Association of Institutions in Higher Education.

European Commission, Eurydice Network (2010) *Focus on Higher Education in Europe 2010: New Report on the Impact of the Bologna Process*. Brussels: European Commission.
European Parliament (2015) *Internationalisation of Higher Education* (Study). Brussels: European Parliament, Directorate General for Internal Policies, Policy Department B, Structural and Cohesion Policies – Culture and Education.
Finardi, K.R. (2014) The slaughter of Kachru's five sacred cows in Brazil: Affordances of the use of English as an international language. *Studies in English Language Teaching* 2 (4), 401–411.
Finardi, K.R. (2016) Globalization and English in Brazil. In K.R. Finardi (ed.) *English in Brazil: Views, Policies and Programs* (pp. 15–36). Londrina, PR: Eduel.
Finardi, K.R. and Archanjo, R. (2018) Washback effects of the Science without Borders, English without Borders and Language without Borders programs in Brazilian language policies and rights. In M. Siiner, F. Hult and T. Kupisch (eds) *Language Policy and Language Acquisition Planning* (pp. 173–185). Cham: Springer.
Finardi, K.R. and Csillagh, V. (2016) Globalization and linguistic diversity in Switzerland: Insights from the roles of national languages and English as a foreign language. In S. Grucza, M. Olpinska-Szkielko and P. Romanowski (eds) *Advances in Understanding Multilingualism* (pp. 59–79). Frankfurt am Main: Peter Lang.
Gimenez, T., Sarmento, S., Archanjo, R., Zicman, R. and Finardi, K. (2018) *Guide to English as a Medium of Instruction in Brazilian Higher Education Institutions 2018–2019*. São Paulo: British Council. See http://faubai.org.br/britishcouncilfaubaiguide2018.pdf.
Green, D. (1994) *What is Quality in Higher Education?* Buckingham: Society for Research into Higher Education (SHRE) and Open University Press.
Grin, F. (2003) *Language Policy Evaluation and the European Charter for Regional or Minority Languages*. London: Palgrave Macmillan.
Grin, F. (2018) Distinguishing internationalisation from Anglicisation in higher education: Diagnosis and strategies. Paper presented at the Ethical Forum of the University Foundation, Brussels, 6 December.
Gvaramadze, I. (2008) From quality assurance to quality enhancement in the European Higher Education Area. *European Journal of Education* 43 (4), 443–455.
Hughes, R. (2008) Internationalisation of higher education and language policy: Questions of quality and equity. *Higher Education Management and Policy* 20 (1), 111–128.
Jenkins, J. (2015) Repositioning English and multilingualism in English as a lingua franca. *Englishes in Practice* 2 (3), 49–85.
Knight, J. (1993) Internationalization: Management strategies and issues. *International Education Magazine* 9 (6), 21–22.
Knight, J. and de Wit, H. (1999) An introduction to the IQRP project and process. In J. Knight and H. de Wit (eds) *Quality and Internationalisation in Higher Education* (pp. 45–59). Paris: OECD.
Lorenzo, F. and Moore, P. (2009) European language policies in monolingual Southern Europe: Implementation and outcomes. *European Journal of Language Policy* 1 (2), 121–135.
Martinez, R. (2016) English as a medium of instruction (EMI) in Brazilian higher education: Challenges and opportunities. In K.R. Finardi (ed.) *English in Brazil: Views, Policies and Programs* (pp. 191–228). Londrina, PR: Eduel.
MECD (Ministerio de Educación, Cultura y Deporte, Gobierno de España (2014) *Strategy for the Internationalisation of Spanish Universities 2015–2020* (English version). See https://studylib.es/doc/4609626/strategy-for-the-internationalisation-of-spanish-universi... (accessed 18 April 2019).
Meneghel, S.M., Camargo, M.S. and Speller, P. (2018) *De Havana a Córdoba: Duas décadas de educação superior na América Latina*. Blumenau: Editora Nova Letra.

Moore, P. and Nikula, T. (2016) Translanguaging in CLIL. In T. Nikula, E. Dafouz, P. Moore and U. Smit (eds) *Conceptualising Integration in CLIL and Multilingual Education* (pp. 211–234). Bristol: Multilingual Matters.

Patel, F. and Lynch, H. (2013) Glocalization as an alternative to internationalization in higher education: Embedding positive glocal learning perspectives. *International Journal of Teaching and Learning in Higher Education* 25 (2), 223–230.

Rajagopalan, K. (2013) Política linguística: Do que é que se trata, afinal? In C. Nicolaides, K.A. Silva, R. Tilio and C.H. Rocha (eds) *Política e Políticas Linguísticas* (pp. 19–42). Campinas, SP: Pontes Editores.

Ricento, T. (2006) *An Introduction to Language Policy: Theory and Method*. Malden, MA: Blackwell.

Robertson, R. (1995) Glocalization: Time-space and homogeneity-heterogeneity. In M. Featherstone, S. Lash and R. Robertson (eds) *Global Modernities* (pp. 25–44). London: Sage.

Rubio-Alcalá, F.D., Arco-Tirado, J.L., Fernández-Martín, F.D., López-Lechuga, R., Barrios, E. and Pavón-Vázquez, V. (2019) A systematic review on evidences supporting quality indicators of bilingual, plurilingual and multilingual programs in higher education. *Educational Research Review* 27, 191–204.

Rubio Cuenca, F. and Moore, P. (2018) Teacher attitudes to language in university bilingual education. *Porta Linguarum (Special Issue 3: Addressing Bilingualism in Higher Education: Policies and Implementation Issues)*, 89–102.

Salimi, E.A. and Safazardeh, M.M. (2018) A model and questionnaire of language education glocalization in Iran. *International Journal of Instruction* 12 (1), 1639–1652.

Santos, B.S. and Meneses, M.P. (2014) *Epistemologias do Sul*. São Paulo: Cortez Editora.

Shohamy, E. (2006) *Language Policy: Hidden Agendas and New Approaches*. New York: Routledge.

Spolsky, B. (2004) *Language Policy*. Cambridge: Cambridge University Press.

Wächter, B. (2000) Internationalisation at home – the context. In P. Crowther, M. Joris, M. Otten, B. Nilsson, H. Teekens and B. Wächter (eds) *Internationalisation at Home: A Position Paper* (pp. 5–13). Amsterdam: EAIE.

Wächter, B., Kelo, M., Lam, Q., Effertz, P., Jost, C. and Kottowski, S. (2015) *University Quality Indicators: A Critical Assessment*. Strasbourg: Directorate General for Internal Policies, Culture & Education.

Woodhouse, D. (1999) Quality and quality assurance. In J. Knight and H. de Wit (eds) *Quality and Internationalisation in Higher Education* (pp. 29–44). Paris: OECD.

4 From EME to SDG: The Journey of a Medical University

Karin Båge and Jennifer Valcke

Introduction: Context of Internationalization Today

As a point of departure for this chapter, the most recent definition of internationalization of higher education will be used and discussed. De Wit *et al.* (2015) have extended the widely accepted definition by Knight (2008: 21), with the new additions marked in *italics*: '[Internationalization of higher education is] the *intentional* process of integrating an international, intercultural, or global dimension into the purpose, functions or delivery of post-secondary education, *in order to enhance the quality of education and research for all students and staff, and to make a meaningful contribution to society*' (de Wit *et al.*, 2015: 281). This extended definition places fresh focus on the *intentionality* of the process of internationalization, on enhancing the quality of education and research and on making a meaningful contribution to society. These dimensions are thus considered to be the result of policies, strategies and other decision-making processes within higher education institutions (HEIs). Striving for mutual understanding in an increasingly intercultural world requires individuals who are ethical and responsible citizens, who appreciate the connections between the local, national, international and global. Disciplines and the labour market are no longer only local or national but are also increasingly regional and in some disciplines even global, and graduate competences should meet the needs of today's world (Mestenhauser *et al.*, 2010). The internationalization of higher education must therefore be viewed as a dynamic process, continuously shaped and reshaped by the international context in which it occurs. As this context changes, so do the purpose, goals, meanings and strategies of internationalization. Globalization is the most important contextual factor shaping the internationalization of higher education, and is characterized by interdependence among nations and manifested in the economic, political, social, cultural and knowledge spheres.

Internationalization is taking place in this radically new, complex, differentiated and globalized context. The change in the context of internationalization is reflected further in how the goals of internationalization are continuously evolving, ranging from educating global citizens and building capacity for research, to generating income from international student tuition fees and the quest to enhance institutional prestige. The balancing of multiple intended outcomes while preserving essential institutional core values and missions is both a challenge and an opportunity for HEIs. The resulting changes in goals, activities and actors require a holistic approach and transformative leadership. A comprehensive international perspective in all activities thus contributes to the attractiveness of HEIs as employers and education providers. For example, activities such as virtual exchange and group work with an element of reflection and intercultural competence development influence the quality of education at individual, programme, institutional, national and international levels. What does this mean for the quality of education?

English-medium education (EME) has emerged as a driver for the internationalization of higher education as a necessary adaptation to the forces of globalization. This chapter will present EME in a broader perspective, whereby *the change in medium of education becomes a means to initiate paradigm shifts in the delivery and services of higher education in order to enhance quality.* The question of language indeed leads university teachers, as well as university leadership, to consider the pedagogical, linguistic and cultural implications of this new context, as well as to rethink the professional development of teaching staff. In the next section, a case study of a university in Sweden will be presented to illustrate the journey of moving from EME to sustainable development goals (SDGs) when it comes to shifting perspectives, understandings and mindsets regarding the internationalization of education, and responding to the urgent need for cultivating global and responsible citizens.

Developing an Internationalized Curriculum: From Action Plan to Constructive Alignment

Karolinska Institutet (KI) is one of Sweden's most prestigious medical universities, perhaps most famous for awarding the annual Nobel prize in Physiology or Medicine. It also boasts high-level research in basic science and trains several thousand students every year in a wide range of different health professions, including speech and language pathology, toxicology, medicine, dentistry, bio-entrepreneurship and public health. Ten of its study programmes are entirely delivered through English. International collaborations in both research and education abound, and students and staff are encouraged to participate in international exchanges as part of their professional development and studies, with options to travel to countries of all income levels on all continents of the world. It is home to many researchers, teachers, students and administrative staff who feel local in many places across the world (Selasi, 2014).

Beyond this, KI is also situated in Stockholm, the capital of Sweden, where around 40% of the Swedish population have an additional cultural or linguistic background (Sweden Statistics, n.d.). Similar to many other countries in Europe and beyond, Sweden has welcomed immigrants throughout the decades since WWII. Most recently, in 2015, it was the country that welcomed the most asylum seekers per capita in Europe (Skodo, 2018). This diversity is reflected in Sweden's student body, as well as in the healthcare sector as a whole. Currently, KI trains dentists, medical doctors and nurses with a licence from outside the EU, making them eligible to work and practise their profession in Sweden. The importance of international partnerships, collaborations and presence is visible in strategies for Swedish universities as a whole, but also in national strategies specifically aimed at education (Bladh et al., 2018). As such, KI is a university with international students, researchers and administrative and teaching staff, which values international partnerships and collaborators, prioritizes these in its research and strategies and trains its future graduates to work in a globalized health sector. However, despite all of these international factors fundamental to the identity of KI, it is only in recent years that a shift in the university's understanding of the internationalization of education has moved beyond that of focusing on mobility and learning through English.

Internationalization of education: From EME to internationalization at home (IaH)

Similar to other universities, KI has intentionally prioritized international research collaborations and, to a smaller extent, education, through agreements regarding exchange opportunities. However, when it comes to the *content* and *delivery* of its education this intentionality is much less, and there is a noticeable gap in study programmes systematically and intentionally integrating internationalization into their curricula. From 2014 to 2018, KI's Board of Higher Education adopted an Action Plan for the internationalization of first- and second-cycle education (henceforth referred to as the Action Plan). It was based on KI's general internationalization strategy (Karolinska Institutet, 2014) and was used as a steering document for the study programmes and departments at KI. It relied on Knight's (2008) definition of internationalization of higher education (see discussion above), and its overall aim was: 'After completion of their studies, all students at KI are to be well prepared for working in a global labour market subject to varying economic and social conditions, and for working in culturally diverse environments. KI is to be an attractive study destination for international students' (Karolinska Institutet, 2013). To achieve this overarching aim, four goals were identified:

- Goal 1: Matters relating to global health are to be integrated into the compulsory components of all study programmes at Karolinska Institutet.
- Goal 2: All study programmes are to offer at least one compulsory course delivered in English carrying 7.5 credit points or more by 2017. All students are thus to take at least one course that is delivered in English during their academic studies at Karolinska Institutet.
- Goal 3: Student and teacher mobility should increase from 2014 to 2018.
- Goal 4: Highly qualified international students should be recruited to courses taught in English and the number of non-EU/EEA students on Global Master's programmes at Karolinska Institutet should increase. KI is to have at least 200 students from non-EU/EEA countries by 2018.

Its implementation was coordinated by the administrative officer in the drafting committee of international affairs of the Board of Higher Education. This was also the main committee to which regular reporting was made by the project coordinators. The Centre for Learning and Knowledge (CLK) in the Department of Learning, Informatics, Management and Ethics (LIME) was given the responsibility of coordinating supporting activities aimed at helping programmes to fulfil Goals 1 and 2 of the Action Plan.

In 2015, an educational developer specializing in EME and international education was specifically recruited to KI to support programmes to implement Goal 2, teaching in English. Another educational developer from the Global and Sexual Health (GLoSH) research group in the Department of Public Health Sciences (PHS) was given responsibility for supporting programmes in implementing Goal 1, where she would get direct advice from and consultations with experts in the field. As Goals 1 and 2 more directly concerned teaching and learning arrangements, the project coordinators for both goals decided early on to synchronize their work in reaching out to study programmes, as well as reporting to university leadership.

Although the university had centred its Action Plan on a broad definition of internationalization, the itemization of the goals illustrated how the understanding of this concept focused primarily on EMI, mobility and recruiting fee-paying international students. However, the coordinating team decided that its implementation demanded a new way of understanding and working with internationalization. Indeed, after engaging with the literature and sharing best practices with international educational developers, as well as realizing the resource and time constraints that teaching staff and study programme directors are under, it became clear that a revised definition that looked at the curriculum was essential. When the instances of internationalized teaching and learning were analysed, many isolated and optional subjects, experiences and activities were found, but nothing was systematically developed with intentionality. If KI was to move away from ad hoc internationalization practices, it had to engage in a planned and systematic evidence-based process in order to provide useful guidelines for everyone on its campuses, through enhancing and sustaining staff motivation by integrating international education holistically. In other words, internationalization of education was more likely to succeed at KI if it was embedded into standard university practice, rather than understood as being developed in parallel to regular university operations.

The Process of Internationalization of the Curriculum

As we have seen so far, the international classroom should be approached as an institutional and organizational change process that requires time and effort, as well as changes at the personal, curriculum and institutional levels. Based on international research (Carroll, 2015; Leask, 2015), and on the initial results from pilot case studies, KI was awarded a Strategic Grant from the Swedish Foundation for International Cooperation in Research and Higher Education to internationalize the curricula of five of its study programmes (from 2017 to 2020). The curriculum is central to Leask's definition of internationalization of the curriculum (IoC), which she defines as: '[...] the incorporation of international, intercultural and global dimensions into the content of the curriculum as well as the learning outcomes, assessment tasks, teaching methods and support services of a study programme' (Leask, 2015: 9). IoC breaks new ground in connecting research-based evidence with practice by applying innovative curricular design to internationalize teaching and learning. The IoC process suggested by Leask is illustrated in Figure 4.1 and comprises five steps: review and reflect, imagine, act, revise and plan, and evaluate. It is an iterative process which allows programme committees to plan short-, medium- and long-term objectives for the internationalization of their curriculum.

Our point of departure for future developments in internationalization of education is that the international classroom is a multilingual and multicultural learning space; it engages all students; it is not language specific; and, it requires special knowledge and reflection (from teachers) to scaffold student learning (Cozart et al., 2015). In sum, the international classroom is characterized by cultural, linguistic and didactic challenges and opportunities that require thinking differently about prioritizing and organizing learning. It requires all stakeholders to change certain assumptions they may make about teaching and learning, namely that to teach is not to transfer knowledge. Instead learning and teaching focus on creating the possibility for the production or construction of knowledge. We must also assume that learning rests on two main principles: experience (Kolb,

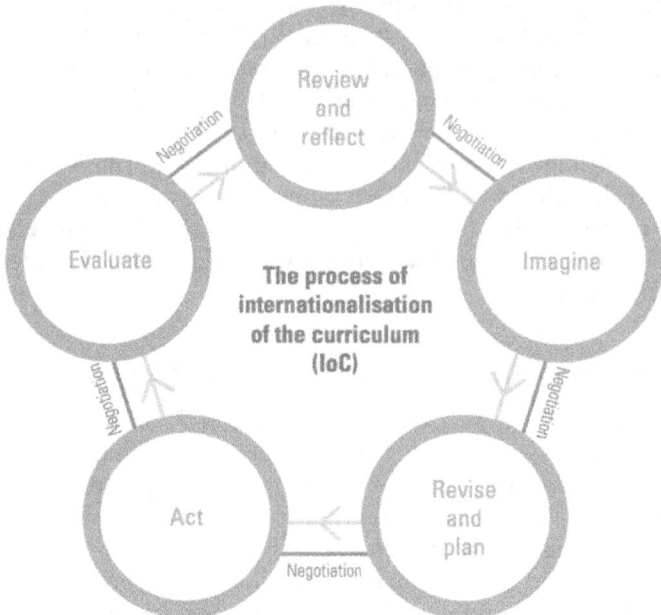

Figure 4.1 The process of internationalization of the curriculum
Source: Leask (2015).

1984) and interaction (Wells, 1981). This entails a radical departure from teacher-fronted practices to student-centred learning practices where teachers and students cooperate and share experiences. In an attempt to move away from individualistic and personal approaches for determining educational practices, teachers are required to base their knowledge and practices on scientific evidence, where traditional ideas are tested and adapted or changed according to accumulated support or refutation. In short, the role of the university teacher is changing and a university teacher today may find that the teaching and learning that they experienced as students, no longer applies to the classrooms in which they teach. As such, the quality of education practices through the continuing professional development of teachers can only be enhanced by favouring research-based scholarship of teaching and learning, and encouraging the use of reflection instead of relying on personal anecdote.

In this context, the concepts of IoC and IaH are particularly useful. They aim to empower all individuals, teachers and students, with linguistic and intercultural competences within domestic learning environments, including in disciplinary learning issues. IaH can be defined as '[...] the purposeful integration of international and intercultural dimensions into the formal and informal curriculum for all students within domestic learning environments' (Beelen & Jones, 2015: 69) and shifts the focus away from incoming mobility. It is clear that mobility can bring substantial benefits to students and staff, and universities around the world are competing to attract a greater number of students. However, internationally mobile students will continue to make up a relatively small percentage of the student body. As such, IaH is a convenient term to designate internationalization activities carried out at home. It is interesting to note that the curriculum is central to this definition of IaH, and is largely inspired by Leask's definition of IoC: '[…] the incorporation of international, intercultural and global dimensions into the content of the curriculum as well as the learning outcomes, assessment tasks, teaching methods and support services of a study programme' (Leask, 2015: 9).

IoC is thus situated at the crossroads between policy and practice. For IoC to be effective, particular attention must be paid to internationalizing learning outcomes, content, teaching and learning activities, and assessment tasks (Leask, 2015: 10). As explained in the previous section, the IoC process allows HEIs to move beyond ad hoc experiences and activities – more typical of EME – to a holistic approach which favours integration and intentionality. Through providing useful guidelines for university leadership, teaching staff and students, IoC opens the discussion of internationalization practices by looking at the curriculum and at student learning (and learning outcomes) through a planned and systematic evidence-based process – which in turn enhances and sustains staff motivation.

IoC is a change process that requires imagining and innovating to transform teaching and learning. This process relies on the engagement of academic staff to take action in order to promote and implement change, and can, at times, be met with resistance. Much recent research has generated valuable insights into what hinders, prevents and discourages staff engagement in IoC; and has resulted in strategies to overcome obstacles to the process. The next section explores some barriers found at the institutional level and at the individual teacher's level. Table 4.1 shows the blockers that can be identified at institutional level (Childress, 2010) and at individual teacher level (Valcke *et al.*, 2011). From this research, it is clear that the importance of local context is paramount, as mentioned previously, and identifying appropriate strategies requires an understanding of the blockers within their context – how promotion procedures work and how workload is calculated, for example. It is evident that internationalizing the curriculum takes time and effort for all those involved since it requires imagination, problem-solving and creative thinking. This is why it is crucial for teaching staff to have an informed and strategic leadership, as well as support: 'In universities where leaders at university level and programme level understood the complexity of internationalization of the curriculum and the need to support it in different ways, academic staff members were more confident, adventurous, and resilient as they worked through the process' (Leask, 2015: 117).

Table 4.1 Blockers at institutional and individual teacher level

Institutional blockers (Childress, 2010)	Individual blockers (Valcke et al., 2011)
(a) Lack of leadership at institutional and 'local' level	(a) Lack of time
(b) Poorly conceived and managed internationalization strategy	(b) Language proficiency of teachers and students
(c) Lack of financial support	(c) Heavy workload
(d) Lack of staff incentives, e.g. recruitment and promotion policies	(d) Lack of motivation
(e) Structural barriers, such as time to meet as a course team	(e) Lack of confidence for EME
	(f) Lack of training for EME and the international classroom
	(g) A preference for working independently
	(h) Lack of desire and/or ability to think outside of traditional disciplinary paradigms
	(i) Don't know where to start
	(j) Lack of incentives

It is clear that the role of teaching staff in HEIs has changed and so have expectations of them. Teachers are asked to teach in increasingly multicultural classrooms, where their students will acquire: ways of thinking (creativity, critical thinking, problem solving, decision making and learning); ways of working (communication and collaboration); tools for working (including information and communications technologies); and skills around citizenship, life and career and personal and social responsibility for success in modern democracies (Schleicher, 2012). This means that todays' teaching staff need the competences to constantly change, innovate and adapt. In turn this demands critical, evidence-based attitudes enabling them to respond to new evidence from inside and outside the classroom, in order to alter their own practices appropriately.

In order to help teachers develop their professional practice under the pressures they face while at the same time making internationalization intentional and explicit, constructive alignment (Biggs, 2003; Biggs & Tang, 2011) can be a practical tool to use. Figure 4.2 shows Biggs's model for constructive alignment, which focuses on ensuring the coherent calibration between intended learning outcomes, teaching and learning arrangements, and assessment and feedback. It provides a clear structure within which to anchor curriculum development systematically. It also enables teaching staff and educational leaders to have an overview of the curriculum and changes within it, in order to plan accordingly.

KI has a longstanding preference for the use of constructive alignment in curriculum design and reform. Motivation for integrating internationalization in the curriculum increased when it became clear that it could be constructively aligned and thus docked into already established ways of working at the university, so avoiding the additional workload involved in designing new elements to fit into an already full curriculum. We rather saw an opportunity to adapt the seemingly fragmented goals of the Action Plan to align with the context, research evidence and established tools for

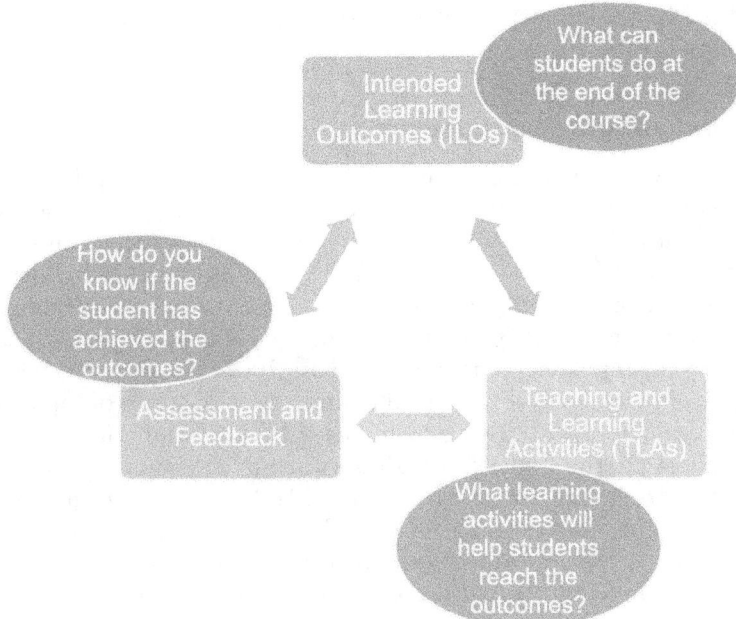

Figure 4.2 John Biggs's (2003) model for constructive alignment

constructive alignment. To do so, the educational team looked at the ICOMs matrix of international competences (ICOMs Project, 2014). ICOMS stands for International Competences in HE Programmes and was born of the collaboration of four Flemish universities led by KU Leuven to define and describe the learning outcomes we can expect from an internationalized curriculum. Figure 4.3 presents four domains

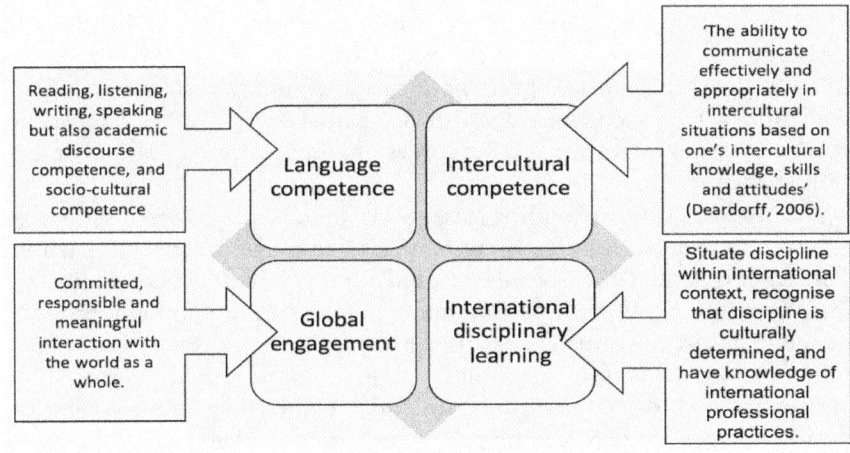

Figure 4.3 The domains of International ILOs
Source: ICOMs Project (2014).

identified by the project as relevant to KI, and we have added our own definitions.

Domain 1: Language competence

Language competence is the first of the ICOMs domains for international competences. It consists of listening, reading, writing and speaking (presenting and interacting). It is important to note that this domain does not only refer to the use of English in the international classroom, and that students can follow an internationalized curriculum in any language. Nonetheless, EME and its spread across Europe in recent years is a well-documented phenomenon (Coleman, 2006; Maiworm & Wächter, 2014; Phillipson, 2015) linked to the internationalization of higher education (de Wit et al., 2015) and to the growing competition between universities in the context of globalization (Altbach et al., 2009). According to Pagèze and Lasagabaster (2018), positions with regard to English-taught programmes vary considerably across the European continent: on the one hand, a maximalist position where English is presented as an inevitable tool for the international diffusion of knowledge (Coleman, 2006; de Swaan, 2001) and, on the other hand, a nuanced language ecology position where attention is paid to the way English coexists with other languages in university programmes and contexts (Harder, 2009). In northern European countries that have a long experience of EME and well-established language policies, the use of English in higher education is considered from the angle of disciplinary and academic cultures and within a certain European idea of multilingualism. Research on EME in Spain and other southern European contexts has reinforced the language ecology approach to EME. This approach highlights how local language identities, local higher education practices and local attitudes to multilingualism are determining factors in the way EME is implemented (Doiz et al., 2013; Nikula et al., 2016). The emergence of EME in national higher education contexts provides an excellent context for exploring glocalization (Robertson, 1995) in education, and a necessary adaptation to the forces of globalization as already mentioned above.

When teaching through a foreign language, an interesting area to investigate as best practice is content and language integrated learning (CLIL). It is 'a dual-focused educational approach in which an additional language is used for the learning and teaching of both content and language. That is, in the teaching and learning process, there is a focus not only on content, and not only on language' (Coyle et al., 2010: 1). This approach enables practitioners to understand the complex relation between language and learning and the linguistic demands of learning academic content with a high cognitive load. Coyle (2012) differentiates between three different dimensions: (a) language *of* learning, which is the language needed for conceptual learning; (b) language *for* learning, which is the language needed for developing metacognitive or learner strategies; and (c) language *through* learning, which is the language needed for applying knowledge, in both disciplinary and transdisciplinary contexts. Through the CLIL approach and because of the heterogeneous language levels of their students, teachers are required to support the development of language learning in terms of academic literacies in their classrooms and pay particular attention to their delivery methods. The CLIL approach fosters high-quality teaching and learning since it is '[...] context-embedded and content-driven yet with specifically-determined target language outcomes. Building on the premise that language is our greatest learning tool, CLIL seeks to connect learners to the realities of using different languages at different times for different purposes' (Coyle, 2015: 86). The challenge for HEIs is therefore to develop pedagogical approaches that integrate content and language in ways that lead to independent successful learners able to live as pluriliterate citizens in tomorrow's world.

'I don't teach English' is a commonly heard utterance from university teachers, and also the title of Airey's (2012) article about physics lecturers. It is clear that the role language plays in learning is usually taken for granted in native-speaking contexts, but it is brought to the fore when the medium of instruction changes. Through our own interactions with university teachers in different European countries and disciplinary contexts, we have come to the conclusion that university teachers do not identify as language teachers because of: (a) the conception of language teaching as being solely comprised of grammar rules and vocabulary lists; (b) the lack of understanding of the difference between English as a foreign language (EFL) and English as a lingua franca (ELF); (c) the lack of prestige associated to language teaching; and (d) misconceptions about the role of university teachers in developing the academic discourse of their students (Ur, 2009).

According to Airey: 'One possible reason for the lecturers' reticence to teach language may be that they do not view language as the main method of meaning making in physics – rather mathematics is seen as a much more important disciplinary resource' (Airey, 2012: 75). This has also been our experience in training teachers from scientific and technological backgrounds, but is a concern for teachers of other disciplines as well, such as law and history where language plays a more predominant role in the discipline (Costa & Mariotti, 2018). Informed choices must therefore be made regarding the subjects to be taught in English, and selection criteria must include, among others, that university teachers be well versed in scaffolding the language students need to understand their discipline (Airey, 2012: 50).

In order to initiate discussions to challenge teachers' attitudes towards their role in their students' language learning, it is interesting to note the status of English in its different varieties around the world. Kachru (1992) focused on the historical context of English, the status of the language and its functions in various regions; he proposed three circles to divide the English-speaking world based on native-speaker norms and the status of English in the country of origin. Today, the sociolinguistic reality of English use is very different. The majority of English speakers are located in the outer or expanding circles, using English for international communication in academia, technology, politics, tourism, entertainment, business and finance, information and interpersonal relationships. Perhaps it is more useful, therefore, to redefine the circles of users of English in terms of their level of competence in the language rather than in terms of where they live and whether or not they are native speakers (Ur, 2009), as exemplified by Figure 4.4.

The user of English as an international language may therefore be either native or non-native, is typically bilingual or multilingual and is likely to be skilled in communicative and comprehension strategies. A reappraisal of our understanding of language competence is therefore necessary. In this respect, Jenkins (2014) suggests that a fully competent speaker of English as an international language is a speaker with a wide vocabulary, accurate grammar and an easily understood accent, and who may or may not originally be a native speaker.

In order for university teachers to develop a teaching persona that is inclusive of the heterogeneous language proficiency present in their classrooms, it seems that debunking myths and preconceptions about language acquisition and language learning is needed. Teachers need to make a mindset change by rethinking the role English plays in their disciplines today and adopt inclusive language practices where the use of a lingua franca is understood and different varieties of English are embraced. Interestingly, this mindset change is also necessary for language experts

Figure 4.4 The world of English today
Source: Ur (2009).

who are often called upon to support content teachers in EME. They must become aware of the norms of English as an international language and shift their focus away from native-speaker norms, in the support they offer university teachers but also in the students' language classrooms. Additionally, misunderstandings and mismatched expectations on behalf of the students can also cause friction in and disturb the learning progression (Huang, 2018). In order to avoid a situation of 'blame-the-student' or 'blame-the-teacher', as well as to create an inclusive environment for all, it is essential that students as well as teachers are made aware of English as a lingua franca and the role that it plays in the contemporary academic and working environments of their specific field of training.

Domain 2: Intercultural competence

Intercultural competence is the second of the ICOMs domains for international competences. It is defined as including the following: cultural self-knowledge, cultural flexibility, cultural resilience, cultural responsiveness, cultural knowledge, cultural connectivity competence, cultural communicative competence, cultural conflict management and multi-perspective approach.

These multiple dimensions are summed up in Gregersen-Hermans's (2016) definition of interculturally competent graduates as being multifaceted. Indeed, she states that graduates are able to understand, evaluate and relate to ambiguous and uncertain situations and to make culturally correct attributions; they also realize the relative validity of their own frame of reference, while being firmly rooted in them, and they are able to select and use communication styles and behaviour that fit a specific local or intercultural context. An intercultural interaction is thus seen as successful when interactants are able to develop shared meaning, while acknowledging their own and others' sociocultural context.

In a world that is increasingly globalizing, healthcare professionals need to have up-to-date, fact-based worldviews, through the development of knowledge, skills and attitudes that help them navigate international, multilingual and multicultural job markets, as well as work environments and patients. Our classrooms have changed and have become superdiverse, as Blommaert and Rampton explain:

> There is a growing awareness that over the past two decades, globalisation has altered the face of social, cultural and linguistic diversity in societies all over the world [...] the multiculturalism of an earlier era has gradually been replaced by what Vertovec calls 'super-diversity' [...] characterised by a tremendous increase in the categories of migrants, not only in terms of nationality, ethnicity, language, and religion, but also in terms of motives, patterns and itineraries of migration, processes of insertion into the labour and housing markets of the host societies, and so on [...]

The predictability of the category *migrant* and of his/her sociocultural features has disappeared. (Blommaert & Rampton, 2011: 2)

According to Gregersen-Hermans (2017), intercultural competence should be conceived as a psychological construct that can be inferred through a set of parameters (cognitions, attitudes, behaviours). Intercultural competence is thus: (a) developmental and reflects the extent to which diversity is included in the construction of daily reality; (b) contextual, combining cultural general and culture-specific elements; (c) context-bound and comes alive in the interaction between culturally diverse individuals and groups; and (d) mediated through verbal and nonverbal behaviour. Key to all of these understandings is that developing intercultural competences is a constant, lifelong process and that learner development is 'not a direct result of solely one experience, such as study abroad' (Deardorff, 2012: 63).

Our classrooms must therefore become culturally rich and inclusive environments, where students' needs come first. This can be achieved through intentional facilitation and guided reflection (through such tools as learner portfolios, for instance), where students engage in behavioural practices through social support and peer learning (Gregersen-Hermans, 2019).

Domain 3: Global engagement

Global engagement is the third of the ICOMs domains for international competences, and requires learners to:

- form their own opinion regarding societal or international topics;
- express their own opinion on societal or international topics;
- show societal involvement.

Global engagement can therefore be understood as students' ability to use fact-based evidence in order to shape informed personal, social and political opinions within a given discipline. It also involves engaging with these opinions and acting upon them accordingly and responsibly. This understanding overlaps to some extent with the concept of global citizenship, a concept much discussed in literature on the internationalization of education (Carroll, 2015: 92–93; Leask, 2015: 58–62). UNESCO (n.d. a) also discusses global citizenship education, and presents it as 'empower[ing] learners [...] to understand' how the world is interconnected by global issues such as 'human rights violations, inequality and [how] poverty still threaten peace and sustainability'; and therefore learners should 'become active promoters of more peaceful, tolerant, inclusive, secure and sustainable societies'. This education 'aims to instil values, attitudes and behaviours that support responsible global citizenship: creativity, innovation, and commitment to peace, human rights and sustainable development'. UNESCO (n.d. b) also emphasizes ethical or globally aware 'agency', i.e. that people can make informed decision for themselves, as well as act upon them so as to contribute to 'resolving global challenges'. For UNESCO, peace, human rights, intercultural education and education for international understanding are core concepts for global citizenship education.

According to Lilley et al. (2013: 144), a global citizen will be able to demonstrate:

- appreciation of, and value and respect for global multicultural and multilingual diversity;
- commitment to engage in informed debate about issues of equity, social justice, human rights and related social, economic and political issues;
- commitment to equality, environmental sustainability and civic obligations;
- commitment to participate in and contribute towards creating an equitable and sustainable community at a range of levels from the local to the global;
- appreciation of the complex interacting factors that contribute to diversity of language, culture and multicultural relationships;
- sensitivity to ... complex human–environment interactions and a willingness to act in a manner consistent with the changing needs and demands facing society;
- a sense of self-identity, self-esteem and belief that people can make a difference in the world.

Hanson summarizes the many discussions on the definition of global citizenship when she writes that it 'involves both inward (awareness and commitment) and outward (action) dimensions, reflecting both social and personal change' (Hanson, 2010: 76).

When implementing the KI Action Plan, global health was linked to the domain of global engagement through the ICOMs model of internationalized intended learning outcomes. Global health was understood to provide the knowledge foundations that students could use in order to form, express and show opinions on international and societal topics related to health and well-being. The Action Plan relied on a definition of global health developed by Koplan et al. (2009) as

> the area of study, research and practice that places a priority on improving health and achieving equity in health for all people worldwide ... it emphasizes transnational health issues, determinants and social solutions; involves many disciplines within and beyond the health sciences and promotes interdisciplinary collaboration; and is a synthesis of population-based prevention with individual level clinical care. (Koplan et al., 2009: 1993–1995).

Although this definition does not directly mention human rights, we saw an opportunity to include the right to health in our work supporting study programmes. The definition has a clear link to the prevention of adverse health outcomes. The right to health 'explicitly transcends access to health care' (Knipper, 2016), and extends to include contributing factors such as housing, water and sanitation, working conditions and nutritious food. It also addresses key components of human rights principles such as non-discrimination, participation and empowerment. The right to health not only makes the broad concept of human rights particularly relevant and tangible to the education of health professions, but it also facilitates the buy-in for internationalization through connectivity to many of the learning outcomes already present in KI study programmes, such as non-discrimination and patient rights. Global health can therefore contribute to students developing the ability to use fact-based evidence to shape informed personal, social and political opinions about the way students practise their discipline and to engage with these opinions as well as to act upon them accordingly and responsibly.

Domain 4: International disciplinary learning

The fourth of the ICOMs domains relates to international disciplinary learning and provides a broad, multidimensional concept of culture, which encompasses the different practices and underlying assumptions and attitudes that university teachers and students bring to the international classroom:

- being able to situate their discipline within the international context;
- recognizing the fact that disciplines are culturally determined;
- having a developed knowledge of the professional activities of their discipline in other countries;
- being aware of relevant international organizations within their field.

As we have seen with the notion of superdiversity mentioned in the previous section, the make-up of university classrooms is increasingly heterogeneous, with growing numbers of students of different abilities, genders, sexual orientations, races and, at times, social class. However, hetero-normativity, whiteness, Eurocentric perspectives, able-body centric classrooms and class privilege reflect the social norms that are still perpetuated in the broader university environment (Kelly & Brandes, 2001; Nkoane, 2012; Stiegler, 2008; Toomey et al., 2012).

Politics has always maintained a great influence over university curricula, as Paulo Freire stated in his 1968 book, *Pedagogy of the Oppressed*: 'all education is political; teaching is never a neutral act' (Freire, 1968: 19). Curriculum is predicated on inherently political questions such as: What is the curriculum for, or what purposes does it serve? How is it determined? How does curriculum change? What makes curriculum relevant? Whose curriculum is it? And, perhaps most of all: Who is it for? Anglo-Western academic traditions are based on Cartesian dualism, which views knowledge as separate from being, where knowledge is based on scientific fact and Western rationality. This notion has been challenged in the so-called postcolonial era, which questions the assumptions that underlie Western scientific paradigms. Such assumptions can be seen as positing the superiority of empirical and detached ways of knowing, to the detriment of other non-Western ways of knowing and the consequent relegation of 'Otherness' as inferior. While referring to the current movement to decolonize the curriculum throughout the African continent (Heleta, 2019; Kamanzi, 2016; Kigotho, 2018; Makoni, 2017), Mbembe characterizes the current time in higher education as a 'negative moment', one that is experienced in all large-scale societal changes: 'a negative moment is a moment when new antagonisms emerge while old ones remain unresolved [...] when contradictory forces – inchoate, fractured, fragmented – are at work but what might come out of their interaction is anything but certain' (Mbembe, 2016: 2). A negative moment, however, also creates the conditions for a deep re-examination of current hegemonies and for a reimagining of how to shape the outcome of that interaction, and in this sense it is important to unpack how the curriculum shapes ways of seeing and doing that may be Anglo-centric to such an extent that it may invalidate students bringing forth other ideas. In this way, HEIs miss out on developing creativity and innovation in ways that only diverse and heterogeneous groups can. We believe that, as scholars and practitioners of international education, we have an obligation to revise existing assumptions such as these, as they lie beneath our current ways of teaching and learning. Critically looking at the individual and institutional values and principles present in our formal and informal curricula are the first steps for change.

Once this is understood, students can be viewed as resources that will legitimize the use of other conceptual frameworks and nomenclatures, as well as open our learning spaces to new ways of seeing and new ways of doing. More so, students become partners in the educational process and provide opportunities to reconsider Anglo-Western norms, and to consider the inclusion of all students (local and global) as fully fledged partners in both the formal and informal curriculum (Haines, 2017).

Aligning with Top Agendas

The understanding of internationalization has moved from focusing on language for the sake of facilitating mobility to integrating international perspectives and dimensions into the curriculum, so as to allow *all* students to benefit from internationalization – and so, where are we now, where to next, and what are the larger visions for internationalization of education? The United Nations has made quality education a top global priority. In Resolution 70/1 of the United Nations General Assembly, *Transforming our World: The 2030 Agenda for Sustainable Development* (UN, 2015), many of the aforementioned issues are tied together. Education is addressed in SDG4, which specifically highlights *quality* education, stating that by 2030 states need to 'ensure inclusive and equitable quality education and promote lifelong learning opportunities for all'.

In SDG4 Target 7, it directly states that education must

> ensure that all learners acquire the knowledge and skills needed to promote sustainable development, including, among others, through education for sustainable development and sustainable lifestyles, human rights, gender equality, promotion of a culture of peace and non-violence, global citizenship and appreciation of cultural diversity and of culture's contribution to sustainable development. (UN, 2015)

The indicators that will ensure that this goal has been accomplished are the following:

> Extent to which (i) global citizenship education and (ii) education for sustainable development, including gender equality and human rights, are mainstreamed at all levels in: (a) national education policies, (b) curricula, (c) teacher education and (d) student assessment. (UNESCO, 2017: 48)

As such, these competences, well aligned with what has been discussed in this chapter (in particular, language competence, intercultural competence, global engagement and international disciplinary learning) can no longer be relegated to elective courses or haphazardly addressed by motivated teachers who happen to be interested in such issues. They need to be *systematically* integrated throughout the curriculum in the intended learning outcomes, the teaching and learning arrangements and finally in the assessment and feedback. Relevant teaching staff *must* be trained if their capacity is to be strengthened for the delivery of quality education, and European and national education policies need to clearly state the importance of these competences for the continuous professional development of teaching staff. If such institutions are at all interested in remaining relevant and making a sincere and meaningful contribution to sustainably developing the world, the arguments presented in this chapter advocate that the quality of education must be developed along these lines.

Conclusion: Lessons Learned and Moving Forward

Although KI's earlier institutional work on EME and global health perspectives in the curriculum has had significant impact in some areas, it was clear that these were not always intentionally integrated within mainstream curricula. In many instances, for example, work in these areas was undertaken largely in personal and professional development modules rather than being linked intentionally to the core knowledge and skills of the subject area. In other cases, this developmental work might have been undertaken in individual modules, but these elements remained unassessed – and could therefore not be monitored and followed up for quality.

Drawing upon Biggs' work on constructive alignment, it quickly became apparent that the key to embedding any of the four domains of international competences within the disciplines would be to ensure that these dimensions were purposefully defined in modules and course learning outcomes. The constructive alignment process would then ensure that content, delivery and assessment would stem from these intended learning outcomes. What is also clear from much of the literature on global citizenship (and related) learning is the need for learning outcomes themselves to reflect more holistic learner development than can typically be the case. In Sweden, at least, significant emphasis is given to constructing learning outcomes that reflect cognitive taxonomies of learning, notably drawn from Bloom's (1956) seminal work. In the development of students as responsible global citizens, however, at least some consideration also needs to be given to their affective and behavioural abilities.

We also recognize the need to ensure that learning outcomes, if they are to effectively drive the curriculum and its assessment, must be constructed in such a way as to present learners and teachers with outcomes that are observable and measurable.

Quality education in the age of SDGs means having the skills, knowledge and values to promote the sustainable development of our societies. For our students, this means being able to work with people they don't know and to be able to communicate effectively both orally and in writing, as well as to find creative solutions to complex challenges (Vaccariello & Haar Siegel, 2018). In addition, they need to be able to advocate and act upon informed fact-based opinions accordingly and responsibly – what UNESCO (2017) calls 'sustainability citizens'.

Although we have addressed reflections undertaken at KI on its internationalization journey, our view is that we will achieve a holistic result through the process of constructive alignment, which underpins good curriculum design, delivery and assessment. Notwithstanding the considerable resource commitment already made in developing appropriate learning outcomes, ongoing staff development and strategic support is essential to enable KI teachers to deliver the student learning opportunities leading to developing language competence, intercultural competence, global engagement and international disciplinary learning. The reflective process detailed above forms the latest stage of the continuous engagement with internationalization at KI which began several years before with the Action Plan in 2014. It is perhaps rare for two education developers to be involved in such an extended process. It is also rare, if not unique, for any institution to be undertaking such a strategic and pervasive approach to IoC. We therefore hope our reflections are useful on what might have been done in hindsight and on the suggested priorities for others who may wish to take forward similar initiatives.

Finally, in light of the current political climates sweeping the globe, the rise of nationalist tendencies and the threat of climate change, we believe that the integration of international, intercultural and global perspectives into the content of university curricula will equip future generations with the skills of mutuality, reciprocity and hospitality they need to live and work creatively and ethically in the world. These ideas can strengthen the foundations of a much more purposeful and deontological approach to internationalization in higher education: one that values internationalization as a means to an end and not an end in and of itself.

References

Airey, J. (2011) Talking about teaching in English: Swedish university lecturers' experiences of changing teaching language. *Ibérica* 22, 35–54.

Airey, J. (2012) I don't teach language: The linguistic attitudes of physics lecturers in Sweden. *AILA Review* 25, 64–79.

Altbach, P., Reisberg, L. and Rumbley, L. (2009) *Trends in Global Higher Education, Tracking and Academic Revolution*. Paris: UNESCO.

Beelen, J. and Jones, E. (2015) Redefining internationalisation at home. In A. Curaj, L. Matei, R. Pricopie, J. Salmi and P. Scott (eds) *The European Higher Education Area: Between Critical Reflections and Future Policies* (pp. 59–72). Cham: Springer.

Biggs, J. (2003) *Teaching for Quality Learning at University: What the Student Does*. Buckingham: Society for Research into Higher Education (SHRE) and Open University Press.

Biggs, J. and Tang, C. (2011) *Teaching for Quality Learning at University*. Maidenhead: Open University Press/McGraw Hill.

Bladh, A., Wilenius, M. and Gaunt, A. (2018) *Internationalisation of Swedish Higher Education and Research – A Strategic Agenda*. Stockholm: Swedish Government Official Reports. See https://www.government.se/48fc30/contentassets/4df6aeabd2bd4f5dbbf69210f786e133/internationalisationagenda.pdf (accessed 15 March 2019).

Blommaert, J. and Rampton, B. (2011) Language and superdiversity. *Diversities* 13 (2), 1–22.

Bloom, B.S. (1956) *Taxonomy of Educational Objectives. Handbook I: The Cognitive Domain*. New York: David McKay.

Carroll, J. (2015) *Tools for Teaching in an Educationally Mobile World*. London and New York: Routledge.

Childress, L. (2010) *The Twenty-First Century University: Developing Faculty Engagement in Internationalisation*. Bern: Peter Lang.

Coleman, J. (2006) English-medium teaching in European higher education. *Language Teaching* 39 (1), 1–14.

Costa, F. and Mariotti, C. (2018) Students' outcomes in English-medium instruction: Is there any difference related to discipline? In F. Costa, A. Murphy and J. Valcke (eds) *Critical Issues in English Medium Instruction in University* (pp. 361–370). Milan: Universita Cattolica del Sacro Cuore.

Coyle, D. (2012) CLIL – a pedagogical approach. In N. Van Deusen-Scholl and N. Hornberger (eds) *Encyclopedia of Language and Education* (2nd edn) (pp. 97–111). New York: Springer.

Coyle, D. (2015) Strengthening integrated learning: Towards a new era for pluriliteracies and intercultural learning. *LACLIL (Latin American Journal of Content and Language Integrated Learning)* 8 (2), 85–103.

Coyle, D., Hood, P. and Marsh, D. (2010) *CLIL*. Cambridge: Cambridge University Press.

Cozart, S., Haines, K., Lauridsen, K. and Vogel, T. (2015) The IntlUni principles for quality teaching and learning in the multilingual and multicultural learning space. In K. Lauridsen and M. Lillemose (eds) *Opportunities and Challenges in the Multilingual and Multicultural Learning Space* (pp. 17–22). Final document of the IntlUni Erasmus Academic Network project 2012–15. Aarhus: IntlUni.

Deardorff, D. (2012) Identification and assessment of intercultural competence as a student outcome of internationalization. In J. Beelen and H. de Wit (eds) *Internationalisation Revisited: New Dimensions in the Internationalisation of Higher Education* (pp. 47–68). Amsterdam: Amsterdam University of Applied Sciences.

de Swaan, A. (2001) *Words of the World: The Global Language System*. Malden: Polity Press.

de Wit, H., Hunter, F., Howard, L. and Egron-Polak, E. (2015) *Internationalisation of Higher Education – Study*. Brussels: European Parliament, Directorate General for Internal Policies. See http://www.europarl.europa.eu/studies (accessed 26 March 2019).

Doiz, A., Lasagabaster, D. and Sierra, J. (2013) Globalisation, internationalisation, multilingualism and linguistic strains in higher education. *Studies in Higher Education* 38 (9), 1407–1421.

Freire, P. (1972) *Pedagogy of the Oppressed*. New York: Herder & Herder.

Gregersen-Hermans, J.W.M. (2017) The impact of an international university environment on students' intercultural competence development. In D.K. Deardorff and L.A. Arasaratnam-Smith (eds) *Intercultural Competence in Higher Education* (pp. 91–106). London and New York: Routledge.

Gregersen-Hermans, J.W.M. (2019) Delivering intercultural competence as a graduate attribute. Keynote address at the Workshop on internationella och interkulturella perspektiv i undervisningen, Association of Swedish Higher Education Institutions, Stockholm, 28 January.

Haines, K. (2017) Students as partners in the international classroom at the University of Groningen, Netherlands. University of Tasmania blog post, 13 November. See https://blogs.utas.edu.au/engaging-students/2017/11/13/students-as-partners-in-the-international-classroom-at-groningen-university-netherlands-by-kevin-haines/ (accessed 27 March 2019).

Hanson, L. (2010) Global citizenship, global health, and the internationalization of curriculum: A study of transformative potential. *Journal of Studies in International Education* 14 (1), 70–88.

Harder, P. (ed.) (2009) *English in Denmark: Language Policy, Internationalisation and University Teaching*. Copenhagen: Museum Tusculanum Press.

Heleta, S. (2019) Dismantling colonisation's 'pedagogy of big lies'. *University World News*, 11 January.

Huang, Y.-P. (2018) Learner resistance to English-medium instruction practices: A qualitative case study. *Teaching in Higher Education* 23 (4), 435–449.

ICOMs Project (2014) *International Competencies and Learning Outcomes (ICOMs): Towards Strong Internationalized Learning Environments*. Project website. See http://www.internationalecompetenties.be/files/List%20of%20ICOMs%20 (2).pdf (accessed 26 March 2019).

Jenkins, J. (2014) *English as a Lingua Franca in the International University: The Politics of Academic English Language Policy*. New York and London: Routledge.

Kachru, B. (1992) World Englishes: Approaches, issues and resources. *Language Teaching* 25 (1), 1–14.

Kamanzi, B. (2016) Decolonizing the curriculum – a student call in context. *University World News*, 27 May.

Karolinska Institutet (2013) *Action Plan for the Internationalisation of First- and Second-cycle Education 2014–2018*. Stockholm: Board of Higher Education. See https://ki.se/sites/default/files/handlingsplan_internationalisering_0216.pdf (accessed 23 March 2019).

Karolinska Institutet (2014) *Strategy 2018 – Roadmap for Karolinska Institutet 2014–2018*. Stockholm: Communications and Publications Office. See https://ki.se/sites/default/files/fullangd_strategy2018_eng.pdf (accessed 23 March 2019).

Kelly, D.M. and Brandes, G.M. (2001) Shifting out of 'neutral': Beginning teachers' struggles with teaching for social justice. *Canadian Journal of Education/Revue Canadienne de L'éducation* 26 (4), 437.

Kigotho, W. (2018) The dangerous rise of neo-liberal universities. *University World News*, 9 November.

Knight, J. (2008) *Higher Education in Turmoil: The Changing World of Internationalisation*. Rotterdam: Sense.

Knipper, M. (2016) Migration, public health and human rights. *International Journal of Public Health* 61, 993–994. doi:10.1007/s00038-016-0893-x

Kolb, D. (1984) *Experiential Learning: Experience as the Source of Learning and Development*. Englewood Cliffs, NJ: Prentice Hall.

Koplan, J.P., Bond, T.C., Merson, M.H., Reddy, K.S., Rodriguez, M.H., Sewankambo, N.K. and Wasserheit, J.N. (2009) Towards a common definition of global health. *Lancet* 373 (9679), 1993–1995.

Leask, B. (2015) *Internationalizing the Curriculum*. New York and London: Routledge.

Maiworm, F. and Wächter, B. (eds) (2014) *English-Taught Programmes in European Higher Education: The State of Play in 2014*. Bonn: Lemmens.

Makoni, M. (2017) Urgent need to decolonise intellectual property curricula. *University World News*, 20 January.

Mbembe, A.J. (2016) Decolonizing the university: New directions. *Arts and Humanities in Higher Education* 15 (1), 29–45.

Mestenhauser, J. (1998) Portraits of an internationalized curriculum. In R.F. Mestenhauser and B. Ellingboe (eds) *Globalizing Education Policy* (pp. 3–39). London and New York: Routledge.

Nikula, T., Dafouz, E., Moore, P. and Smit, U. (2016) *Conceptualising Integration in CLIL and Multilingual Education*. Bristol: Multilingual Matters.

Nkoane, M.M. (2012) Discomforting truths: The emotional terrain of understanding social justice in education. *Journal for New Generation Sciences* 10 (2), 3–13.

Pagèze, J. and Lasagabaster, D. (2018) Teacher development for teaching and learning in English in a French higher education context. In F. Costa, A. Murphy and J. Valcke (eds) *Critical Issues in English Medium Instruction in University* (pp. 289–310). Milan: Università Cattolica del Sacro Cuore.

Phillipson, R. (2015) English as threat or opportunity in European higher education. In S. Dimova, J.K. Hultgren and C. Jensen (eds) *English-Medium Instruction in European Higher Education: English in Europe, Vol. 3*. Berlin: De Gruyter Mouton.

Robertson, R. (1995) Glocalization: Time-space and homogeneity-heterogeneity. In M. Featherstone, S. Lash and R. Robertson (eds) *Global Modernities* (pp. 25–44). London: Sage.

Schleicher, A. (ed.) (2012) *Preparing Teachers and Developing School Leaders for the 21st Century: Lessons from around the World*. Paris: OECD. See https://www.oecd.org/site/eduistp2012/49850576.pdf (accessed 26 March 2019).

Selasi, T. (2014) Don't ask where I'm from, ask where I am local. *TedGlobal* video. See https://www.ted.com/talks/taiye_selasi_don_t_ask_where_i_m_from_ask_where_i_m_a_local?language=en (accessed 26 March 2019).

Skodo, A. (2018) Sweden: By turns welcoming and restrictive in its immigration policy. *Online Journal of the Migration Policy Institute*, 6 December. See https://www.migrationpolicy.org/article/sweden-turns-welcoming-and-restrictive-its-immigration-policy (accessed 27 March 2019).

Stiegler, S. (2008) Queer youth as teachers: Dismantling silence of queer issues in a teacher preparation program committed to social justice. *Journal of LGBT Youth* 5 (4), 116–123.

Sweden Statistics (n.d.) Website. See https://www.scb.se/en/finding-statistics/statistics-by-subject-area/population/population-composition/population-statistics/ (accessed 28 March 2019).

Toomey, R.B., McGuire, J.K. and Russell, S.T. (2012) Heteronormativity, school climates, and perceived safety for gender nonconforming peers. *Journal of Adolescence* 35 (1), 187–196.

UN (2015) *Transforming our World: The 2030 Agenda for Sustainable Development*. A/RES/70/1. See https://sustainabledevelopment.un.org/post2015/transformingourworld/publication.

UNESCO (2017) *Education for Sustainable Development Goals: Learning Objectives*. Paris: UNESCO.

UNESCO (n.d. a) *Global Citizenship Education*. See https://en.unesco.org/themes/gced (accessed 27 March 2019).

UNESCO (n.d. b) *Relationship between Sustainable Development Goal 4 and the Education 2030 Framework for Action*. See http://www.unesco.org/culture/pdf/edu/SDG4-Ed2030-relationship.pdf (accessed 26 March 2019).

Ur, P. (2009) English as a lingua franca and some implications for English teachers. Handout. See https://www.tesol-france.org/uploaded_files/files/Coll09-Ur_Plenary_Handouts.pdf (accessed 18 March 2019).

Vaccariello, L. and Haar Siegel, S. (2018) Brave new world. *Denison Magazine*, Winter. See https://denisonmagazine.com/opening_page/brave-new-world-winter-2018/ (accessed 27 March 2019).

Valcke, J., Bartik, K. and Tudor, I. (2011) Practising CLIL in higher education: Challenges and perspectives. In D. Marsh and O. Meyer (eds) *Quality Interfaces: Examining Evidence & Exploring Solutions in CLIL* (pp. 140–154). Eichstätt: Eichstätt University.

Wells, G. (1981) *Learning through Interaction*. Cambridge: Cambridge University Press.

5 The Role of Languages in the Internationalization of Higher Education: Institutional Challenges

Víctor Pavón Vázquez

Introduction

Probably as a result of a process as far back as the dawn of the new century, the internationalization of higher education has become a central concern for educational policy makers (Byram, 2012; Chan & Dimmock, 2008; Knight & de Wit, 1995). The process of globalization affecting the world of science at this level and the need to disseminate knowledge and to create networks of collaboration, together with the elaboration of policies aspiring to foment student and teacher mobility, have resulted in the appearance of linguistic demands regarding the promotion of languages as vehicles of communication for this international scenario, namely English as the lingua franca of the scientific community (Hamel, 2007) and of higher education (Brumfit, 2004; Coleman, 2006; Seidlhofer, 2001; Smit, 2013).

One of the most obvious ways to increase the linguistic levels of the members of a given society is to build a solid educational programme for languages starting in the early stages of education. This is the case in Europe, which has placed the English language in a dominant position in primary and secondary education (Eurydice, 2005). However, the problem may be that these programmes fail to produce positive outputs (European Commission, 2012). Even if standardized tests reveal that these programmes are successful, the levels of achievement may not necessarily be commensurate with the requirements of the professional market or the competences that the workforce needs in order to function effectively in specific professional areas: 'during primary and secondary school [...] there is little exposure to and practice of the academic language expected in university settings' (Crossman, 2018: 565). For this reason, educational authorities and policy makers are now looking to universities to raise the linguistic standards of students through English-taught programmes (Dearden, 2014; Marsh & Laitinen, 2005; Ritzen, 2004; Wächter & Maiworm, 2008, 2014). The implementation of such programmes is not an indispensable measure to improve the international profile of universities, but it is increasingly becoming a means to address some of the different facets of the internationalization process (Doiz et al., 2014; Knight, 2004, 2009; Rizvi, 2007). For example, the increase in the number of studies offered in English may attract international students, and the enhanced linguistic command of teachers and students will undoubtedly help expand potential mobility and collaboration between universities. Also, the need to adapt to the new challenges can be a decisive factor for the improvement of the university as a whole (Doiz et al., 2011). Whether the *Englishisation* of universities (Kirkpatrick, 2011) may be viewed negatively as a 'pandemic' process (Phillipson, 2009) or as an undesirable effect of the aspiration to enhance the international profile of universities, we must concur that it is an unstoppable wave which is changing the characteristics and traditional dynamics of many universities.

Interest in internationalization has grown dramatically in recent decades, leading to what Knight (2012: 4) calls 'the centrality of internationalization in the current world of higher education'. This process is mainly due to the purported positive effects of the proposal: 'The benefits of internationalisation appear obvious, as it encourages academic cooperation and staff and student exchange' (Kirkpatrick, 2011: 3). However, we should acknowledge that this process is also influenced by what Coleman (2006: 4) calls 'the Microsoft effect': 'once a medium obtains a market share, it becomes less and less practical to opt for another medium'.

In general, there are several recognizable forces shaping what could be labelled as the road map to internationalization in higher education (Altbach & Knight, 2007; Wächter & Maiworn, 2014). Firstly, supranational policies and regulations may exert a notable influence on the delineation of national or, more directly, institutional university policies (Holdsworth, 2004). In this sense, if the target is to tighten social and professional cohesion between members of a supranational entity, as happens within, for example, the European Union (European Commission/EACEA/Eurydice, 2018; High Level Group on Multilingualism, 2007), then these directives have an unequivocal effect on the countries and on universities. We should not forget, however, that it is possible that some universities may be reluctant to follow these norms, arguing that what may be valid in an international context may not be applicable to their settings. Secondly, universities may use specific marketing strategies to attract students from other countries, with the objective that increasing the number of international students will automatically raise the international profile of the university (Bolsman & Miller, 2008). Thirdly, and closely connected to the latter, a relevant drive for the improvement of internationalization comes from enabling student and staff mobility (Wächter & Maiworm, 2008). However, as Mellion (2008) points out, there are other factors contributing to the enhancement of the international profile of universities that are probably more important than student mobility. Along this line, a fourth decisive factor has to do with upgrading the quality of research, taken to mean essentially the dissemination of scientific discoveries and knowledge in general by means of reputed channels of communication (Hamel, 2007). Finally, another crucial factor for internationalization is the promotion of networking between academics and professionals (Marsh *et al.*, 2013). The possibility of networking internationally, of collaborating with other colleagues and of working together with selected academics from other countries offers a significant opportunity for professional development.

Together with all these forces, there is a mid-level drive stemming from the initiatives promoted at a national level. In the case of Spain, educational authorities have formulated a strategy to increase the number of degrees, courses or modules of which one-third will be offered in English by 2020 (Ministry of Education, Culture and Sports, 2014). Developing the internationalization of universities has also become a priority in the Spanish context, and the role of languages is of paramount importance in this process (Ramos, 2013). However, in general, universities have been taking decisions without a framework of reference in the Spanish context as 'each university tends to develop a different model' (Johnson, 2012: 50), and there are specific challenges that require shared solutions. Consequently, there seems to be a need for a common comprehensible set of actions, or at least suggestions and recommendations, in order to help universities structure a language policy in the service of internationalization. In this context, the Board of Rectors of Spanish Universities (henceforth, CRUE) has established a series of guidelines and regulations with regard to the promotion of a given line of action in higher education (Bazo *et al.*, 2017). The characteristics and significance of the suggestions and recommendations included in the document elaborated by CRUE are aligned with the necessity to establish common lines of action with regard to the elaboration of a language policy specific to each university. The recommendations posited in the document cover three main areas: the linguistic accreditation of students; the qualifications of staff teaching in a different language; and the support needed by the administrative staff to face the challenges of internationalization. In this section, we will describe and analyse the conditions for establishing a language policy aimed at enhancing the international profile of universities. Our attention will be directed mainly at the institutional challenges that this process may entail, and to the decisions and actions that may be taken in order to achieve successful results.

The Role of the Foreign Language and the Mother Tongue in the Process of Internationalization in Higher Education

The significance of languages (in plural) in internationalization

When analysing the role of languages in universities that aspire to enhance their international profile, Byram (2012: 377) states that the promotion of languages in higher education 'is only one element' in the list of reasons addressed when delineating a road map for internationalization. However, if we recognize the role of languages as a significant element and if we are to answer the question 'why is it advisable for universities to have a language policy?', the response appears to be somewhat obvious, because for languages to be used effectively we would need 'a desire or intention to develop English language learning skills' (Dearden, 2014: 12) at all levels and for all purposes. Needless to say, this includes a sound command of all the languages present in the university for teaching staff, local and international students, and administrators (Bazo et al., 2017). This also requires universities to create sufficient mechanisms to ensure that all stakeholders involved are provided with the necessary training and support, and with initiatives that can make this effort a sustainable process (van der Walt, 2013).

Before returning to the idea that languages should be dealt with appropriately, it is worth considering the languages that might be part of the internationalization procedure. It is evident that if one of the objectives is to increase the number of courses taught in a foreign language, global attention to the language of teaching is vital, 'not only to subject-specific language use but specially to classroom discourse, in both native and non-native speaking contexts' (Mancho-Barés & Arnó-Macià, 2017: 270). In the majority of cases in the European context, including Spain, English is the foreign language that is commonly accepted as the instrument to promote internationalization: 'what emerges unambiguously is that in the Bologna process, internationalization means English-medium higher education' (Phillipson, 2009: 37). This leads us to the need to implement ways of raising the standard of this language for all stakeholders. Both teachers and students should have an adequate linguistic level so that the quality of the teaching is not compromised. In essence, this requires equipping students with linguistic competences to help them perform effectively in international enterprises (Kremer & Valcke, 2014), be it mobility, publications or research ventures. Furthermore, administrators should be prepared to deal with international teachers and students, international projects and all other managerial requirements: 'any institution adopting English-medium instruction must also extend its administration and support services to cater to a new heterogeneous student and faculty body in English' (Bradford, 2012: 10).

Revitalizing the role of the mother tongue

While special attention must be paid to the role of foreign languages in universities, it is also essential to consider the position of the mother tongue: 'there is a common concern about the effects of EMI [English-medium instruction] on the many different spheres of higher education and how EMI impacts on the ecology of languages at each university' (Doiz *et al.*, 2014: 173). Providing teaching through English may not attract all international students, although this language is the most widespread international language. Students may be motivated to study in a foreign country because they are interested in learning its language(s) and about its culture, and are genuinely motivated to study through the local language. Secondly, the reasons to study in a foreign country may be associated with the degree of specialization of the chosen studies and the quality of expertise in a particular area that these studies may offer. Thus the decision to study at a given university may be due to its prestige and the desire to deepen knowledge to the maximum level in a particular area. Thirdly, one of the main reasons to support the academic profile of the mother tongue in the process of internationalization stems from consideration for this language; hence, the international market for some countries may demand the utilization of the mother tongue and not a foreign language. It might be the case that a great number of potential international applicants come from countries with a shared mother tongue of the host country. Such is the case of the Spanish-speaking world, which opens up the possibility of a huge market for internationalization. Here we find a more than obvious reason to protect and dignify the role of the mother tongue in the process of internationalization in higher education. This fact would apparently reduce the importance of implementing English-taught programmes in certain countries, for example in Spain, and is used on some occasions to dissuade efforts to promote these studies: 'the move towards English medium education and need to publish in "international" journals may present serious threats to local languages' (Kirkpatrick, 2011: 3).

However, perhaps the discussion, as in the case of Spain, should not be limited to the amount of attention paid to foreign languages. Rather, the focus should be on engaging universities to undertake a careful analysis of the possibilities of attracting international students, and on making an effort to recognize and identify the strengths of each university, irrespective of their origin and of the language that would ultimately be used. In addition, the implementation of partial English-taught programmes, or bilingual programmes, with English and the mother tongue coexisting within the curriculum, maintains the relevance of the mother tongue with respect to the 'international' foreign language (Preisler, 2009), without mentioning the pedagogical benefits of keeping the use of the L1: 'The theories associated to input and interaction in the L2 have been put in the shade by those advocating code-mixing, use of the L1, and translanguaging' (Macaro,

2020: 272). Therefore, policy makers might proceed accordingly to delineate a road map for internationalization that takes into account the potential of every university, the possible applicants for the courses offered and the languages that may be needed.

Language Policies: Institutional Challenges

Is a language policy necessary?

Perhaps the most obvious concern in identifying problems associated with the elaboration of a language policy for the whole university is the need to understand why it is necessary (Tollefson & Tsui, 2004). Maybe the consideration of languages as purely instrumental (Wright, 2004) largely dismisses the necessity to think of a language policy as a strategic priority for universities. It may be argued that what matters is that the academic content is transmitted adequately. However, this assumes that the language used as a vehicle of communication is used correctly. As a consequence, the importance of language, not only the foreign language but also the mother tongue, is overlooked and very little or no attention is paid to the characteristics of the language utilized as a medium of instruction (Aguilar & Muñoz, 2014). This omission may have negative consequences since the construction of meaning depends entirely on the quality of the language that is used to transmit knowledge: 'By acquiring the language of a subject and reflecting on it consciously, all learners, independent of their background, will master the content and accompanying tasks more successfully' (Council of Europe, 2015: 10). Correspondingly, paying little or no attention to the language will certainly have a negative effect on the acquisition of content.

The second problem is a lack of appreciation, or perhaps ignorance in some cases, of what a language policy consists of and its potential benefits. Although we can find numerous documents and recommendations regarding the implementation of language policies at the supranational level in Europe and 'the advance in language policies, both at the Council of Europe and at the European Commission, has been recurrent during the last 35 years' (Julián de Vega & Ávila, 2018: 20), it seems as if these suggestions have not filtered down to the strategies and regulations of the universities. On a larger scale, in a study on the global growth of English as a medium of instruction, Dearden (2014: 12) points out the surprising fact that less than half of the participants were aware of the existence of a policy in their universities: 'the majority of the teachers interviewed suspected that there was a strategy but it was not explicit and believed that the lack of official policy was perhaps due to the fact that EMI was new'. Even if language policies are explicitly or implicitly considered in an internationalization strategy, universities should be aware that the areas of influence of a language policy cannot be limited to defining the levels of the language when used for different purposes such as teaching or management, or to regulate the certifications that allow teachers and students to attain a certain accreditation in language proficiency (Ramos & Pavón, 2018). On the contrary, a language policy covers all the circumstances in which the language is involved, both academic and non-academic. Therefore, the issues needing to be addressed range from the complex academic material of a lesson to enhancing the teachers' and students' competences to perform in the international sphere (Wilkinson, 2018) – from, for example, coordinating the departments related to all the languages present in the university academic life (Zappa-Hollman, 2018) to learning to deploy resources such as language centres or schools (Julián de Vega & Ávila, 2018).

Benefits of a language policy

This absence of an appreciation of language policies may emanate in some cases from unfamiliarity with the benefits of a language policy. Whether national, regional or local, language policies are useful instruments which, on the one hand, value the significance of languages in the process of internationalization of universities (Cancino *et al.*, 2011) and, on the other, draw attention to the relation between content and language (Fortanet-Gómez, 2013), vital for the success of any teaching programme, as previously mentioned. A language policy also serves to establish a common framework of lines of action, without which the level of efficacy of universities to expand their international profiles and different schools, colleges and institutions would be seriously compromised (Lauridsen, 2013). For example, when taking into account the characteristics of universities, careful consideration should be paid to the definition of accreditation levels, validation of certifications, productive training programmes for teachers and students, and initiatives to support all the stakeholders in all aspects related to language (Ramos, 2013). We may conclude that the elaboration of a language policy should be approached from a global perspective if we wish to outline a strategy for the whole university, but at the same time it should be noted that these policies should also allow space for universities to modify and adapt the regulations to their own particular profiles and objectives (Pavón & Gaustad, 2013).

English-taught Programmes: Institutional Challenges

Organization

An analysis of the challenges affecting the implementation of English-taught programmes (Bradford, 2012; Valcke & Wilkinson, 2017; Wilkinson & Walsh, 2015) is inextricably linked to many of the previously discussed misconceptions and possible confusions associated with these programmes. Unfortunately, the conceptualization of the very nature and characteristics of English-taught programmes may directly affect the way in which universities face the challenges of their implementation.

The most visible misunderstanding derives from the idea that the main objective of these programmes is to boost the linguistic level of the students; therefore, the main instrument to achieve this target is to offer a given number of subjects that assure this improvement. However, as Dearden (2014) states, even though the increase in the levels of language proficiency may be a reasonable target, we should also include more specific objectives such as the necessity to balance the acquisition of receptive and productive skills, and the obligation to cope with a broader learning of the language together with the academic language connected to the content material. Another problem is that students should possess a minimum level of competence that allows them to progress adequately in these subjects (Jäapinen, 2005). This might change the significance of the primary objective, as this should not only be that the students improve, but that they should have previously acquired the necessary baseline level (Kremer & Valcke, 2014). It is also claimed that, if language proficiency is the primary target, the objective should really be that these programmes equip students with linguistic, multicultural and professional competences that will be extremely useful for their professional development in a globalized market (Stier, 2006). When planning English-taught programmes we should decide if this is exactly what students need, and consequently identify what universities should provide and not focus so much on improving language proficiency. Unfortunately, the desire to enhance the international profile of universities has provoked a rush to offer studies in English, leading to a situation where decisions regarding the implementation of these programmes are not well defined nor founded with respect to the significance of languages (Alexander, 2008; Sercu, 2004).

Besides possible misunderstandings about the objectives and benefits of English-taught programmes, other aspects require careful consideration if we are to tackle the institutional challenges and threats that need resolution (Costa & Coleman, 2012; Evans & Morrison, 2011; Tatzl, 2011). First of all, from a general perspective, universities have to decide if the decisions, including the control of the volume and type of these programmes, will follow a top-down or a bottom-up strategy, or maybe a mixture of both (Dafouz, 2018). That is, the university may decide to create a language policy that includes the prerequisites for implementing English-taught programmes which is to be applied to all the faculties and schools. Perhaps the university may simply provide legal cover and possible support to proposals designed and implemented in certain faculties and schools. Or, as a third option, the university can elaborate a global language policy with all the necessary dimensions clearly defined but with a certain degree of flexibility (Marsh et al., 2013). This would allow some particular proposals to benefit from shared actions such as common training and incentives programmes, but also allow them to pursue their own specific objectives.

Objectives

A second institutional challenge connects the existence of a language policy with the implementation of English-taught programmes, in the sense that if such a university policy exists there should be a clear definition of the programme objectives (Madrid & Julius, 2017). In addition, the decision regarding which studies could be offered in English must be based on a careful analysis of the benefits and academic gains for the students and the university (Pavón & Gaustad, 2013), which will ultimately lead to prioritizing some studies over others. Needless to say that the decision should be driven by an exploration and identification of the intrinsic challenges in each particular case. The aforementioned flourishing of these programmes in many universities suggests favouring a process which prioritizes the quality of teaching and not the number of studies offered in English (Macaro *et al.*, 2018). Finally, with regard to the relationship between language policies and English-taught programmes, any plan aiming to achieve positive results must consider the financial implications with a special focus on the investment in human resources: 'funding for designing international curricula is pivotal for material development [...], and staff stability, recruitment and training' (Méndez García & Casal, 2018: 49). Whether specifically intended for the upgrading of the qualifications of existing teaching staff or to facilitate hiring teachers who already possess the necessary linguistic and methodological competences, the university must accept that the most essential component in ensuring quality in the teaching process is the human factor: 'lack of attention to language lies not only in lecturers' low levels of proficiency, but also in a lack of training in language teaching, which would, in turn, involve a lack of language awareness' (Arnó-Macià & Mancho-Barés, 2015: 71). Consequently, universities should provide all resources to ensure that highly qualified and appropriately experienced staff can teach effectively.

Model

A third challenge regards the type of model of teaching through English that is going to be implemented. On the one hand, we may opt to choose a simple and straightforward instruction in English, commonly known as English-medium instruction (EMI) (Dearden, 2004). On the other hand, we may focus on facilitating the integration of language and content in a similar way to that being done at other stages of education (Marsh, 2003). This approach is known as the integration of content and language in higher education (ICLHE) (Wilkinson & Walsh, 2015), often proposed as a refined version of EMI. The decision as to whether to choose EMI or ICLHE is crucial, since this determines the importance given to the language in the programme. As Schmidt-Unterberger (2018: 528) puts it, the difference between EMI and ICLHE is 'more than just a terminological consideration'. In EMI, for example, the attention to the development of the language is minimal or completely non-existent as the students are assumed to possess the necessary linguistic proficiency in the language of instruction. In contrast, in the ICLHE model there is an explicit intention to promote the development of the academic language of the students. In an attempt to balance the combination of grammar and content in this second model, Walenta (2018: 580) suggests the adoption of content-based structured input (CBSI), a proposal in which students receive 'full processing instruction *and* explicit information about the target form'.

What is relevant here is that the choice of one or the other model will have a direct influence on the effectiveness and quality of the teaching offered (Smit & Dafouz, 2013). Therefore, the option as to whether to implement EMI or ICLHE must be based on an explicit decision involving the appropriate screening of the proficiency of the students and an identification of the objectives of the programme (Karabinar, 2008).

Benchmarking

A fourth dimension that has to be closely studied relates to the issue of benchmarking (Haines & Ashworth, 2008). The comparison of results of courses taught in English with those taught in the mother tongue is probably one of the most frequent concerns for policy makers, teachers and students: 'instructors need to make constant adaptation to their lectures, and this affects the quality and quantity of content' (Bradford, 2012: 9). Thus, it is very common for stakeholders to experience a degree of anxiety concerning the possible lowering of content objectives (Johnson, 2012). It is reasonable to assume that students' (and teachers') lack of proficiency in the language may result in a deterioration in the quality of the content material (Fortanet, 2008). Firstly, this is because the time devoted to covering the content in English is longer than when the same task is carried out in the mother tongue, as the teachers need to deploy a variety of methodological strategies that take more time (Airey, 2004). Secondly, since the students' capacity to deal with complex material is not as high in the foreign language as it is in the mother tongue, their capacity to understand may consequently be reduced (Rubio-Cuenca & Moore, 2018).

In general, it should also be noted that the increased richness of teachers' pedagogy is of paramount importance: 'A key challenge faced in university teaching is how to actively engage students in the course material and learning objectives' (Walker, 2009: 214). In these programmes, in particular, the level of attention and engagement entailed in using a foreign language has a noticeable effect on the learning of the content material (Aguilar & Muñoz, 2014; Wong, 2010). The outcomes of this change are the students' increased capacity to store and recall information (Cots, 2013). In these contexts, benchmarking of results is a reasonable concern but the benefits deriving from a more effective way to acquire content material should be considered alongside linguistic achievement.

The problem is that, despite the wide array of topics covered when analysing the characteristics of EMI programmes, specifically the teaching and learning process (Kremer & Valcke, 2014) and the role of language in the classroom (Sánchez-Pérez, 2020), there is little evidence or empirical results of the outcomes of these programmes: 'a small number of studies in the literature review actually presented empirical evidence to underpin their impact' (Kremer & Valcke, 2014: 1438). Furthermore, when they exist, systematic reviews show that many lack the necessary rigour according to scientific standards: 'it cannot be stated that the majority of the evidences found are reliable from a purely scientific point of view' (Rubio-Alcalá *et al*., 2019: 199). It seems clear that if we are aiming to establish whether or not EMI programmes may produce satisfactory results there should be proof of the outcomes, that is, 'there is an urgent need for a research-driven approach which consults key stake-holders at a national and international level and which measures the complex processes involved in EMI and the effects of EMI' (Dearden, 2014: 2). Also, it would be more than welcome if language and content specialists could conduct EMI research collaboratively; as Macaro (2020: 274) puts it, 'there has to be a research partnership between researchers in applied linguistics and researchers in those disciplines which are being taught through the medium of English'. What we cannot pretend is to rely only on the purported benefits, in many cases well documented, of English-taught programmes in other levels of education: 'insights drawn from research conducted in secondary education cannot simply be transferred to the tertiary level of education' (Schmidt-Unterberger, 2018: 528).

Language proficiency entry levels

A fifth challenge is associated with the linguistic prerequisites that teachers and students require in order to participate in this type of programme: 'Limitations in university teachers' linguistic competencies also pose challenges for program quality' (Bradford, 2012: 9). This is a problematic area due to the complexity of determining the necessary linguistic proficiency, as 'practice shows that EMI teaching competence is extremely difficult to define in linguistic terms' (Gustafsson, 2018: 2). Regarding the linguistic qualifications of the teaching staff, it is commonly agreed in the literature (Lasagabaster & Ruiz de Zarobe, 2010: 288) that a C1 or a C2 level should be the linguistic level required for teachers using a foreign language, in accordance with the Common European Framework of Reference for Languages (Council of Europe, 2001). In most cases, C1 or C2 evidences a linguistic level appropriate for teaching, but it is impossible to say that linguistic level alone is proof of being capable of teaching through a language (O'Dowd, 2018), as the teachers' methodological competences not included in linguistic certification are decisive for effective teaching (Chappel, 2015; Klaassen, 2008). This leads us to the necessity to equip teachers not only with communicative awareness and knowledge of cultural and multicultural aspects (Gustafsson, 2018), but with a pedagogic understanding of what teaching through English really entails. Contero *et al.* (2018: 133) state that 'certain methodological aspects need to be included in bilingual teacher development activities designed for lecturers' which, at the same time, suggests the creation of a training programme to cover this area: 'any university which is offering any number of subjects through English should be preparing training and development courses for their teachers involved in this activity' (O'Dowd, 2018: 561).

With regard to students, another decision that has to be taken cautiously is the prerequisite for establishing a minimum entry level to enrol on English-taught programmes (Lynch *et al.*, 2001). This is another controversial decision based on an often erroneous assumption that students should possess a proficiency in the language that allows them to learn in the foreign language: 'Although we see how English as a medium of instruction might positively affect students' English mastery level, other studies show how this hinders content learning' (Kremer & Valcke, 2014: 1432). In view of this assumption, some universities may be tempted to introduce a certain degree of flexibility leading to a lowering of the entry level to facilitate the enrolment of students. Needless to say, this is a dangerous decision which will obviously increase the number of enrolments but will seriously compromise the quality of teaching (Norris & Phillips, 2003). Lack of attention to such an important aspect may result in a possible withdrawal of teachers who become frustrated that lessons cannot be conducted in English. It may also result in a possible withdrawal of students, who sooner or later will notice that the quality of the teaching is considerably lower compared to lessons conducted in the mother tongue.

Teachers' professional development

A final important challenge that is frequently relegated to a lower level of consideration is the personal profile and professional development of the teachers participating in these programmes (Ruiz de Zarobe & Lyster, 2018; Smith, 2004). In general, we could say that being involved in these programmes is something that university teachers appreciate; as Dafouz (2018: 546) puts it, 'lecturers in this setting usually view EMI as an investment in their own professional identity and a means to strengthen their agency in international circles'. We should be aware, however, that the linguistic conditions, mainly due to the proficiency level of students as well as teachers, automatically entail teaching that will be different from when the mother tongue is used (Airey & Linder, 2008; Johnson, 2012). Thus, teachers may be concerned about the changes that are likely to occur when teaching through English (Ellison *et al.*, 2017) and how the experience is going to affect them personally and professionally, especially in relation to a lack of confidence when they are lecturing in English: 'This weakness puts our highly experienced lecturers in an uncomfortable situation' (Doiz *et al.*, 2019: 159). This also includes their ability to cope with the new situation (Aguilar & Rodríguez, 2012; Jensen & Thogersen, 2011), including the amount of extra work involved or the evaluation procedure now that language has a vital role in the acquisition of content. In the case of students, they may experience a similar degree of discomfort caused by the additional difficulties of learning through English, especially if their level of English is lower than required (Gu, 2014). They may also show resentment in situations where teachers are not proficient enough in the foreign language (Lasagabaster *et al.*, 2019).

Conclusion

The implementation of English-taught courses has become an unstoppable process in European higher education as well as in many other parts of the world. It is one of the most ground-breaking initiatives to promote the international profile of universities. The rush to offer studies in English can be seen as a seismic movement which has taken its toll on many universities unprepared for the enterprise of managing the transition to becoming more international. Consequently, they may be unsure as to how best to proceed with regard to the important decisions that need to be taken. In some cases, this process has triggered a series of initiatives at the organizational level. However, implications for human resources as well as a lack of clear objectives and a sound structure have the potential to lead to unexpected and undesirable results. The aspiration to increase the number of courses taught in English has also uncovered numerous unforeseen problems at a time when universities feel obliged to introduce English-taught studies in the belief that this will enhance their international dimension.

English is now recognized as the lingua franca in the worlds of science, technology, business, tourism, etc., and at the same time it is acknowledged that the movement towards internationalization is triggering a process of *Englishization* in higher education institutions. Despite the existence of a clear line of action derived from supranational and national policies, and the fact that the duality of going international and offering English-taught programmes has become a strategic priority for the majority of universities, university policy makers should carefully consider the impact of all this. For internationalization, universities should review their decisions concerning the role and significance of both the foreign language and the mother tongue. For example, in Spain, Spanish-taught programmes may have a comparable market to English-taught programmes, and overemphasis on the latter may have a profound social and cultural influence on the acquisition of competences by students. Multiculturality and interculturality will obviously be developed through these programmes, but it is necessary to consider the balance with regard to possible damage to the local culture and language.

Another issue that has to be resolved is whether favouring the implementation of English-taught programmes should be part of a global university-wide strategy or if the target should rather be to offer support to small-scale initiatives launched by schools, faculties, colleges or departments. Experience has shown that bottom-up proposals initiated at these levels may come to nothing in the medium and long term if they are not consistently supported by a university-wide policy, no matter how correctly ideated. For example, the elaboration of a programme of incentives for both teachers and students (teaching load reduction or recognition of studies, to name but two) requires funding and organizational regulations that can only be obtained from top-down initiatives. Absence of incentives may result in initial discomfort, and potentially in programme abandonment. The same importance must be attached to decisions concerning the model to be implemented. We have seen that the benefits of implementing content and language integrated learning (CLIL) at non-university levels has prompted the desire to implement a similar model (ICLHE) in higher education. However, the complexity of this second proposal and probably the lack of understanding of how to coordinate language and content effectively by content specialists has led the majority of universities to adopt an EMI model. A realistic blunt assessment of the situation might be that language specialists may want to choose ICLHE as a model, but the reality is that most universities finally choose EMI due to its ease of implementation, the presence of organizational difficulties and a lack of interdepartmental coordination, thus avoiding possible resistance by teachers and students. Universities therefore need to be aware of the differences between these two models and to be able to choose that which best adapts to their characteristics and needs.

The language proficiency of both teachers and students is another important factor that should be treated with caution, as the effective use of the language of instruction determines the effectiveness of the programme. For this reason, this aspect should be very high on the list of priorities. Expecting teachers to exhibit a given level of proficiency to perform in the foreign language, together with the necessary possession of certain pedagogical skills, are requirements for a minimum degree of quality, as is the identification of obligatory entry levels for the students enrolled in these studies. Finally, when analysing the relevance of these institutional challenges, we cannot forget the concerns of teachers and students, specifically regarding the emotional dimension of being involved in English-taught programmes. These include the fear of a possible lowering of the quality of the content and concern about the additional difficulties for students, as well as the extra amount of work for teachers. Universities would do well to diagnose and explore the diverse kinds of extrinsic and intrinsic motivations that lead teachers and students to participate and, perhaps more importantly, their levels of satisfaction after being involved for some time. What is also clear is that there is an urgent need to give account of the outcomes of these programmes. Universities are urged to present substantial evidence of progress and results by conducting research in all these areas. Mere speculation cannot be allowed to dominate when it comes to identifying areas that require special attention.

References

Aguilar, M. and Muñoz, C. (2014) The effect of proficiency on CLIL: Benefits in engineering students in Spain. *International Journal of Applied Linguistics* 24 (1), 1–18.

Aguilar, M. and Rodríguez, R. (2012) Implementing CLIL at a Spanish university: Lecturer and student perceptions. *International Journal of Bilingual Education and Bilingualism* 15 (2), 183–197.

Airey, J. (2004) Can you teach it in English? Aspects of the language choice debate in Swedish higher education. In R. Wilkinson (ed.) *Integrating Content and Language: Meeting the Challenge of a Multilingual Higher Education* (pp. 97–108). Maastricht: Maastricht University.

Airey, J. and Linder, C. (2008) Bilingual scientific literacy? The use of English in Swedish university science courses. *Nordic Journal of English Studies* 7 (3), 145–161.

Albatch, P.G. and Knight, J. (2007) The internationalisation of higher education: Motivations and realities. *Journal of Studies in International Education* 11 (3), 290–305.

Alexander, R.J. (2008) 'International' programmes in the German-speaking world and englishization: A critical analysis. In R. Wilkinson and V. Zegers (eds) *Realizing Content and Language Integration in Higher Education* (pp. 77–95). Maastricht: Maastricht University.

Arnó-Macià, E. and Mancho-Barés, G. (2015) The role of content and language in content and language integrated learning (CLIL) at university: Challenges and implications for ESP. *English for Specific Purposes* 37, 63–73.

Bazo, P., Centellas, A., Dafouz, E., Fernández, A., González, D. and Pavón, V. (2017) *Documento marco de política lingüística para la internacionalización del sistema universitario español* [Towards a Language Policy for the Internationalisation of Spanish Universities: A Framework of Reference]. Madrid: CRUE-IC. See https://is.muni.cz/do/rect/metodika/VaV/vyzkum/hr4mu/CRUE_DMPL_14.10.16_EN.pdf.

Bolsman, C. and Miller, H. (2008) International student recruitment to universities in England: Discourse, rationales and globalisation. *Globalisation, Societies and Education* 6 (1), 75–88.

Bradford, A. (2012) Challenges in adopting English-taught programmes. *International Higher Education* 69, 8–10.

Brumfit, C. (2004) Language and higher education: Two current challenges. *Arts and Humanities in Higher Education* 3, 163–173.

Byram, M. (2012) A note on internationalisation, internationalism and language teaching and learning. *Language Learning Journal* 40 (3), 375–381.

Cancino, R., Dam, L. and Jaeger, K. (2011) *Policies, Principles, Practices: New Directions in Foreign Language Education in the Era of Educational Globalization*. Cambridge: Cambridge Scholars.

Chan, W. and Dimmock, C. (2008) The internationalisation of universities: Globalist, internationalist and translocalist models. *Journal of Research in International Education* 7, 184–203.

Chappel, J. (2015) Teaching English is not necessarily the teaching of English. *International Education Studies* 8 (3), 1–13.

Coleman, J.A. (2006) English-medium teaching in European higher education. *Language Teaching* 39, 1–14.

Contero, C., Zayas, F. and Arco-Tirado, J.L. (2018) Addressing CLIL lecturers' needs: Reflections on specific methodological training. *Porta Linguarum (Special Issue 3: Addressing Bilingualism in Higher Education: Policies and Implementation Issues)*, 121–135.

Costa, F. and Coleman, J.A. (2012) A survey of English-medium instruction in Italian higher education. *International Journal of Bilingual Education and Bilingualism* 16 (1), 3–19.

Cots, J.M. (2013) Introducing English-medium instruction at the University of Lleida, Spain: Intervention, beliefs and practices. In A. Doiz, D. Lasagabaster and J.M. Sierra (eds) *English-Medium Instruction at Universities: Global Challenges* (pp. 106–128). Bristol: Multilingual Matters.

Council of Europe (2001) *Common European Framework of Reference for Languages*. Cambridge: Cambridge University Press.

Council of Europe (2015) *The Language Dimension in All Subjects*. Strasbourg: Language Policy Unit.

Crossman, K. (2018) Immersed in academic English: Vocabulary and academic outcomes of a CLIL university preparation course. *International Journal of Bilingual Education and Bilingualism* 21 (5), 564–577.

Dafouz, E. (2018) English-medium instruction and teacher education programmes in higher education: Ideological forces and imagined identities at work. *International Journal of Bilingual Education and Bilingualism* 21 (5), 540–552.

Dearden, J. (2014) *English as a Medium of Instruction: A Growing Phenomenon*. London: British Council.

Doiz, A., Lasagabaster, D. and Sierra, J.M. (2011) Internationalisation, multilingualism and English-medium instruction. *World Englishes* 30 (3), 345–359.

Doiz, A., Lasagabaster, D. and Sierra, J.M. (2014) What does 'international university' mean at a European bilingual university? The role of languages and culture. *Language Awareness* 23 (1–2), 172–186.

Doiz, A., Lasagabaster, D. and Pavón, V. (2019) The integration of language and content in English-medium instruction courses: Lecturers' beliefs and practices. *Ibérica: European Association of Languages for Specific Purposes* 38, 151–176.

Ellison, M., Araújo, S., Correia, M. and Vieira, F. (2017) Teachers' perceptions of need in EAP and ICLHE contexts. In J. Valcke and R. Wilkinson (eds) *Integrating Content and Language in Higher Education: Perspectives on Professional Practice* (pp. 59–76). Frankfurt: Peter Lang.

European Commission (2012) *Eurobarometer 2012: Europeans and their Languages*. Brussels: European Commission.

European Commission/EACEA/Eurydice (2018) *The European Higher Education Area in 2018: Bologna Process Implementation Report*. Luxembourg: Publications Office of the European Union.

Eurydice (2005) *Key Data on Teaching Languages at School in Europe*. Brussels: European Commission.

Evans, S. and Morrison, B. (2011) Meeting the challenges of English-medium higher education: The first-year experience in Hong Kong. *English for Specific Purposes* 30, 198–208.

Fortanet, I. (2008) Questions for debate in English medium lecturing in Spain. In R. Wilkinson and V. Zegers (eds) *Realizing Content and Language Integration in Higher Education* (pp. 21–31). Maastricht: Maastricht University.

Fortanet-Gómez, I. (2013) *CLIL in Higher Education: Towards a Multilingual Language Policy*. Bristol: Multilingual Matters.

Gu, M. (2014) From opposition to transcendence: The language practices and ideologies of students in a multilingual university. *International Journal of Bilingual Education and Bilingualism* 17 (3), 310–329.

Gustafsson, A. (2018) Capturing EMI teachers' linguistic needs: A usage-based perspective. *International Journal of Bilingual Education and Bilingualism* (online), 1–12.

Haines, K. and Ashworth, A. (2008) A reflective approach to HE language provision: Integrating context and language through semi-structured reflection. In R. Wilkinson and V. Zegers (eds) *Realizing Content and Language Integration in Higher Education* (pp. 201–212). Maastricht: Maastricht University.

Hamel, R.E. (2007) The dominance of English in the international scientific periodical literature and the future of language use in science. *AILA Review* 20, 53–71.

High Level Group on Multilingualism (2007) *Final Report.* See https://op.europa.eu/en/publication-detail/-/publication/b0a1339f-f181-4de5-abd3-130180f177c7.

Holdsworth, P. (2004) EU policy on language learning and linguistic diversity as it relates to content and language integrated learning and higher education. In R. Wilkinson (ed.) *Integrating Content and Language: Meeting the Challenge of a Multilingual Higher Education* (pp. 20–27). Maastricht: Universitaire Pers Maastricht.

Jäppinen, A.K. (2005) Thinking and content learning of mathematics and science as cognitional development in content and language integrated learning (CLIL): Teaching through a foreign language in Finland. *Language and Education* 19 (2), 148–166.

Jensen, C. and Thøgersen, J. (2011) Danish university lecturers' attitudes towards English as the medium of instruction. *Ibérica* 22, 13–34.

Johnson, M. (2012) Bilingual degree teachers' beliefs: A case study in a tertiary setting. *Pulso* 35, 49–74.

Julián de Vega, C. and Ávila, J. (2018) Políticas lingüísticas europeas y españolas: el camino hacia el cambio en la educacion terciaria [European and Spanish language policies: The road to changing tertiary education]. *Porta Linguarum (Special Issue 3, Addressing Bilingualism in Higher Education: Policies and Implementation Issues)*, 17–30.

Karabinar, S. (2008) Integrating language and content: Two models and their effects on the learners' academic self-concept. In R. Wilkinson and V. Zegers (eds) *Realizing Content and Language Integration in Higher Education* (pp. 53–63). Maastricht: Maastricht University.

Kirkpatrick, A. (2011) Internationalization or Englishization: Medium of instruction in today's universities. Working Paper No. 2011/003. Hong Kong: Hong Kong Institute of Education.

Klaassen, R. (2008) Preparing lecturers for English-medium instruction. In R. Wilkinson and V. Zegers (eds) *Realizing Content and Language Integration in Higher Education* (pp. 32–42). Maastricht: Maastricht University.

Knight, J. (2004) Internationalization remodelled: Definition, approaches, and rationales. *Journal of Studies in International Education* 8 (1), 5–31.

Knight, J. (2009) Internationalization: Unintended consequences. *International Higher Education* 54, 8–10.

Knight, J. (2012) Five truths about internationalization. *International Higher Education* 69, 4–5.

Knight, J. and de Wit, H. (1995) Strategies for internationalisation of higher education: Historical and conceptual perspectives. In H. de Wit (ed.) *Strategies for Internationalisation: A Comparative Study of Australia, Canada, Europe and the United States of America* (pp. 5–32). Amsterdam: European Association for International Education (EAIE).

Kremer, M. and Valcke, M. (2014) Teaching and learning in English in higher education: A literature review. In *Edulearn14 Proceedings* (pp. 1430–1441). Valencia: IATED.

Lasagabaster, D. and Ruiz de Zarobe, Y. (eds) (2010) *CLIL in Spain: Implementation, Results and Teacher Training.* Newcastle upon Tyne: Cambridge Scholars.

Lasagabaster, D., Doiz, A. and Pavón, V. (2019) Undergraduates' beliefs about the role of language and team teaching in EMI courses at university. *Rassegna Italiana di Linguistica Applicata – RILA* 2 (3), 111–127.

Lauridsen, K. (2013) *Higher Education Language Policy.* Strasbourg: European Language Council.

Lynch, A., Klee, C.A and Tedick, D.J. (2001) Social factors and language proficiency in postsecondary Spanish immersion: Issues and implications. *Hispania* 84 (3), 510–524.

Macaro, E. (2020) Exploring the role of language in English medium instruction. *International Journal of Bilingual Education and Bilingualism* 23 (3), 263–276.

Macaro, E., Curle, S., Pun, J., An, J. and Dearden, J. (2018) A systematic review of English medium instruction in higher education. *Language Teaching* 51 (1), 36–76.

Madrid, D. and Julius, S.M. (2017) Quality factors in bilingual education at the university level. *Porta Linguarum* 28, 49–66.

Mancho-Barés, G. and Arnó-Macià, E. (2017) EMI lecturer training programmes and academic literacies: A critical insight from ESP. *ESP Today* 5 (2), 266–290.

Marsh, D. (2002) The Emergence of CLIL in Europe 1958–2002. In E. Kärkkäinen, J. Haynes and T. Lauttamus (eds) *Studia Linguistics ar Literaria Septentrionalia*. Studies presented to Heikki Nyyssönes (pp. 205–225). Finland: University of Oulu.

Marsh, D. and Laitinen, J. (2005) *Medium of Instruction in European Higher Education: Summary of Research Outcomes of European Network for Language Learning amongst Undergraduates (ENLU) Task Group 4*. Jyväskylä: UniCOM, University of Jyväskylä.

Marsh, D., Pavón, V. and Frigols, M.J. (2013) *The Higher Education Languages Landscape: Ensuring Quality in English Language Degree Programmes*. Valencia: Valencian International University.

Mellion, M.J. (2008) The challenge of changing tongues in business university education. In R. Wilkinson and V. Zegers (eds) *Realizing Content and Language Integration in Higher Education* (pp. 212–227). Maastricht: Maastricht University.

Méndez García, M.C. and Casal, S. (2018) Towards an identification of provisos for the implementation of plurilingualism in higher education. *Porta Linguarum (Special Issue 3, Addressing Bilingualism in Higher Education: Policies and Implementation Issues)*, 47–60.

Ministry of Education, Culture and Sports (2014) *Estrategia para la Internacionalización de las Universidades Españolas 2015–2020 [Strategy for the Internationalisation of Spanish Universities]*. Madrid: Secretaría General Técnica, Centro de Publicaciones.

Norris, S.P. and Phillips, L.M. (2003) How literacy in its fundamental sense is central to scientific literacy. *Science Education* 87 (2), 224–240.

O'Dowd, R. (2018) The training and accreditation of teachers for English medium instruction: An overview of practice in European universities. *International Journal of Bilingual Education and Bilingualism* 21 (5), 553–563.

Pavón, V. and Gaustad, M. (2013) Designing bilingual programmes for higher education in Spain: Organisational, curricular and methodological decisions. *International CLIL Research Journal* 1 (5), 82–94.

Phillipson, R. (2009) English in higher education: Panacea or pandemic? *Angles on the English-Speaking World* 9, 29–57.

Preisler, B. (2009) Complementary languages: The national language and English as working languages in European universities. *Angles on the English-Speaking World* 9, 10–28.

Ramos, A.M. (2013) Higher education bilingual programmes in Spain. *Porta Linguarum* 19, 101–111.

Ramos, A. and Pavón, V. (2018) The linguistic internationalization of higher education: A study on the presence of language policies and bilingual studies in Spanish universities. *Porta Linguarum (Special Issue 3, Addressing Bilingualism in Higher Education: Policies and Implementation Issues)*, 31–46.

Ritzen, J. (2004) Across the bridge: Towards an international university. In R. Wilkinson (ed.) *Integrating Content and Language: Meeting the Challenge of a Multilingual Higher Education* (pp. 28–40). Maastricht: Universitaire Pers Maastricht.

Rizvi, F. (2007) Internationalisation of curriculum: A critical perspective. In M. Hayden, J. Levy and J. Thompson (eds) *The Sage Handbook of Research in International Education* (pp. 390–408). London: Sage.

Rubio-Alcalá, F.D., Arco, J.L., Fernández, F., Barrios, E. and Pavón, V. (2019) A systematic review on evidences supporting quality indicators of bilingual, plurilingual and multilingual programs in higher education. *Educational Research Review* 27, 191–204.

Rubio-Cuenca, F. and Moore, P. (2018) Teacher attitudes to language in university bilingual education. *Porta Linguarum (Special Issue 3: Addressing Bilingualism in Higher Education: Policies and Implementation Issues)*, 81–102.

Ruiz de Zarobe, Y. and Lyster, R. (2018) Content and language integration in higher education: Instructional practices and teacher development. *International Journal of Bilingual Education and Bilingualism* 21 (5), 523–526.

Sánchez-Pérez, M.M. (ed.) (2020) *Teacher Training for English-Medium Instruction in Higher Education*. Hershey, PA: IGI Global.

Schmidt-Unterberger, B. (2018) The English-medium paradigm: A conceptualization of English-medium teaching in higher education. *International Journal of Bilingual Education and Bilingualism* 21 (5), 527–539.

Seidlhofer, B. (2001) Closing a conceptual gap: The case for a description of English as a lingua franca. *International Journal of Applied Linguistics* 11, 133–158.

Sercu, L. (2004) The introduction of English-medium instruction in universities: A comparison of Flemish lecturers' and students' language skills, perceptions and attitudes. In R. Wilkinson (ed.) *Integrating Content and Language: Meeting the Challenge of a Multilingual Education* (pp. 547–555). Maastricht: Maastricht University.

Smit, U. (2013) Learning affordances in integrating content and English as a lingua franca ('ICELF'): On an implicit approach to English medium teaching. *Journal of Academic Writing* 3 (1), 15–29.

Smit, U. and Dafouz, E. (eds) (2013) *Integrating Content and Language in Higher Education: An Introduction to English Medium Policies, Conceptual Issues and Research Practices across Europe*. AILA Review 25, 1–12. Amsterdam: John Benjamins.

Smith, K. (2004) Studying in an additional language: What is gained, what is lost and what is assessed? In R. Wilkinson (ed.) *Integrating Content and Language: Meeting the Challenge of a Multilingual Higher Education* (pp. 78–93). Maastricht: Universitaire Pers Maastricht.

Stier, J. (2006) Internationalisation, intercultural communication and intercultural competence. *Journal of Intercultural Communication* 11, 1–12.

Tatzl, D. (2011) English-medium masters' programmes at an Austrian university of applied sciences: Attitudes, experiences and challenges. *Journal of English for Academic Purposes* 10, 252–270.

Tollefson, J.W. and Tsui, A.B.M. (eds) (2004) *Medium of Instruction Policies: Which Agenda? Whose Agenda?* Mahwah, NJ: Lawrence Erlbaum.

Valcke, J. and Wilkinson, R. (eds) (2017) *Integrating Content and Language in Higher Education: Perspectives on Professional Practice*. Frankfurt am Main: Peter Lang.

van der Walt, C. (2013) *Multilingual Higher Education: Beyond English-Medium Orientations*. Bristol: Multilingual Matters.

Wächter, B. and Maiworn, F. (2008) *English-taught Programmes in European Higher Education*. Bonn: Lemmens.

Wächter, B. and Maiworn, F. (eds) (2014) *English-taught Programmes in European Higher Education: The State of Play in 2014*. Bonn: Lemmens.

Walenta, M. (2018) Balancing linguistic and extra-linguistic gains in CLIL: A case for content-based structured input. *International Journal of Bilingual Education and Bilingualism* 21 (5), 578–590.

Walker, C. (2009) Teaching policy theory and its applications to practice using long structured case studies: An approach that deeply engages undergraduate students. *International Journal of Teaching and Learning in Higher Education* 20 (2), 214–225.

Wilkinson, R. (2018) Content and language integration at universities? Collaborative reflections. *International Journal of Bilingual Education and Bilingualism* 21 (5), 607–615.

Wilkinson, R. and Walsh, M.L. (2015) *Integrating Content and Language in Higher Education: From Theory to Practice*. Peter Lang: Maastricht.

Wong, R. (2010) The effectiveness of using English as the sole medium of instruction in English classes: Student responses and improved English proficiency. *Porta Linguarum* 13, 119–130.

Wright, S. (2004) *Language Policy and Language Planning: From Nationalism to Globalisation*. London: Palgrave Macmillan.

Zappa-Hollman, S. (2018) Collaborations between language and content university instructors: Factors and indicators of positive partnerships. *International Journal of Bilingual Education and Bilingualism* 21 (5), 591–606.

6 A Key Development Indicator Matrix for Systemizing CLIL in Higher Education Environments

David Marsh and Wendy Díaz Pérez

Introduction

Identifying key actions and conditions by which to leverage quality in higher education programs held in an additional language became an area of interest during a period of rapid internationalization in Finland during the 1990s. As with the introduction of immersion in Canada in 1965, which was linked to sociocultural forces prevalent at that time, the shift towards partial teaching through English in Finnish higher education was, in part, driven by a strategic need to respond to a demanding situation facing the country.

During the early 1990s, Finland faced a difficult financial situation caused partly by the breakup of the Soviet Union alongside a banking crisis resulting from erroneous decision making during an economic boom in the 1980s. In response, higher education institutions embarked on swift and wide-scale internationalization processes. These included the introduction of teaching through the medium of English.

In Finland, development work on testing and operationalizing quality assurance processes to support the introduction of teaching and learning through an additional language started in 1992 (see, for example, Marsh *et al.*, 1996; Oksman-Rinkinen & Marsh, 1993, 1994). This period saw the emergence of the educational approach in Finland known as content and language integrated learning (CLIL), with respect to basic, vocational and higher education.

The introduction of programs in an additional language took place during the 1990s in higher education institutions in other European countries as well, including in particular Germany, the Netherlands and France. This trend was also seen in other countries in Europe after the 1998

Sorbonne Declaration, which set the agenda for the formation of a European Higher Education Area (EHEA) which was eventually launched in 2010.

A survey report on medium of instruction in European higher education was conducted through the auspices of the European Language Council (Marsh, 2005). This study explored the intentions and experiences of universities across Europe in respect of providing courses in an additional language. The report was one part of a set of studies that examined the impact on undergraduate studies in relation to the harmonization of the EHEA architecture.

The report found that there were commonalities in how universities were preparing for and responding to the challenges of the Bologna Process and the EHEA with respect to languages. These were mainly reported in relation to governance, and less on the capacity to deliver programs through the medium of an additional language. At this time it appeared to be a case of 'strategy by assumption' in that little expertise was being applied to the complexities of providing programs in another language, and to some extent there was an implied understanding that once decisions were made, processes would follow fairly smoothly.

A major focus of the EHEA was to reform, strengthen and support cooperation between universities in Europe in compliance with standards and guidelines for quality assurance. Some features of the reform were to introduce innovative teaching and learning practices, enable active collaboration between universities in different countries and extend outreach beyond Europe. Reviewed in 2018 (Paris Communiqué – European Conference of Ministers of Higher Education, Fifth Bologna Policy Reform; EHEA, 2018), issues relating to the mobility of students and staff, the introduction of innovative teaching and learning practices, active collaboration between universities in different countries and extending outreach to universities beyond Europe remained key imperatives. Actions such as these invariably raised the issue of which languages were to be used, where and when.

In 2013, *The Higher Education English Landscape: Ensuring Quality in English Language Degree Programmes* (Marsh *et al.*, 2013) described factors that should be addressed when seeking to introduce programs in English. This was followed by *Teaching through English in Higher Education: Realizing Internationalization in Practice* (Díaz Pérez & Marsh, 2017) and *Shaping the Future: A Framework for Building CLIL Environments in Higher Education* (Marsh & Díaz Pérez, 2018).

While drawing on the internationalization processes experienced in Finnish higher education during the 1990s, these later publications draw on experiences from a range of other countries in which English has been introduced as the medium of teaching and learning. Interest in teaching and learning in English as an additional language has continued to be approached from different angles over a recent period. These include:

discussion on policy (Byun *et al.*, 2011; Hu & Lei, 2014); teaching competences (Dafouz & Núñez-Perucha, 2009); impact on other languages (Kirkpatrick, 2017); conceptual issues (Airey, 2016; Cenoz, 2015; Smit & Dafouz, 2012; Toh, 2016); challenges (Doiz *et al.*, 2013); impact (Choselidou & Griva, 2014; Galloway *et al.*, 2017; Sanchéz Peréz, 2016); teachers' and students' beliefs (Macaro *et al.*, 2018); and models (Díaz Pérez *et al.*, 2019).

The title of this chapter includes the term CLIL, which is an acronym for content and language integrated learning. 'CLIL is a dual-focused approach in which an additional language is used for the learning and teaching of both content and language' (Marsh, 1994). Discussion on teaching through English in higher education may be centered around the term EMI (English as the medium of instruction). Whereas CLIL can be considered as a bilingual teaching and learning methodology, EMI can be viewed as a monolingual methodology. 'In EMI programs... lessons are often taught as if students are already competent users of English, with little or no language support' (Chalmers, 2019: 8). 'In CLIL, the medium of instruction is English, but the goals of classroom pedagogy include a focus on the development of English as well as the growth of academic knowledge' (Chalmers, 2019: 28).

This chapter describes an approach developed as part of a quality assurance process created to guide the introduction of higher education programs, or parts of programs, in an additional language. Examples relate to the adoption of English as an additional language, and a case example from a large public university in Mexico is introduced for the purposes of reflection.

Case: KDI Development in the Guadalajara Context 2010–2019

The University of Guadalajara in Mexico (*c.*127,330 students) has 14,985 faculty members. Alongside provision of higher education, the university (UdeG) also has responsibility for the administration of 71 high schools. It has 15 campuses and is the second largest in a country of 120 million inhabitants. The environment within and outside the university is Spanish speaking and essentially monolingual. The number of students learning additional languages has traditionally been low, as has the perceived competence of academic staff to work in languages other than Spanish. Heritage languages, although recognized and respected, are not widely used in the university environment.

In 2010–2012, recognition of the weakness and deficit in learning and using languages other than Spanish was increasingly recognized. This led to enhanced intra-university discussion and cooperation on reaching agreement on the scale of the problem, and the identification of needs and pathways towards solutions.

In 2013, operations started in an independent unit, but in cooperation with the language and other departments at the university. Diagnostics were conducted to form an evidence base on curricula, teacher capacity, learner performance and the potential for additional language learning across the university. International benchmarking and outreach processes were operationalized which led to the identification of CLIL as a significant potential educational solution.

A specialized Foreign Language Institutional Program (FLIP) was created in 2015. At the outset FLIP designed the first university Language Policy (1.0) and embarked on CLIL professional development programs for academic teaching staff wishing to teach through the medium of English.

In 2016, a CLIL communications plan was designed for the professional, academic and administrative community within the university, in order to further articulate how strategies in the Language Policy were being implemented. A key function, however, was to communicate the opening steps of what was intended to be a constructive and collaborative change management process with regard to the position of languages within the university.

Recognizing that one reason for the languages deficit at the university was the low language learning performance of students entering from high schools, FLIP also engaged with setting up across-the-curriculum projects in English which combined CLIL with phenomenon-based learning (PhBL). Having become an instrumental part of the Finnish national curriculum from 2016 onwards, PhBL involves the integration of different subject fields to create a single learning experience where students look at a phenomenon from different real-world/academic perspectives (Marsh et al., 2019).

Finally, 2016 saw the realization of one major imperative which was to combine alternative ways of learning English (such as through CLIL and PhBL) with the introduction of opportunities to learn Chinese, French, German, Italian and Japanese.

In 2017, FLIP became a permanent university unit with 20 full-time staff and continued to act as a form of innovation incubator to support an active multilingual strategy throughout the university. CLIL professional development programs for academics continued alongside CLIL community building across faculties and between academics, and continuous monitoring of data diagnostics to support evidence-base building.

The period 2015–2018 saw continuous upward trajectories in various annual performance data. The professional upskilling of university language teachers increased steadily year on year from 249 teachers in 2015 to 307 in 2018. Likewise, certification in professional competences rose from 141 in 2015 to 1222 in 2018. However, one figure stands out from the others, namely an increase in the number of university students studying languages. In 2012 this figure was 6787 students; by 2018 it had risen to 43,946 students.

In 2018, FLIP examined ways of having university-level students learn Chinese, French, German, Italian and Japanese using CLIL-type pedagogical principles. Complementing this move towards language learning innovation involving different languages, CLIL learning projects were piloted for students of English in high schools. Finally, during this year emphasis was given to quality assurance processes resulting in the creation of a key development indicator (KDI) matrix, and the introduction of a certification test for academics who teach through English (Teaching through English in Higher Education Certificate, University of Jyväskylä, Finland).

In 2019, the FLIP objectives were to: enable wider recognition of heritage and sign languages within the university by exploring usage and methods by which these are taught and learnt; engage in inter-university dialogue on means by which to enhance multilingual strategies through CLIL; increase the capacity of language teachers to develop competences and qualifications; and increase the number of students learning languages.

The background rationale can be summarized as follows:

- The future of higher education learning institutions partly depends on the ability to respond to challenges, needs and opportunities, some of which relate to multilingualism.
- Universities can be highly complex organizations which are resistant to certain forms of change.
- The changing global higher education landscape places renewed pressure on teaching through an additional language, particularly English.
- Successfully introducing a multilingual strategy including teaching through an additional language such as English into a longstanding monolingual university environment is a major challenge.
- Implementing such a strategy can be facilitated by having language and non-language expertise work together to design and lead initial processes.
- In the UdeG case, a systemic approach has been adopted to launch and embed the multilingual strategy into the everyday life of the university. This involves time-sensitive coordinated and calibrated interrelated actions which enable efficiency in terms of development and implementation outcomes.
- This approach has been systemized using a KDI matrix.

Introducing the Key Development Indicator Matrix

A matrix can be considered as a visual representation of a social environment in which the means that enable something to develop and intersect are embedded with one another. A KDI matrix comprises a set of indicators which provides a systemized set of actions to realize a strategy, in this case an institutional multilingual strategy (see, for example, Aubrey, 2016; Badaway *et al.*, 2016; Star *et al.*, 2016). The function of KDIs is to articulate and show the interrelatedness of key development areas in order to enable systemic change to materialize in an effective and successful way. Identifying progress on separate yet interlinked issues is useful in highlighting what is absent, emergent or advanced in terms of development of the main objective.

This objective is to enable programs, or parts of programs, to be taught through the additional language while minimizing investment needs and maximizing both pace of change and quality. A KDI matrix is useful when introducing innovation into a large and complex ecosystem such as a university. This is because it functions as a single tool enabling management of possibly complex and overlapping processes in a coordinated way. It is different from performance measurement systems such as those based on key performance indicators (KPIs). These tend to focus on what has been achieved, often quantitatively, and not on what is actively developing, or otherwise in need of either development or process harmonization, as with KDIs (see, for example, Areana et al., 2009).

Constructing the Key Development Indicator Matrix

The KDI matrix is formed by first identifying the goal, for example, enabling quality education through English which complements teaching through the first language, and which supports realization of the university strategy. Next is the identification of key factors that can support, or hinder progress being achieved (e.g. governance, management, praxis, and outcomes). Then, finally, selection of the key development questions. Based on these, the indicators are formed to gain deeper understanding of the answers to these questions. (Marsh & Díaz Pérez, 2018: 12)

Design of a KDI matrix will differ from one university to another. Size, type of organizational structure, resources and the position that the institution has in relation to the use of additional languages are just some factors that influence how a matrix is formed and used in different universities. However, there are four parameters that tend to remain constant. These are governance, management, praxis and outcomes. A representation of how these parameters evolve over time can be seen in Figure 6.1.

Governance concerns decisions that are usually made and directed from within the central administration of a university. Management generally involves faculty- or department-level decision-making processes. Praxis covers teaching and learning approaches and design of learning environments. Outcomes are generally described in terms of metrics and other means by which to benchmark performance.

Some examples of KDIs are now introduced. For the purposes of exemplification, an accompanying comment is provided on the application of each of these in the context of the University of Guadalajara, Mexico (UdeG), over the period 2010–2019.

A Key Development Indicator Matrix for Systemizing CLIL in HE Environments 121

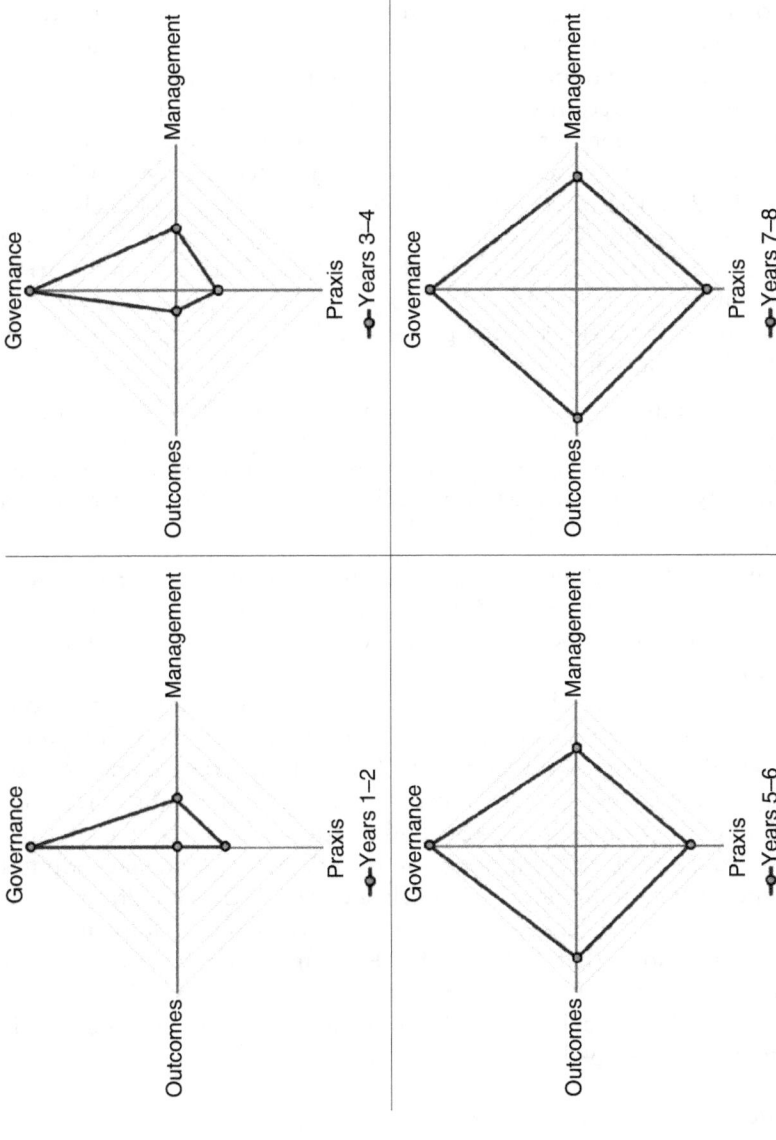

Figure 6.1 Representation of the evolution of KDI parameters in a university

Parameter 1: Governance

Language policy

An ineffective language policy is merely a statement of intent. An effective university language policy states the position of the organization on the recognition and use of different languages, as this determines practices that promote academic quality, equity and social cohesion. It is subject to periodic renewal (anything between one and three years) and carries action statements. These action statements concern 'aims – what is intended; actions – what is done to realize the aims; and intended outcomes – what is realized within the university as a result of these actions' (Marsh & Díaz Pérez, 2018: 20). These actions are then reviewed at the end of each policy time frame, possibly with some removed and others added. The policy requires an executive body to oversee it and enable its communication throughout the organization, and to ensure that budget and other policies are aligned for the actions in the period specified. Drafting of the policy needs to be multidisciplinary:

> a frequent mistake has been to assume that language specialists working alone should take responsibility for constructing a plan. The problem here is that both policy and plan may have far-reaching impact on the university community, and thus interdisciplinary central level actors need to be involved. (Marsh *et al.*, 2013: 14)

In relation to teaching through an additional language (TAL), a language policy needs to be aligned to the university international strategy. If there is disjuncture between these, the quality of each may be compromised.

Adoption of the English language acronym TAL in communications within the university was intentional. Firstly, it emphasizes the long-term multilingual strategy of the university. Secondly, the movement towards teaching in languages other than Spanish was not restricted to the adoption of English without pedagogical adaptation as in EMI. Thirdly, it is used to avoid specifying that adoption of a vehicular language assumes that a specific methodological approach such as CLIL or integrating content and language in higher education (ICLHE) is being implemented. TAL merely denotes that an additional language is used as a medium of teaching and learning. In the UdeG environment the term CLIL refers to a situation in which teaching and learning in an additional language is according to specific pedagogical principles.

Case UdeG

The university Language Policy (1.0) was conceived over a three-year period leading up to 2015. The initial development involved considerable discussion on structure, definitions, purpose and implementation. This first policy contained basic concepts and linguistic goals and was mainly focused on English as an additional language. Issued with a built-in review required after three years, one assumption was that the second version would be extended to include languages other than English.

Implementation during the first three years was not straightforward. Overcoming challenges in securing localized endorsement of its purpose and significance required continuous effort and communications. A key success factor was in having official recognition of the unit responsible (FLIP) as a coordination unit within the university. Over 2015–2019, explicit acknowledgement through communications by the university leadership was particularly important in enabling recognition and support from within the university community.

Alignment with university international strategy

As with a language policy, a university international strategy may be something that exists within the institution but that does not actively serve as a means by which to formalize and activate strategic processes. A challenge surfaces if there is disjuncture between the coordination of internationalization and cooperation within a university which, for example, manages mobility, and those academic departments involved with introducing TAL. There needs to be fusion between each if TAL is to further support the realization of higher education internationalization strategies.

The introduction of TAL can be linked to mobility, but it can also support a range of interrelated outreach activities. These include higher frequency publishing in English, joint degree programs, shared teaching (often through e-learning and electronic means) and shared student learning opportunities (collaborative learning across institutions in different countries). It can also influence the provision of opportunities for cross-sector and other research and development initiatives which indirectly support what are traditionally considered as being international activities. If TAL is seen as a key driver for leveraging a range of internationalization activities, it requires the attention and direction of central administration, and international or, where available, innovation and teacher training units within the university.

Case UdeG

At the start of the Language Policy construction process, the offices responsible for internationalization were involved with forging the conceptual links between policy and strategy. However, this unity of purpose between separate units did not impact on implementation to any significant extent.

This was due in part to some disconnectedness between the entities involved. One reason for this could have been partly due to these units not being accustomed to cross-sector cooperation and interdisciplinary convergence. At the start, the disconnection was evident in operationalizing the Language Policy, and in finding synergies by which cooperation could be of benefit for the internationalization office, the coordination unit, and other key stakeholder units within the university such as those involved with teaching languages and preparing language teachers.

This issue of realignment between international strategy and implementation of not only the Language Policy but also a consequence of that policy, namely TAL, presented a key issue of disjuncture which was steadily addressed by all concerned. The initial lack of an articulated and sustained recognition between strategy and TAL was clearly disadvantageous in enabling swift progress to be achieved, particularly with respect to the introduction of new practices and quality assurance.

Resourcing and staff incentives

There are inevitably faculty set-up costs and the likelihood of a substantial increase in time-on-task by academics who opt for TAL. The set-up costs can apply to having access to professional development programs, equipment, international library and other services and, in some cases, infrastructure. Recognition of the time and effort required to switch the language of teaching and learning by academics also means that forms of staff incentive are necessary.

Engagement with TAL may be supported by academics having intrinsic motivation because the individuals can see that TAL could be personally rewarding. Career development may be one of these. At the outset, such rewards may not be obvious and may include: the opportunity for pedagogical development (learning how to teach in new ways); ease of publishing in international forums and participating in events; working across disciplines within the university and creating new learning environments; career development; and the satisfaction of providing an added value for students on certain programs.

Extrinsic motivation is where the university needs to play a role, particularly during the introduction of TAL. This can be provided in terms of recognition, reduction in normal teaching and other workload for TAL preparation purposes, and remuneration. Provision of support for language development, upskilling in writing and publishing, access to subject-specific resources, international mobility and employment of temporary support staff may also be facilitated through central administration.

Case UdeG

Motivating academic staff to prepare and implement TAL raised issues of incentivization. For those staff undergoing preparatory professional development there was clear recognition that teaching through English would require substantially more preparatory work than teaching through Spanish. This soon led to discussions about not only recognition (primarily for effort at the outset) but also compensation (primarily for time) which had not been previously considered at the university.

The time-lag in agreeing on incentives is understandable given the size of the university and the complexity involved in tracking and evidencing individual involvement with TAL (large or small scale and so forth). By 2018 involvement with TAL was included in the standard annual individual 'bonus' system for certain teaching staff, and this was facilitated by the introduction of an external certification process for showing competence to teach through English (TEHE).

Even though academics readily recognized that there could be certain advantages for themselves as professionals in teaching through English at UdeG, the initial challenges faced also required extra effort and to some extent risk (e.g. students avoiding courses held in English because they considered that it would be harder to gain credits; how students would manage standard course feedback forms designed for teaching through Spanish; acquiring resources in English). This again raised issues of incentives, recognition and compensation.

Impact on university international ranking systems

International ranking systems can have a profound impact on university life. Combined with national higher education and professional organization ranking systems, these international systems exhibit an 'increasing protagonism as quality measurement instruments' (Nyssen, 2018: 158) and are currently of major significance to universities worldwide. Recognition that globalization and the information age are driving the need for educational and organizational transformation, the statistics generated by the ranking systems are being cited as evidence of levels of quality, even if the means by which the statistics are generated can be controversial.

Measuring, in one way or another, academic reputation, proportion of international faculty, proportion of students from other countries, international outlook, research citations and indexes and the number of research papers published by each faculty member are among the many performance indicators applied in these ranking systems. Some link directly to the availability of teaching and learning opportunities in an additional language, such as international outlook, international faculty and students, research, and feedback from students on the quality of teaching on courses at the university.

Case UdeG

Currently UdeG is not well positioned internationally. QS World Rankings 2019 position it as seventh place in Mexico and 47th place in Latin America. Internationally it is ranked between 751 and 800. There are various reasons for this, including not only how international ranking systems such as QS manage key data but also the fact that this is a large public sector university with a strong social responsibility mandate. Social responsibility invariably involves a university investing in activities of high importance which may not be recognized in standardized international ranking surveys. One example could be using university expert time to support medical procedures in universities, which could otherwise be used to conduct and report on research. In relation to TAL, publishing in English is a key factor for future reference in having the potential to strengthen the ranking position of the university. Another relates to teaching quality. Although the ratio of professors to students is rated rather low, TAL has introduced, often for the first time, awareness of and skills building in teaching and learning methodologies suitable for higher education. In time, these are foreseen as likely to have a positive impact on overall academic reputation.

Programming linked to research and development

> One of the surprising insights we have gained from research and consultancy over the years is that degree programs may be provided in English without specific objectives explicitly established. The most frequent word used to answer 'why are we running this programme' is internationalization. But this word often lacks substance. (Marsh *et al.*, 2013: 14)

In the 1990s when universities started embarking on TAL, a key objective was to raise the language and communication standards of students in the domestic environment. During the late 1990s this then turned to accommodating students for short-term academic exchange visits. Now, some 20 years later, a *primus motor* is to raise quality standards in a department or faculty by attracting high-caliber international faculty and students with a view to raising standards of research and development. This, after all, is a basic reason for the existence of universities. However, raising quality standards also relates to competitiveness, sourcing of funding and the need to score well in international ranking systems.

TAL is by no means a necessity, but it often plays an important role in facilitating these processes. For many years universities in certain countries have been able to attract aspiring students from around the world, developing their language skills through pre-program, first- and second-cycle language studies, and to strengthen university research and development profiles by having these students complete doctoral studies. In the past the objectives have been partly political, by educating the 'future sociopolitical elite' of certain developing countries. Now it may be more pragmatic, namely, to attract and retain those individuals who show signs of academic excellence.

TAL can be applied for many reasons, whether through short-term transversal learning modules that cross different disciplines or full-scale degree programs. But one imperative is to bring added value to departments that specialize in leading-edge fields of research and development, and to create flagship international programs moderated through an additional language. One single university may not have the capacity to do this by itself without either international academic input or working in close collaboration with universities in other countries. Introducing TAL is one means by which to enable this to happen.

Case UdeG

Linking programs to research and development, nationally and internationally, remains a confusing and difficult challenge due to Mexico's current critical safety and security problems. Attracting academics and students from other countries to live in Guadalajara is challenging and is likely to remain so until the overall situation improves. This is happening while industry, especially international concerns, are increasing the demand for personnel who can work in more than one language. TAL is viewed as having the potential to equip national students with competences to develop language skills and, as of now, this needs to be done without the added value of having non-Spanish speaking academics and students physically located at the university. In addition, moves are being made to raise the international academic and student input through virtual means during this period when personal security remains a critical issue for parts of the country.

Parameter 2: Management

Staff language competences

Teaching complex content using academic language requires specialized use of language alongside appropriate methodologies. Methodologies are such a significant factor in TAL quality assurance that it is one of the four parameters in the KDI matrix. 'Developing linguistic competence in an additional language to teach and learn complex subject matter that is cognitively demanding is an ongoing process. As with using the first language, educators constantly need to give attention to eloquence, communication and accuracy in their use of language' (Marsh *et al.*, 2013: 16). This issue can become one of contentious debate within a university. Higher education staff may not respond well to undertaking language testing to show evidence of proficiency, and standardized tests such as TOEFL and IELTS may not be sophisticated enough to identify competences for teaching in the language at this level of education. Procedures for ensuring that academic staff do have prerequisite language competences are needed if quality is to be assured, but these should be managed internally, and preferably be subject to peer review. The role of methodology is crucial because if an academic does not use methods that provide some degree of language support in understanding, for example, concepts in the first language, they may be unlikely to use such methods when teaching through TAL.

Case UdeG

Academics expressing an interest in teaching through English were invited to undertake language tests. Results from these tended towards lower than desired score levels. Language learning support was then made available for those staff already teaching, and those intending to prepare for TAL. As was anticipated, oral competences in English lagged behind other skills such as reading which can be highly advanced among academics. English language teaching in Mexico has been widely based on grammar-based language instruction, and thus some form of reformative language development was expected to be required for certain teaching staff prior to embarking on TAL.

Coordinated staff teamwork

'Sharing understanding of the genre and culture of different subjects, and how these can be taught and understood by students, can be the basis for developing significant methodological solutions and overall readiness for TAL' (Marsh & Díaz Pérez, 2018: 24). In some countries, universities have traditions where academics tend to work in isolation from others, even those within the same department. This isolation is particularly the case in respect of subject specialists and those involved with language teaching.

Universities worldwide differ considerably in respect of the role of language specialists. 'In some environments there is a clear separation between academic and service-oriented departments of languages. This inevitably leads to diverse positioning on organizational status and hierarchies' (Marsh *et al.*, 2013: 19). Academic language departments do not necessarily take responsibility for language teaching, which may be subcontracted to external entities or internal language centers.

There is an opportunity for the realignment of language teaching expertise within a university with TAL. This requires a sometimes considerable systemic change of attitude towards how language specialists are perceived, and how they can work as an integral part of academic teamwork that leads to successful TAL. If language teaching is viewed as a service that produces value which is primarily intangible and is not regarded as main core, opportunities may be lost in maximizing both efficiency and quality.

In an 'information age', the role of language has evolved in such a way that teaching a language as a discrete subject has become questionable, as is assuming that programs such as 'languages for specific purposes' can fulfil student learning needs in contemporary universities worldwide. The following have all played a part in remolding the position of languages in the lives of students: understanding of the neurological, cognitive, motivational and social bases of language learning; human technologies that support learning; representations of knowledge and information in the new media; reshaped working life cultures; new knowledge and competence demands; and scientific and technological innovation.

Asikainen *et al.* (2010) stated:

> We are entering an age where the added value of learning languages, linked with the development of interrelated electronic literacies, is becoming profoundly important ... and educational priorities emphasize the development of key competences for life-long learning many of which are language-based. As educational practice builds on social connectivity, the development of communication competences becomes a shared responsibility across all disciplines. (Asikainen *et al.*, 2010: 3)

This repositioning is important for TAL in two ways. Firstly, students in universities have generally experienced high exposure to integrated technologies which impacts on how their minds process information. Secondly, it invites language specialists to be repositioned within a university. This can mean shifting from teaching language as a discrete subject or as an associated competence through to integrating language learning deeply within the learning of other subjects as through forms of CLIL.

Case UdeG

Coordinated staff teamwork has not been a regular feature of academic life in the university. Of course there are exceptions, some of which are longstanding, but the general trend has been for academics to manage the responsibilities of their posts on an individual basis. The idea of changing the status quo with respect to team work as in building communities of practice (Lave & Wenger, 1991) has been a focus of development in respect of TAL, but it has not been easy to establish. This is not only because of the traditional separation of subjects and disciplines, but also because UdeG university campuses are spread throughout the region, and only recently has cross-disciplinary research and course design become increasingly developed. One strategy has been to form a single CLIL community within the university. This has been successful in bringing together academics from diverse backgrounds who have been trained in CLIL and who are able to identify and communicate their common interests. Having members of the CLIL community advancing arguments on TAL and articulating purpose and requirements has been seen to have been important in promoting the TAL strategy. This is particularly significant because in pursuit of a long-term multilingual strategy the CLIL community is envisaged as increasingly including academics who teach through languages other than English.

Teaching and learning resources support

Allocating teaching and learning software and materials for academics and students is a resourcing issue for university management. TAL invariably involves academics needing to access teaching and learning resources in the additional language which are not readily available at a university library. Alternative forms of support for academics working with TAL such as for travel or for the purchase of specialized equipment may also be necessary.

Case UdeG

As the CLIL community evolved, it became evident that academics did not have knowledge of certain resources, or the means by which to access resources, which already existed at the university. Focus on TAL enabled these persons to become aware of support materials, processes and services already available, and to identify other support which they required as necessary for maximizing quality teaching and learning.

International networking, partnerships and ventures

International networking is linked to the potential for collaborative joint ventures and partnership agreements, research and publishing. 'When faculty become involved with teaching through an additional language their enhanced professional profiles may lead to an increase in global networking. This can provide added value for the university and is best served through acknowledgement and support by management' (Marsh & Díaz Pérez, 2018: 25). This type of networking can be in the form of collaborative ventures in the public and private sectors, transnational organizations, and especially between universities and other institutes of higher education and research.

Case UdeG

UdeG has a long tradition of international networking with North America and Europe and within Latin America. Participation in such networks was often by individual academics or at a departmental level. The work on TAL enabled these academics and others to look at international connections already existing, identify those sectors and geographical areas that needed further exploration and share knowledge that could lead to institutional collaboration.

Academic staff professional development

'The predominance of lecture monologue, originating in Europe when printing was unfeasible, remains a chief methodology in some countries' (Marsh & Díaz Pérez, 2018: 26). The use of extended lectures as a form of 'one-way information transmission' has a role in certain types of higher education context. However, in TAL, due to the increased factors that need to be considered (e.g. heterogeneous levels of student additional language competence; diverse educational backgrounds according to where students have studied previously; and greater need for language support in understanding concepts), higher education staff need to be able to apply a range of methods depending on purpose, context and intended learning objectives.

It is possible to consider academic professional development with respect to three ongoing trends and realities: students in universities have a long experience of media-rich environments; competence building in teaching and learning methods is not commonly part of the professional development of academic staff in universities; and TAL frequently requires skills in facilitating multifaceted types of interaction if learning is to be successful.

Case UdeG

The move towards introducing TAL involved commissioning purpose-designed professional development programs. Having examined what was available from national and international suppliers, UdeG opted for a customized process. This involved: fusion with international higher educational expertise coordinated through Finland to develop professional development processes which combined competence building in CLIL methodological skills; understanding how to use English in TAL contexts; individual learning paths for developing fluency in English; confidence building and the design of CLIL models which would suit an individual, or group of individuals, for their subject field and perceived level of readiness; use of digital media to support TAL; teamwork; and foresight planning in scoping and focusing on the potential added value of TAL at individual and department levels.

Systemized student intake

Student intake from both the domestic environment and from other countries depends heavily on the reasons why a university implements TAL. If the primary purpose is revenue generation, the ways in which students are selected will differ from other intentions including those that are largely altruistic. The types of students selected for a TAL program can be of significance in relation to achieving high levels of quality overall. If a selection process is flawed, especially with regard to the competence of the students in the additional language and their cognitive ability and capabilities for intercultural adaptation, this can have long-term and potentially serious consequences for all involved. This may be in respect of teaching workload, personal well-being of teaching staff and students, student satisfaction rates and overall performance outcomes.

Case UdeG

This has remained recognized as a significant KDI, but due primarily to the national security situation and the gradual emergence of modules and programs in TAL, international student intake has been at minimal levels. National student intake has been largely on a fully voluntary basis and more remains to be done to determine 'terms of engagement' for students, whether national or international.

Parameter 3: Praxis

Teaching and learning methodologies and learning environments

> There is a significant difference between teaching in an additional language (where little explicit attention is given to language and communication), and teaching through an additional language (where extra language support is provided through integrated forms of scaffolding). (Marsh & Díaz Pérez, 2018: 29)

If TAL is taught in English through a primarily monolingual frame of reference '… as if students are already competent users of English, with little or no language support' (Chalmers, 2019: 8), then it can be described as an example of EMI. If the word 'instruction' is understood as relating to directives, demands, rulings, specifications, orders and 'imparting information', this implies teaching that is largely transmission based, not teaching and learning that is interactional and dialogic. Apart from specializations such as in vocational and professional education, or some subjects in higher education, 'teaching as instruction' is no longer compatible with the demands of much higher education in the present day (van der Linden & Renshaw, 2004).

If a TAL course or program is designed using CLIL, the intended learning outcomes are likely to include identifiable language, content and communication objectives. If a TAL course is implemented using CLIL-type activities, the methods used will tend towards bilingual rather than monolingual and involve focus on language, cognition and concept formation.

The deepening of concept development is central to university education as learning demands become increasingly abstract and cognitively challenging. Scaffolding is a set of support mechanisms that enable students to progressively move towards successful understanding of content. Use of scaffolding is equally important in higher education for teaching and learning in the first language, just as in an additional language. The main difference is in the frequency, scope and intensity of scaffolding which is likely to be more extensive in TAL than in education through the first language. 'TAL requires a blend of both content and language scaffolding if success is to be achieved' (Marsh & Díaz Pérez, 2018: 30). These are use of language and conceptual scaffolding, interactional and dialogic methods, and other language-support processes and mechanisms which may be outside the immediate face-to-face teaching environment.

Case: UdeG

Few of the academics attracted to TAL since 2015 report having had prior experience of professional development in higher education teaching and learning methods. Thus, the subsequent preparatory program provided on TAL may have been the first time that these individuals had experienced 'training in how to teach'. This clearly had a bearing on their perceptions of themselves as educators and their understanding that techniques for TAL could also be applied to teaching through Spanish. Having completed professional development processes and starting teaching through TAL, academics have identified a range of aspects relating to pedagogical and communicative processes. The effective and sustained use of a variety of language-supportive scaffolding and dialogic methods have been identified as particularly significant in achieving success, as is an awareness of the need to adapt situationally to the demands of different teaching contexts through the flexible and creative use of techniques.

Parameter 4: Performance Outcomes

Performance outcomes generally involve comparing the academic output of courses through TAL with equivalent courses that are or have been taught through the first language. Using metrics and other measures, these processes are necessary to ensure that the same or higher levels of quality are being achieved through TAL. It is necessary to reformulate certain existing measures due to the changes of dynamics resulting from TAL. This is particularly the case with the use of standardized end-of-course evaluation processes such as those used for evaluating teacher quality and learning performance.

Some of the performance outcomes that may be both monitored and evaluated for the purposes of quality assurance are: number of international students participating in courses; student language competence; accredited levels of staff language competence; the experimental and possibly unorthodox nature of teaching and learning techniques especially during start-up; added value relating to number of published studies in prestigious journals, international collaboration and engagement; and impact on processes that contribute to the international dynamics of the university.

Case UdeG

Evaluation processes have been active from the outset in terms of professional development processes, and the introduction of modules, courses or programs through CLIL. Identifying evidence of the impact of TAL in a large-scale organization like UdeG has been regarded as taking an estimated 5–10 years from the start-up of TAL processes in 2015. There are development actions that can be monitored, such as in types of formative assessment built into the professional development programs for staff, but measuring the overall impact requires time and coordination. What is positive in this respect is not only the initial reporting on various aspects of TAL, as well as the reporting of challenges, but also the recognition that this is a significant innovation with regard to longstanding teaching, learning and linguistic traditions. This recognition means that we carry out certain baseline studies so that eventually it is easier to see if and how TAL has impacted positively or otherwise on university operations.

Conclusion

Teaching courses or programs through an additional language such as English in a Spanish-speaking higher education environment presents substantial challenges. If quality assurance is to be achieved, there are a range of cross-sector factors that need to be monitored, adapted and sometimes made subject to major change. Viewing the university as an ecosystem has been invaluable in identifying interlocking actions, strengths and weaknesses which can support or hinder quality issues. Some of these relate directly to conventions, practices and norms associated with use of the first language. Others may already exist or be generated by the introduction of an additional language into university life.

The use of a KDI matrix has been of value at the University of Guadalajara. It has enabled those persons at the core and periphery of teaching in English as an additional language to understand and recognize how a systemic approach provides value which impacts on different features of university operations. Universities can be complex organizations and the potential for innovation can easily be squandered if it does not fit into the culture of organizational structures. The university as an ecosystem does not only consist of the organizational structures, but also those forces, longstanding or emergent, which exist between these structures, and which can enhance or block the potential for innovation.

TAL can present a significant challenge to the status quo in a university. If it does not fit smoothly into the organization as an ecosystem, achieving quality input and output during implementation is likely to be challenging. The use of a KDI matrix comprising indicators on governance, management, praxis and outcomes is a tool that helps those responsible to manage processes and to communicate what is happening with those processes to key stakeholders in the university community.

References

Airey, J. (2016) EAP, EMI or CLIL? In K. Hyland and P. Shaw (eds) *The Routledge Handbook of English for Academic Purposes* (pp. 71–83). London: Routledge.

Areana, M., Arnabaldi, M., Azzone, G. and Carlucci, P. (2009) Developing a performance measurement system for university central administrative services. *Higher Education Quarterly* 63, 237–263.

Asikainen, T., Bertaux, P., Frigols Martin, M., Hughes, S., Marsh, D. and Mehisto, P. (2010) *Talking the Future: CCN Foresight Think Tank Report on Languages in Education*. Jyväskylä: CCN.
Aubrey, B. (2016) *Measure of Man: Leading Human Development*. New York: McGraw Hill Education.
Badaway, M., Abd El-Aziz, A., Idress, A., Hefny, H. and Hossam, S. (2016) A survey on key performance indicators. *Future Computing and Informatics Journal* 1, 1–2, 47–52.
Byun, K., Chu, H., Kim, M., Park, I., Kim, S. and Jung, J. (2011) English-medium teaching in Korean higher education: Policy debates and reality. *Higher Education* 62 (4), 431–449.
Cenoz, J. (2015) Content-based instruction and content and language integrated learning: The same or different? *Language, Culture and Curriculum* 28 (1), 8–24.
Chalmers, H. (2019) *The Role of the First Language in English Medium Instruction*. Oxford: Oxford University Press.
Choselidou, D. and Griva, E. (2014) Measuring the effect of implementing CLIL in higher education: An experimental research project. *Procedia – Social and Behavioral Sciences* 116, 2169–2174.
Dafouz, E. and Núñez-Perucha, B. (2009) CLIL in higher education: Devising a new learning landscape. In E. Dafouz and M.C. Guerrini (eds) *CLIL across Educational Levels: Experiences from Primary, Secondary and Tertiary Contexts* (pp. 101–112). London and Madrid: Richmond.
Díaz Pérez, W. and Marsh, D. (2017) *Teaching through English in Higher Education: Realizing Internationalization in Practice*. Montreal: Inter-American Organization for Higher Education.
Díaz Pérez, W., Ellison, M., Harumi, I., et al. (2019) *Implementing Internationalization of Academia: Teaching, Learning and Research through English*. Guadalajara: University of Guadalajara.
Doiz, A., Lasagabaster, D. and Sierra, J.M. (2013) Future challenges for English-medium instruction at the tertiary level. In A. Doiz, D. Lasagabaster and J.M. Sierra (eds) *English-Medium Instruction at Universities: Global Challenges* (pp. 213–221). Bristol: Multilingual Matters.
EHEA (European Higher Education Area) (2018) *Paris Communiqué – European Conference of Ministers of Higher Education, Fifth Bologna Policy Reform, 25 May*. See http://www.ehea.info/media.ehea.info/file/BFUG_Meeting/48/8/BFUG_BG_SR_61_4_FinalDraftCommunique_947488.pdf.
Galloway, N., Kriukow, J. and Numajiri, T. (2017) Internationalisation, higher education and the growing demand for English: An investigation into the English medium of instruction (EMI) movement in China and Japan. ELT Research Paper No. 17.02. London: British Council.
Hu, G. and Lei, J. (2014) English-medium instruction in Chinese *higher education*: A case study. *Higher Education* 67, 551–567.
Kirkpatrick, A. (2017) The languages of higher education in East and Southeast Asia: Will EMI lead to Englishization? In B. Fenton-Smith, P. Humphreys and I. Walkinshaw (eds) *English Medium Instruction in Higher Education in Asia-Pacific. Multilingual Education* (pp. 21–36). Cham: Springer.
Lave, J. and Wenger, E. (1991) *Situated Learning: Legitimate Peripheral Participation*. Cambridge: Cambridge University Press.
Macaro, E., Curle, S., Pun, J., An, J. and Dearden, J. (2018) A systematic review of English medium instruction in higher education. *Language Teaching* 51 (1), 36–76.
Marsh, D. (1994) *Bilingual Education & Content and Language Integrated Learning: Language Teaching in the Member States of the European Union (Lingua)*. Paris: University of Sorbonne, International Association for Cross-cultural Communication.

Marsh, D. (2005) *Medium of Instruction in European Higher Education: The Lisbon Strategy and Education & Training 2010*. Berlin: ENLU Research Group, European Network for Language Learning amongst Undergraduates, European Language Council.

Marsh, D. and Díaz Pérez, W. (2018) *Shaping the Future: A Framework for Building CLIL Environments in Higher Education*. Guadalajara: University of Guadalajara.

Marsh, D., Oksman-Rinkinen, P. and Takala, S. (1996) *Mainstream Bilingual Education in the Finnish Vocational Sector*. Helsinki: National Board of Education.

Marsh, D., Pavón Vazquéz, V. and Frigols Martin, M. (2013) *The Higher Education English Language Landscape: Ensuring Quality in English Language Degree Programmes*. Valencia: Valencia International University.

Marsh, D., Díaz Pérez, W. and Escarzaga Morales, M. (2019) Enhancing language awareness and competence-building through a fusion of phenomenon-based learning and content and language integration. *Journal of e-Learning and Knowledge Society* 15 (1), 15–25.

Nyssen, J.M. (2018) The social dimension and university rankings. In A. Curaj, L. Deca and R. Pricopie (eds) *European Higher Education Area: The Impact of Past and Future Policies* (pp. 155–170). New York: Springer.

Oksman-Rinkinen, P. and Marsh, D. (1993) *Internationalization Strategies of the Jyväskylä Vocational Teacher Education Polytechnic*. Jyväskylä: University of Jyväskylä.

Oksman-Rinkinen, P. and Marsh, D. (1994) *Internationalization Strategies of North Karelia Polytechnic*. Jyväskylä: University of Jyväskylä.

Sanchéz Peréz, M. (2016) The written production of university students in a bilingual higher education context: A multidisciplinary study. PhD thesis, University of Almería.

Smit, U. and Dafouz, E. (eds) (2012) *Integrating Content and Language in Higher Education: An Introduction to English Medium Policies, Conceptual Issues and Research Practices across Europe*. AILA Review 25, 1–12. Amsterdam: John Benjamins.

Star, S., Russ-Eft, D. and Braverman, M. (2016) Performance management and performance indicators: A literature review and a proposed model for practical adoption. *Human Resource Development Review* 15 (2), 151–181.

Toh, G. (2016) *EMI in Higher Education: Initiatives, Practices and Concerns. English as Medium of Instruction in Japanese Higher Education*. Basingstoke: Palgrave Macmillan.

van der Linden, J. and Renshaw, P. (eds) (2004) *Dialogic Learning: Shifting Perspectives to Teaching, Instruction and Teaching*. Dordrecht: Springer.

7 AGCEPESA Project: Designing a Tool to Measure the Quality of Plurilingual Programmes in Higher Education

Javier Ávila-López, Francisco Rubio-Cuenca and Rocío López-Lechuga

Introduction

Spanish universities are currently going through a period in which the development of an international profile and the desire to provide students with specific skills to work in a globalized environment are promoting initiatives aimed at offering studies taught in a foreign language (Dafouz & Núñez, 2009; Ramos-García, 2013), particularly in English. English is a language that has acquired the status of lingua franca, as it facilitates global academic exchange, advancement of knowledge, career advancement and mobility in international scientific settings (Coleman, 2006: 4). Therefore, universities all over Europe are offering English-medium instruction (EMI) or content and language integration programmes (integrating content and language in higher education, ICLHE) (Doiz et al., 2013; Fortanet-Gómez, 2013; Hellekjaer & Wilkinson, 2009; Smit & Dafouz, 2013; Wilkinson, 2004; Wilkinson & Walsh, 2015; Wilkinson & Zegers, 2008), with the aim of providing students with the necessary linguistic understanding and skills that allow them to adapt to these global needs.

The globalization of professional areas demands the development of a series of specific competences of a holistic, creative and innovative nature. The universities, therefore, are becoming aware that not only must they equip their students with a deep understanding and knowledge in each of their fields, but they must also provide them with cross-cutting skills, among which multilingual communicative and intercultural competences can greatly enrich their academic and professional profile (Lorenzo *et al.*, 2011). In line with these proposals, plurilingual programmes seek to develop linguistic competence in English through the increase of credits taught in this language or through the implementation of plurilingual English-Spanish degrees or even degrees taught entirely in English (Pavón & Gaustad, 2013).

Some aspects related to the implementation of a plurilingual education model are needed to carefully define the objectives of the programme, the existence of a clear language policy or the selection of adequate initiatives and strategies to guarantee the successful outcome of the programme (Marsh *et al.*, 2013). Needless to say, the role played by lecturers, together with their professional profile, has a profound impact on the quality of this type of programme (Escobar, 2013). Moreover, it becomes imperative that the linguistic and pedagogical dimensions, as the most relevant factors, should be addressed for quality assurance.

Taking into account all these factors, which we will deal with in detail in the different sections of this chapter, a number of researchers from eight Andalusian (southern Spain) universities started the AGCEPESA (Analysis and Quality Assurance of Plurilingual Studies in Higher Education in Andalusia) Project (2014–2019). With the primary goal of designing a tool to measure the good practices and quality of bilingual and plurilingual programmes in Andalusian universities, the project undertook the task of drawing a map of the current state of affairs regarding the implementation of bilingual and plurilingual programmes in Spanish universities, focusing on the Andalusian higher education territory. Some key issues were considered for the analysis, such as motivation for the implementation of plurilingual degrees, the teaching model undertaken, both the general and specific objectives of the programmes and, finally, the drawbacks and challenges found in the process. For that purpose, AGCEPESA designed a systematic review of the literature concerning evidence-based studies on the impact of the implementation of bilingual and plurilingual programmes in higher education institutions (HEIs) globally. The results were very poor, both worldwide and, more specifically, in Andalusian universities, demonstrating the exiguous number of robust studies on the issue. Based on the findings of the systematic review, the Quality Assurance Inventory for Plurilingual Programs in Higher Education (QAIPPHE) was designed – a tool ready to be administered to Andalusian universities and, by extension, to HEIs across Spain and other countries. We will devote the final section of this chapter to explaining the project in detail.

The sections below consider some of the main issues in bilingual/plurilingual programmes in higher education as they emerged from the systematic review. They will be analysed in detail before proceeding to elaborate on the QAIPPHE itself.

The Implementation of the Bilingual/Plurilingual/Multilingual Modality in Spanish Universities

The increase in the number of students joining public plurilingual schools in Spain rose from 240,154 in the period 2010–2011 to 1.1 million (an increase of 360%) in the period 2016–2017, according to data from the Education Ministry. Moreover, 95% of Spanish students enrolled in plurilingual schools chose English as the language of instruction (Torres Menárguez, 2018).

This statement, where 'plurilingual teaching' is synonymous with teaching through English and Spanish, is in line with the growth of plurilingual university teaching in Europe (Doiz et al., 2013: 173). Spanish universities are making a remarkable effort to promote their internationalization through a set of initiatives which range from the inclusion of courses oriented towards the development of oral and written communication skills in the English language to a proposal for plurilingual academic studies (Halbach et al., 2013: 111). Ramos-García (2013) and Ramos-García and Pavón (2018) point out a list of the plurilingual degrees that can be found in Spanish universities, highlighting bachelor's degrees related to business administration, business, engineering, political science and social sciences. On the other hand, Halbach et al. (2013) feature bachelor's degrees in journalism, law, administration and business management as those most common in plurilingual education in Spain. Toledo et al. (2012: 216) describe three plurilingual modalities offered at Spanish universities: (1) a gradual approach to teaching courses through a foreign language; (2) an option to study for the degree either in Spanish or in a foreign language; and (3) agreements with foreign universities to carry out some courses abroad.

The variety of plurilingual degrees offered with the support of universities and regional educational authorities, together with the minimum-level English language requirement, contributes to increasing the heterogeneity of language policies in Spanish HEIs. However, there are studies that confirm the general lack of empirical research that underpins linguistic, academic or political decisions in higher education (Fernández-Costales & González-Riaño, 2015). We should therefore set a series of criteria, goals and homogeneous procedures leading to general language policies shared by all Spanish universities. However, following the publication of the *Documento Marco de Política Lingüística para la Internacionalización del Sistema Universitario Español* (Framework Document of Language Policy for the Internationalization of Spanish Universities; Bazo et al., 2017), there seems to be a slight tendency towards homogenizing the implementation of plurilingual programmes in many HEIs throughout Spain.

Motivation for implementing plurilingual degrees

Social phenomena are reconfiguring the world in a way that suggests the paramount importance of the internalization phenomena of universities. It is internally acknowledged that the main drive behind the process is economic but, incidentally, against the background that social media and fake news promote, this internationalization process cannot but help society to grow.

One of the constituents of the internalization process is that of developing plurilingual degrees and/or increasing the number of credits taught in a foreign language to make the programmes more attractive for international students. Delicado Puerto and Pavón (2015) call this type of internationalization 'obvious'. They distinguish it from other processes, namely the 'invisible', where it is the international character of the publications that supports the internalization process, and the 'necessary' creation of collaborative international working networks.

There may be additional motivations. As Balfour (2007: 37) points out, the higher education programme may be 'mediated, shaped, and even distorted by the influence of globalization, illuminating the complexity of the national, regional, and global interface'. These motivations range from improving students' competence in foreign languages, to the benefits of academic performance and the competencies derived from managing high-level skills in a foreign language. Higher education innovative policies are also supported by the supranational regulations of the European Union, with content and language integrated learning (CLIL) and EMI as highlighted approaches (Delicado Puerto & Pavón, 2015).

Which plurilingual teaching model?

The selection of the plurilingual model will always be a function of the university language policy plan at both local and national levels, so that universities can invest in the quality of their plurilingual programmes.

Deciding which model to offer is a crucial aspect of implementing a plurilingual teaching programme. However, as Coyle (2005: 2) puts it, 'there is no single model for CLIL. Different models all share the common founding principle that in some way the content and the language learning are integrated'. As Delicado Puerto and Pavón (2015) state:

> the logical option in European higher education institutions would be the EMI model, for teaching through English. Another option would be to start an ICLHE programme, with the commitment to transfer the benefits of the CLIL approach from primary and secondary education to university education. While EMI is often the chosen option in contexts in which the development of language competence in the target language is not a primary objective or even an objective to be considered, ICLHE is a more frequent choice when there is a clear intention to help improve the students' command of the foreign language. (Delicado Puerto & Pavón, 2015: 42)

Rubio-Cuenca and Moore (2018: 98) state that the distinction between EMI and ICLHE stems from the role accorded to the L1 in the learning process: 'While EMI ... is conceptualized, in theory at least, as English-only, ICLHE is taken to factor the L1 into the equation'. The selection of the approach has a direct influence on the different elements of the teaching curriculum, from method and activities to coordination and materials development. General organizational aspects at the macro-level (i.e. affecting the whole institution) of plurilingual programme implementation are gathered by the first QAIPPHE macro-indicator, particularly those organizational aspects measured by Quality Indicators 1, 2 and 3.

Defining objectives: Difficulties and challenges

To finish this overview of the key issues of the implementation of plurilingual plans, we should pay attention to the identification and definition of both global objectives for the whole plurilingual degrees and specific objectives for each of the courses offered in the foreign language:

> The programme objectives need to be linked to the skills and competences resulting from participation, and the spin-off activities such as staff publishing in English, mobility, and collaborative teaching input (increasingly inter-institutional and using VoIP-type technologies). If a nursing programme is taught through English in a German institution, financed mainly through federal/national funds, then the objectives will clearly differ from those of an engineering doctoral programme in the Netherlands financed through student fees. The key issue here is to be explicit on the programme goals. These may include income-generation for the university as a whole, benefits for students and staff, international ranking, and added value for the surrounding environment. (Marsh *et al.*, 2013: 14)

As for the specific objectives, we cannot offer the full range of possibilities here. However, Mehisto's (2012: 7) list of objectives, although not addressed at university degrees, seems translatable to higher education programmes that try to achieve:

(1) age-appropriate levels of L1 competence in reading, writing, speaking and listening and age-appropriate levels of advanced proficiency in L2 reading, writing, speaking and listening;
(2) grade-appropriate levels of academic achievement in non-language subjects taught primarily through the L2 and in those taught primarily through the L1;
(3) an understanding and appreciation of the L1 and L2 cultures;
(4) the capacity for and an interest in intercultural communication;
(5) the cognitive and social skills and habits required for success in an ever-changing world. (Mehisto, 2012: 7)

The linguistic qualifications of the lecturers as well as the linguistic competences of the students are two of the challenges that fostered the third macro-indicator of the tool. As for the linguistic qualifications of lecturers (Pérez-Cañado, 2013), a Common European Framework of Reference for Languages (CEFRL; Council of Europe, 2001) C1 level is considered the minimum level required for lecturers in plurilingual degrees (Lasagabaster & Ruiz de Zarobe, 2010: 288), as the identification of a minimum linguistic level seems to be a basic measure to support the quality of teaching. On the other hand, students are recommended to certify a minimum CEFRL B2 level of knowledge and use of the language of instruction in order to access a plurilingual programme.

Another challenge is the need, in many cases, to clarify concepts and eradicate the false beliefs of students and lecturers, especially regarding any reduction of content when taught through a foreign language. However, some studies demonstrate that the amount of content learned may be consolidated in a more effective way than the same content taught through the mother tongue (Serra, 2007; Wode, 1999); other studies show no impairment in the outcome of essential learning objectives (Admiraal *et al.*, 2006; Bergroth, 2006; Stehler, 2006) as objectives regarding language skills and competences increase exponentially.

Experience has shown that verification is a key element for the effective functioning of degrees, where assessment and evaluation procedures are the safety net of innovation procedures; the case of plurilingual programmes is no exception. This is in line with Quality Indicator 28 of our tool, i.e. to check whether the institution has a plan to evaluate academic achievement in order to compare academic outcomes between bilingual and non-bilingual groups.

Actions and Initiatives for the Implementation of Bilingual/Multilingual/Plurilingual Degrees

Following preliminary consideration of the decision to implement plurilingual degrees, we will try to summarize some key additional decisions for universities to make in order to eventually offer quality academic training in a foreign language.

Coordination and information

In this section, recommendations that emerge from the research are presented. In order to guarantee successful implementation of plurilingual degrees, the design of an organizational framework is of paramount importance; it needs to work 'as a backbone of the programme to coordinate and provide support for the full array of resources and actions which … must be put into operation' (Pavón & Gastaud, 2013: 88). Within this framework, all stakeholders (the vice-rectorates involved, the managing board for each faculty, lecturers and students) have to be informed about the needs and challenges facing the university as a whole. To these ends, the different vice-rectors involved should understand the importance of a coordinated effort to contribute the necessary actions and resources. The general language policy and the strategic plan regulate teamwork among vice-rectorates, faculties and language centres, a key factor in providing support by designing tailor-made language courses for both lecturers and students. All these general issues should be checked by the first macro-indicator on organizational aspects of the institution.

Lecturers should work collaboratively when planning, adapting and searching for didactic materials while sharing resources for their courses. Ideally, they should be coordinated by a fellow mentor, a linguistically and methodologically competent teacher in close contact with the general coordinator or coordinating board of the school or faculty. The general coordinator features as the central element for the internal organization of the plurilingual programme, being in charge of staff training, teacher and student support, detecting the most problematic areas and applying resources efficiently (Delicado Puerto & Pavón, 2015). The figure of a general faculty or school coordinator or coordinating board for the bilingual programme, although not directly mentioned as a specific quality indicator in our tool, parallels that of our Quality Indicator 3, in the sense that the coordinator or coordinating board will be in charge of the language policy for their faculty or school in the same way as the general language policy coordinator and commission act for the whole institution.

The teaching staff should be trained to realize the implications of teaching in a foreign language, a process that, as mentioned above, not only involves a change in the language of instruction, but also requires approaching classroom management from a new perspective, with a specific pedagogical apparatus, redesigning the use of materials and resources and redefining assessment, taking into account linguistic competence and the capacity to understand and verbalize academic content (Delicado Puerto & Pavón, 2015: 45).

Finally, the offer of plurilingual degrees should be clearly stated on each university's website in order to inform students about the possibilities and benefits of choosing plurilingual academic paths. As plurilingual plans have not been regulated in Spanish universities thus far, they should be offered as an option – not as compulsory education – to students. Newcomers should be informed about the academic options before enrolment, at the welcome meeting and by lecturers in each course presentation lesson. International incoming students should also have direct access to all this information prior to their arrival. Whether each faculty or the whole institution has a structured plan for the dissemination of and information about the programmes will be checked by Quality Indicator 6.

Teacher training

There is a commonly acknowledged axiom in the profession that high language level accreditation will automatically lead to a quality education.

However, regardless of the accredited level in the foreign language, lecturers participating in a plurilingual degree need to be equipped to explain academic content in the foreign language easily and safely, producing adapted materials by simplifying texts and making them more attractive and affordable for students. They also need to identify the language that students require in order to understand and produce knowledge derived from the subject-matter content (Arnold, 2010).

The introduction of a plurilingual programme may lead to methodological changes based on pair, group work and cooperative learning, identifying the appropriate learning strategies, applying adequate error-handling techniques and helping students to maintain their motivation and self-confidence (Stryker & Leaver, 1997). For all these reasons, universities must find a way to select and train the most qualified lecturers, those who combine linguistic and pedagogical skills meeting basic quality standards (Mohan & Slater, 2005). Hence, training programmes should be designed to cover this double linguistic and methodological function.

Fernández-Costales and González-Riaño (2015) show how lecturers rate the training received as positive. However, they all concur that the number of courses offered is insufficient and does not necessarily help them to improve their methodological competence for a plurilingual degree. On the other hand, they demand more support for participating in plurilingual degrees: more help for producing authentic materials in English, a greater reduction in teaching hours and a greater control over the quality of plurilingual programmes.

Along these lines, it will be the role of programme coordinators to devise support measures aimed at strengthening linguistic and pedagogical capacities, such as to provide personalized pedagogical advice, to focus on academic use of language, to manage classroom grouping, to increase the use of authentic materials, to adapt assessment to the new teaching context, etc. The designation of an expert for teaching and language support and advice is listed as Quality Indicator 19 in the macro-indicator on lecturers' incentives. Moreover, teacher training courses should include methodological strategies such as task-based teaching (Escobar & Sanchez, 2009), anchoring to previous knowledge, pre-lesson tasks, topic contextualization, maximization of redundancy, use of glossaries and graphic organizers, predominance of visual materials, fostering cooperative work (Pastor, 2011), group work (Dörnyei, 1997) and project work (Bonnet, 2012). To foster correct linguistic production, Valcke and Pavón (2015) suggest working on aspects of pronunciation and applying scaffolding techniques for both language (modelling, connection, contextualization, reuse and adaptation) and content (rewording, redundancy, exemplification, circular explanation, comparison, use of synonyms and antonyms, etc.) (van de Pol *et al.*, 2010). Training support for teaching staff is paramount for the success of plurilingual programmes, which should include teacher training plans backed by teaching innovation projects for which participants should get a recognized certificate. The macro-indicator on language level and methodology checks whether the institution has a language training and accreditation plan (Quality Indicator 12) together with a methodological training plan for lecturers (Quality Indicator 13).

Support measures for lecturers

One of the aspects that lecturers most appreciate is help with producing adapted materials. According to Arnold (2010: 230), the distinction made by Cummins (1984) between basic interpersonal communication skills (BICS) and cognitive academic language proficiency (CALP) is reflected in textbook materials, as English language teaching textbooks are supported by BICS, whereas non-linguistic textbooks are supported by CALP. The combination of these two types of language is essential for the success of plurilingual education. It is also important to point out that CLIL is not a translation of activities from L1 to L2, as both languages are complementary (Pinter, 2006).

As additional measures to support teaching staff, one could also consider purely linguistic support from highly skilled professionals. However, research across Europe has focused on literacy and discourse practices in plurilingual settings. Meyer et al. (2015: 43) address the issue within the context of formal academic subject discourses and state: 'Thus, the need to shift teacher and learners' attention towards academic literacies development opens up new pathways towards deep learning.' The Graz Group's pluriliteracies model (Meyer et al., 2015) is especially relevant for higher education since it establishes strong links between the conceptual and the communication continua, and the student progresses from basic cognitive discursive functions towards a mastery of various academic discourses.

On the other hand, universities could also initiate or strengthen a structure of cooperation and collaboration with other lecturers, providing support for collaboration networks with foreign language lecturers, including contact with lecturers from foreign HEIs working in plurilingual programmes. Teacher training and foreign language expert support go hand in hand in a plurilingual programme. Contero (2018: 14–15) lists three key roles in which foreign language specialists should use their expert knowledge within the new bilingual teaching paradigm, namely, coordinator of the bilingual programme, CLIL trainer and pedagogic advisor.

Linguistic support for students

Plurilingual-based degrees not only require qualified lecturers, but also support for students in order to cope successfully with difficulties and challenges. Initially, students need to be independent users of the language. B2 seems to be the most common required or recommended level for students (Bazo et al., 2017: 14). However, a common perception of lecturers participating in plurilingual degrees is that students show a lower linguistic competence than expected, resulting in a barrier to efficient learning. Fortunately, the number of students coming from plurilingual primary and secondary schools with a certified B1 or higher level in English has increased exponentially during 2010–2020 (Rubio-Cuenca, 2019). For quality assurance purposes, our tool checks for a minimum B2 level requirement for students involved in plurilingual programmes (Quality Indicator 14).

It is important to analyse error correction in the plurilingual classroom, given the emphasis on the discursive exchanges that occur among the different participants (García, 2009). Plurilingual programmes require a more active stance from students, participation in cooperative learning strategies, choice of topics and activities, etc. (Pavón & Rubio-Alcalá, 2010).

Regardless of whether a minimum entry level is required, it seems advisable to regulate actions aimed at strengthening the linguistic competence of the students. This may require putting into action measures to try to compensate for a supposed linguistic deficit on their part. One of these could be to offer linguistic support in the form of personalized advice from students with a certificate level of C1 from the degrees related to foreign languages or with translation and interpretation. Another measure could be for university language centres to offer courses specifically aimed at students who are studying plurilingual degrees, with the stipulation that courses focused on language development should be connected with the subjects taught in those degrees. For both purposes, some institutions are hiring language assistants who are native or near-native speakers of the programme's target language. Specifically oriented courses for students should be financed or aided by the institution by means of grants or a reduction in course fees. As a student incentive, Quality Indicator 22 is the provision of grants for language-specific courses and accreditation exams for students. Moreover, the designation of an expert for language learning support and advice is also listed as Quality Indicator 24 in the macro-indicator on students' incentives.

Main Factors Affecting Plurilingual Programmes in Higher Education

HEIs all over Europe, pioneered by Finnish universities (Saarinen & Nikula, 2013: 134), are increasingly introducing internationalization procedures in their general strategic plans. A consequence of the application of these procedures has been the expansion of plurilingual education programmes together with the emergence and rapid growth of CLIL and EMI, despite the lack of a clearly identified theoretical model, the lack of empirical research on plurilingualism in higher education and the paucity and unproved quality of this research.

Coleman (2006) has been more specific, proposing seven drivers or reasons impelling HEIs and educational authorities to introduce programmes and courses taught through English: CLIL, internationalization, student exchanges, teaching and research materials, staff mobility, graduate employability and the market in international students.

With regard to this line of pressure for internationalization, universities are increasingly offering undergraduate and postgraduate programmes through the medium of English (Lasagabaster *et al.*, 2014) and other languages such as Spanish, French or German. Additionally, student mobility programmes have largely contributed to an increase in the number of students enrolled outside their country of citizenship: from 0.8 million worldwide in 1975 to 4.6 million in 2015, with inflows towards European countries and the United States increasing by 5.0% and 7.5%, respectively (OECD, 2017). In this vein, Wächter and Maiworm's (2014) study reveals a 239% growth in bachelor's and master's programmes over a seven-year period: from 2389 in 2007 to 8089 in 2014.

This rapidly emerging phenomenon has led to a new educational paradigm variously known by the terms bilingual degree programmes, bilingual or plurilingual learning, bilingual education or bilingual MOOCs (Arco-Tirado *et al.*, 2018). In this regard, exploratory research shows variability found in bilingual, plurilingual or multilingual practices and programmes (simplified hereafter to bilingual programmes or BPs), ranging from EMI, which basically entails the delivery of instruction in English, to other approaches such as ICLHE. ICLHE is a variation of the form of plurilingual education known as CLIL which has developed in compulsory education (Arco-Tirado *et al.*, 2017). Concurrently, the variability in the use of these terms could arguably be attributed to the absence of a commonly shared definition of the concept, as discussed in the Council of Europe's (2007) document entitled *From Linguistic Diversity to Plurilingual Education: Guide for the Development of Language Education Policies in Europe*. Indeed, this document comprises a comprehensive effort to justify and frame the development of plurilingual education policies by emphasizing consensus around linguistic, sociological or economic arguments rather than theoretical and/or empirical evidence from evaluation research.

Concerning curricular development, BPs encompass the same curricular components as monolingual ones, with additional components related to the use of more than one vehicular language. The introduction of language goals and outcomes thus increases curricular complexity from the teaching, learning and research perspectives. In this regard, whereas some authors like Marsh *et al.* (2013) or Soltero and Ortiz (2012) identify several levers conditioning BPs' quality at the macro-level, other authors, such as Short (2006), focus on the components for effective plurilingual content lessons at the micro-level.

All in all, the quality and effectiveness of BPs may be determined by these components and their potential interactions, and therefore represent a complex range of research targets for evaluation studies. The main goal of these studies is to identify the extent to which those 'high-quality' components are supported by credible evidence. However, although these key components may be justifiable from a theoretical perspective, there is a need for evidence to support whether their contribution to BPs is really effective from an empirical evaluation standpoint.

In this context, from a quality of teaching and learning perspective, the lecturers have to face basic educational and instructional decisions around those key dimensions of the curriculum for which no systematic reviews on evidence-based practices or very little on practice-based evidence are available (Arco-Tirado et al., 2017). For example, while authors like Dafouz et al. (2014) suggest that BPs (which make use of some native language instruction) do not significantly differ from English-only programmes in their impact on standardized test performance, other authors like Arco-Tirado et al. (2018) provide empirical evidence, using a counterfactual impact evaluation design. They suggest that there is a cost for plurilingual students in academic performance compared to their monolingual counterparts. Therefore, in this paradoxical and pressing context of delivering high-quality educational practices without enough evaluation research data and results, lecturers and staff have had to turn their research efforts towards studies that allow them to apply intervention effects accurately and reliably (Arco-Tirado & Fernández-Martín, 2018).

The Council of Europe uses 'Languages of Schooling' as a language teaching framework to refer to three main components: language as a subject (LS), language across the curriculum (LAC) and language curriculum (LC), referring to the language needs of students. CLIL is closely related to LAC, based on LS, and it is a constituent part of LC (Martyniuk, 2008).

A basic premise of CLIL is that any subject can be taught in a foreign language without it negatively impacting on the acquisition of contents (Wilkinson & Zegers, 2008). However, the majority of the research on the topic has been carried out in primary and secondary education and reliable studies on the working of university programmes are still needed (Rubio-Alcalá et al., 2019).

Pre-university research, however, is not conclusive on the quality of content learning. Aguilar and Muñoz (2014) indicate that it affects the natural construction of knowledge in the students; on the other hand, primary and secondary education studies show a clear progression in L2 linguistic competence (Aguilar & Muñoz, 2014).

In higher education, CLIL involves three basic requirements for success: mastery of the foreign language, an effective method and the development of learner attitudes (Aguilar & Muñoz, 2014); however, Mellion (2008) goes further in the description of the conditions for successful CLIL programmes:

(1) sociopolitical dimensions – society and government support regarding internationalization programmes and language policy in higher education;

(2) language policies at the universities;
(3) CLIL funding (translating services, hiring specialized lecturers and assistants, training programmes, etc.);
(4) guaranteed connection in the different stages of the process, from the design of training programmes to the administration and publications of the outcomes (Mellion, 2008);
(5) collaboration among the different stakeholders and especially lecturers from the different areas (Pavón *et al.*, 2015a);
(6) a settled procedure to assess the programme at the different stages.

Bilingual education models

As addressed above, in the section entitled 'Which plurilingual teaching model?', the selection of the most appropriate model, CLIL, EMI or ICLHE, will determine the further development of the whole programme. Marsh (2008: 236) described CLIL as 'a wide range of educational practice', and Mehisto *et al.* (2008: 236) consider CLIL an umbrella term covering a dozen or more educational approaches. In fact, the debate approach/method has not been resolved yet. With that level of specificity, it is a complex task to develop a stable and homogeneous model to teach content subjects through a foreign language.

The main differences in ways of finding the most appropriate model involve the degree of integration the foreign language has in the educational context. On the one hand, there is complete integration, where all the courses and subjects are taught in the foreign language (Karabinar, 2008) and it is taken for granted that people involved in the process enjoy a high command of the CLIL language (Alexander, 2008). The Netherlands and Finland have developed this model. On the other hand, in the partial integration model, some courses are taken in a foreign language (Alexander, 2008; Karabinar, 2008) using a language replacement (language shift, language transfer or language assimilation), as in Poland. In the Norwegian case, CLIL is used as a complement to rather than a replacement for the courses taught in the mother tongue, whereas in Germany some institutions use the foreign language as an additional language to facilitate the access of international students to the courses offered in German (Alexander, 2008; Karabinar, 2008).

Course selection

CLIL appears to condition the selection of courses. Learning a subject through a foreign language means that students have to make an extra effort to acquire content; besides, if there is just one group in the degree course, some problems might occur if the students do not have the opportunity to take the subject in the L1 (Fortanet, 2008). In cases where there is more than one group, concern about the quality of the contents and group ratio might affect the development of the project.

Some contexts allow for a full CLIL implementation in every year of the degree. However, some lecturers show concerns regarding the early stages of the degree. Other universities prefer the first contact with integrated learning to occur during the postgraduate programme (Aguilar & Muñoz, 2014; Fortanet, 2008). In these cases, the students may take preparatory subjects in the first years of the degree (English for academic purposes (EAP) or English for specific purposes (ESP); see Fortanet, 2008). Researchers suggest designing and developing a step-by-step programme, mainly in those subjects where CLIL is clearly needed.

Lecturers and students

Mellion (2008) outlines key competences to develop in a CLIL programme. Students need to develop linguistic competence, entailing not only knowledge of the language but also development of a positive attitude towards language and culture. Lecturers need to develop not only their linguistic and methodological competences but also those competences directly related to their roles as lecturers. These include pedagogical competence, organizational and collaborative competences, reflective competence and all those competences related to their professional development (Lorenzo et al., 2011). Lecturers also need to transfer their original L1 teaching competences into CLIL competences. Higher education leaders must pay special attention to the development of intercultural competence, with dialogue and active learning pervading the whole process to involve international students.

Aguilar and Muñoz (2014) analyse the need to set a threshold level for students before enjoying the benefits of CLIL. They conclude that CLIL methodology is more effective for those students with lower competence in their L2. Students also need to develop a number of skills in order to give presentations and write academic essays (Zegers, 2008). Likewise, the optimal command of the L2 for lecturers must be set out. Committed and coordinated lecturers have been shown to be key components in plurilingual development (Pavón et al., 2015a, 2015b). Education is a complex activity which requires the active participation of the different stakeholders. Shifting the education vehicle towards a new and initially unstable one will need not only an extra effort on the part of each participant, but also special attention to how these driving forces are attuned within the CLIL orchestra.

Extrinsic as they may seem, bonus schemes have been shown to be effective in terms of, for example, acknowledging lecturers' involvement in the quality of education, with a reduction in their teaching load or priming CLIL innovation projects, as well as Erasmus+ applications and visiting professors (Fortanet, 2008). Similarly, a C1 accreditation in the CLIL language may be considered as a requirement for accessing new teaching positions (Klaassen, 2008). Good practices exchanges and seminars can also be of great help.

Apart from bonus schemes and exchanges, another important component is that of teacher training within and outside the home university, such as methodological courses and seminars, language courses towards C1 language level (Klaassen, 2008) and training in intercultural competence. A scaffolding framework should also be built for the CLIL teacher, with services ranging from lesson templates to linguistic reviewing of the materials (language centres, translation faculties) (Aguilar & Muñoz, 2014).

Finally, cooperation among different content and language lecturers (Friedenberg & Schneider, 2008) together with specific quality control measures (Kling & Hjulmand, 2008) may lead to a fruitful development of CLIL programmes.

Methodology

The objectives, expectations and outcomes of the programme have to be clearly set. A good starting point might be detailing the needs of the students (Zegers, 2008). CLIL classroom dynamics ask for a very specific methodology in terms of attention span and learning pace. We provide below some key ideas to take into account during course planning and implementation. Along these lines, designing alternative working methods that promote class interaction seems to be an interesting option (Klaassen, 2008). The mother tongue does not need to be neglected in class interaction, especially in the early stages of the programme, with the use of compensation strategies such as non-verbal communication, visual contact, the introduction of new terms and different ways to tackle new concepts (Klaassen, 2008). In this context, translanguaging (and the use of code-switching) is a valuable learning strategy in higher education for integrating the mother tongue and the target language; its specialized use of the language and high demands may seem hard to master at the beginning, but the technique has proved effective (Kontio & Sylvén, 2015; Nikula, 2007).

Academic skills in the target language have to be stressed, fostering the ability to present orally (Kling & Hjulmand, 2008) or providing the necessary scaffolding for academic reports and research projects (Lim, 2008).

Finally, materials design and development is a time-consuming activity; as Ball (2018: 224) points out, the main problem for practising lecturers is a lack of time. Biggs (2003) and Ball (2018) advocate a constructive alignment for the creation and distribution of CLIL materials; Ávila-López (2020) proposes the task-based content through language teaching (TBCLT) approach, which 'offers a number of indications to develop task-based EMI materials taking into account the potential of a text-driven syllabus that includes integrated project work as a staple diet of classroom dynamics' (Ávila-López, 2020: 298).

Friedenberg and Schneider (2008) propose 'sheltered instruction', an approach to teaching English language learners which integrates the development of content knowledge, language proficiency and academic skills, at the same time. Sheltered instruction was developed in the United States in the mid-1980s by linguists and educators who sought ways to integrate L2 learning theories and strategies with content instruction for secondary schools, in the absence of bilingual instruction. It uses simplified speech, graphic organizers (Kagan, 2001; Parks & Black, 1992), hands-on activities, cooperative learning, visual aids, demonstrations, hand movements and reiteration to help students acquire both language and appropriate grade-level content simultaneously (Friedenberg & Schneider, 2008: 156). Within this approach, the language and the content teacher should work together as a way to ease the learning process linguistically but to retain the intellectual scope of the material. Friedenberg and Schneider recommend the sheltered alternative for immigrants or international students. Finally, ICT may be really helpful to scaffold language (Koenraa *et al.*, 2008); there are an endless number of ICT resources on the internet to help students in that process.

AGCEPESA's Quality Assurance Inventory for Bilingual Programmes in Higher Education (QAIPPHE)

The project

AGCEPESA (Analysis and Quality Assurance of Plurilingual Studies in Higher Education in Andalusia) is a project endorsed by the Junta de Andalucía, Spain (2014–2019) in its 2012 Incentive Plan, 'Projects of Excellence' (P12-SEJ-1588). It is made up of researchers from public Andalusian universities who, aware of the need for a common frame of reference for the implementation of plurilingual education plans, undertook the task of drawing a map of the current state of affairs. The first draft showed autonomous programmes scattered across the Andalusian higher education territory. In this context, a quality assurance plan emerged to diagnose the need for a tool to evaluate quality and promote good multilingual practices in higher education. The original plan intended to generate a tool drawn from the different plurilingual experiences in Andalusia. The criteria for good practices were established, and 'quality indicators' were drawn from the analysis, integrating the quality tool, Quality Assurance Inventory for Plurilingual Programs in Higher Education (QAIPPHE), whose results can guide the implementation of plurilingual plans with scientific quality criteria. The outcome of the project is available in a joint publication by Moore, Rubio-Alcalá and Pavón (2018), where the different working teams of AGCEPESA published their analysis and insights on the bilingual programmes in the Andalusian higher education area.

Systematic review

The main objective of this project was to generate a framework that could serve as a reference for the implementation of plurilingual plans in higher education. For that purpose, work dynamics were structured by alternating small operational groups working on specific topics with executive meetings where the main decisions were taken. Operational definitions of the variables involved emerged from this interaction: multilingualism, linguistic policies and quality indicators. The need for a systematic review of the studies published on the topic was identified. Studies based on evidence constituted the central corpus of the evaluation tool, QAIPPHE.

The review team adapted a systematic review protocol based on *Campbell Systematic Reviews: Policies and Guidelines* (Campbell Collaboration, 2015. Last update 2019). The detailed results of this review were published in Rubio-Alcalá *et al.* (2019).

The following search criteria were used for this systematic review. Educational practices and programmes in which two (or more) languages are used as a medium of instruction (Council of Europe, 2007) were defined as independent variables. Dependent variables were learning outcomes, second language proficiency and employment, on the one hand, and attitude or motivation, on the other. Eligible participants were university students with no time, geographical or cultural restrictions. The eligible research designs were pre-experimental, quasi-experimental, experimental, correlational and *ex post facto* (as classified by Campbell & Stanley, 1963).

Two types of search were carried out. A primary search was made through three search engines and their corresponding databases (Proquest, Web of Science and Scopus). This primary search was carried out simultaneously at the University of Huelva, the University of Granada and the University of Málaga, yielding a result of 7476 records. A complementary search, consisting of published and unpublished studies from Google Scholar, specialized journals, website platforms, etc., was made according to relevance for the study. It was carried out following different methods: search in other resources, manual search in relevant websites, snowball method and personal contacts with experts. The outcome of both the primary and complementary searches was 8914 records.

These records went through a selection process: duplicates were removed, as well as those belonging to unrelated fields or topics, leaving 4566 primary search records and 168 complementary search records. After reading titles and abstracts, those that did not focus on the variables defined for the search were removed, resulting in 966 primary search records and 168 for the complementary search. The second stage consisted of reading the complete texts, and those that were not based on plurilingual or multilingual practices or programmes, or on attitude or motivation were discarded, yielding 20 primary search records and 158 complementary search records. The third and last stage consisted of a new full reading of the texts, leaving a final selection of 62 records (see Figure 7.1).

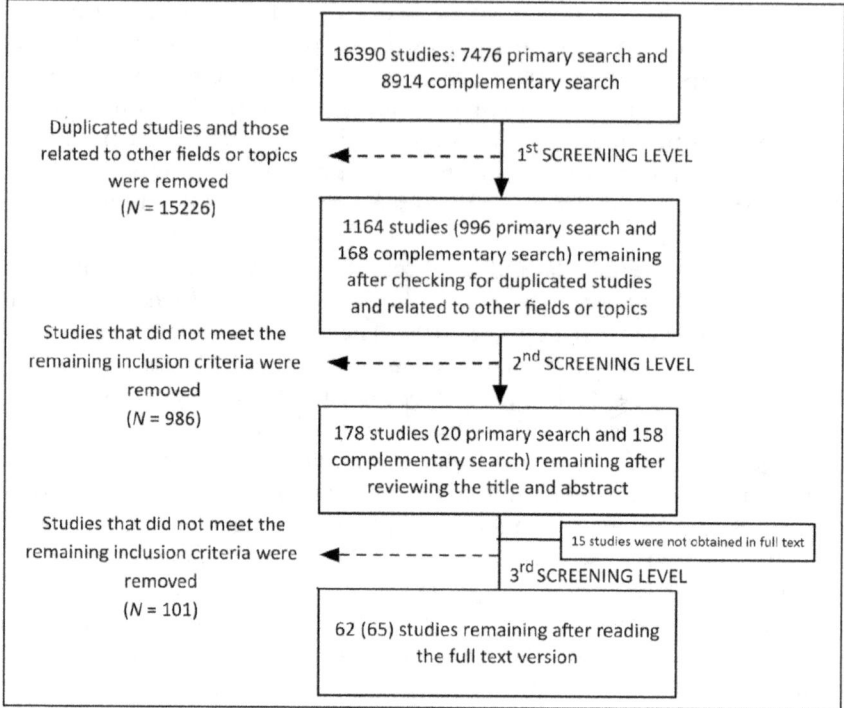

Figure 7.1 Flow chart for the literature search and screening
Source: Rubio-Alcalá *et al.* (2019: 203).

The studies and the data were coded in variables related to study methods, independent variables, variable results, characteristics of the samples, results and conclusions. The results were published in Rubio-Alcalá *et al.* (2019), in which they analysed a total sample of 202,685 participants from the studies of 21 countries, published between 1995 and 2016, in English and Spanish.

The results demonstrate the dearth of high-quality and robust research and evaluation designs and are therefore insufficient to demonstrate the causality between the programmes and/or practices and the results (Rubio-Alcalá *et al.*, 2019).

Quality indicators

From the aforementioned work, 30 quality indicators were specified, which are grouped into six macro-indicators that refer to the areas involved in this process: organizational aspects; curriculum; language level and methodology; lecturers' (and staff) incentives; students' incentives; and quality assurance (evaluation plan – sustainability – impact) (see Table 7.1).

Table 7.1 Quality assurance inventory for bilingual programmes in higher education (QAIPPHE)

No.	Quality indicators	Yes	No	Observations	Evidences
Macro-indicator: Organizational aspects					
1	There is a general framework of linguistic policy approved by the governing board of the university.				
2	There is a document in which the objectives are clearly set out (degrees, target language(s), language levels required, etc.).				
3	There is a Language Policy commission, a general coordinator at the university and coordinators in faculties.				
4	There is a document with a list of all the lecturers in the faculty that may participate.				
5	There is a document with a budget for the programme (whether in the faculty or institution).				
6	There is a plan for information and dissemination of the programme (website, posters, etc.) (whether in the faculty or institution).				
7	There is a protocol for administrative procedures (change of class, enrolment, etc.).				
Macro-indicator: Curriculum					
8	There is a *verified* certification of the bilingual degree (approved by an external academic committee).				
9	There is an itinerary with the sequence of courses in the foreign language along the degree.				
10	The credit load of courses in the foreign language is between 40% and 60% in the degree.				
Macro-indicator: Language level and methodology					
11	The minimum language level required for lecturers to participate is C1.				
12	There is a language training and accreditation plan for lecturers.				
13	There is a methodological training plan for lecturers.				
14	The minimum language level required for students to participate is B2.				
Macro-indicator: Lecturers' (and staff) incentives					
15	Lecturers have priority or advantages for mobility programmes (Erasmus Teaching, etc.).				

16	Lecturers and staff have grants (€) for language and/or methodological formation.				
17	Lecturers have teaching load reduction (minimum 1.5 ECTS out of 6).				
18	The university board certifies lecturers' participation in the programme.				
19	Lecturers and staff have a designated expert available for advice about teaching and language learning.				
20	Lecturers have priority to choose the same course for the next course year.				
Macro-indicator: Students' incentives					
21	Students have priority or advantages for mobility programmes (Erasmus Study, etc.).				
22	Students have grants (€) for language learning and/or accreditation exams.				
23	Students have the courses taken in the foreign language certified in the SET (European Degree Title Supplement).				
24	Students have a designated expert available for advice about language learning.				
Macro-indicator: Quality assurance – evaluation plan – sustainability – impact					
25	There is a plan to diagnose language levels at the first and last year of the programme.				
26	There is a plan to assess students' satisfaction.				
27	There is a plan to assess lecturers' satisfaction.				
28	There is a plan to evaluate academic achievement to compare between the bilingual group and the non-bilingual group.				
29	There is written commitment from the institution for continuity of the programme.				
30	There is a plan to analyse students' employability when finishing the degree.				

Source: Rubio-Alcalá et al. (2018).[1]

Conclusion

Spanish universities are immersed in a deep transformation regarding the main vehicle for communication in the classroom. Accordingly, language policies are having a deep impact on faculties and curriculums, with English becoming complementary to Spanish in an attempt at internationalizing higher education across the country. This transformation is not free of challenges, ranging from a clear definition of how the role of the teacher has to evolve to fit into the new language milieu, to structural and economic measures required to tackle the new learning scenario. Different factors have been identified as having a determinant role on the operation of the plurilingual programmes: the linguistic integration model inspiring the programme, the courses involved, coordination of lecturers from linguistic and non-linguistic areas, linguistic support for students, and the teacher training plan which is directly linked to the methodology used in the classrooms.

The systematic review protocol applied to the evidence-based literature on the topic has been used by the AGCEPESA team as a springboard to generate an evaluation tool with 30 quality indicators specifically selected for the assessment of plurilingual programmes, analysing aspects such as organization, curriculum, language level and pedagogical implementation, or how lecturers and students are extrinsically motivated to enrol and stay involved.

The tool allows for the evaluation of bilingual programmes and the necessary steps towards evidence-based programmes that may develop more robust, better designed, effective bilingual, plurilingual or multilingual programmes.

Note

(1) Arco, J.L., Ávila-López, F.J., Barrios, E., Carretero, A., Casal, S., Coyle, D., Fernández, F.D., Fonseca, M.C., Hermosín, M., Julián de Vega, M.C., Marsh, D., Méndez, M.C., Moore, P.F., Morales, F., Nieto, J.M., Pavón, V., Romero, E., Rubio-Alcalá, F.D., Rubio-Cuenca, F., Salaberri, S., Sánchez, M., Vélez-Toral, M., Villoria, J. and Zayas, F.

References

Admiraal, W., Westhoff, G. and de Bot, K. (2006) Evaluation of bilingual secondary education in the Netherlands: Students' language proficiency in English. *Educational Research and Evaluation* 12 (1), 75–93.

Aguilar, M. and Muñoz, M. (2014) The effect of proficiency on CLIL benefits in engineering students in Spain. *International Journal of Applied Linguistics* 24 (1), 1–18.

Alexander, R.J. (2008) International programs in the German-speaking world and Englishization: A critical analysis. In R. Wilkinson and V. Zegers (eds) *Realizing Content and Language Integration in Higher Education* (pp. 77–95). Maastricht: Maastricht University.

Ament, J.R. and Pérez-Vidal, C. (2015) Linguistic outcomes of English medium instruction programs in higher education: A study on economics undergraduates at a Catalan university. *Higher Learning Research Communications* 5 (1), 47–68. doi:10.18870/hlrc.v5i1.239

Arco-Tirado, J.L. and Fernández-Martín, F.D. (2018) Systematic review protocol example on effective plurilingual higher education programs. Unpublished manuscript, Department of Developmental and Educational Psychology, University of Granada.

Arco-Tirado, J.L., Fernández-Martín, F.D. and Hernández-Moreno, N. (2017) Skills learning through a bilingual mentors programme in higher education. *International Journal*

of *Bilingual Education and Bilingualism* 21 (8), 1030–1040. doi:10.1080/13670050.201
6.1228601
Arco-Tirado, J.L., Fernández-Martín, F.D., Ramos-García, A.M., Littvay, L., Villoria, J. and
Naranjo, J.A. (2018) A counterfactual impact evaluation of a bilingual programme on
students' grade point average at a Spanish university. *Evaluation and Programme
Planning* 68, 81–89. doi:10.1016/j.evalprogplan.2018.02.013
Arnold, W. (2010) Where is CLIL taking us? *Pulso* 33, 227–233.
Ávila-López, J. (2020) Materials development: A constituent element of teacher training for
EMI in higher education. In M. Sánchez-Pérez (ed.) *Teacher Training for English-
Medium Instruction in Higher Education* (pp. 298–319). Hershey, PE: IGI Global.
Balfour, R.J. (2007) University language policies, internationalism, multilingualism, and
language development in South Africa and the UK. *Cambridge Journal of Education*
37 (1), 35–49.
Ball, P. (2018) Innovations and challenges in CLIL materials design. *Theory into Practice*
57 (3), 222–231. doi:10.1080/00405841.2018.1484036
Bazo, P., Centellas, A., Dafouz, E., Fernández, A., González, D. and Pavón, V. (2017)
*Documento marco de política lingüística para la internacionalización del sistema uni-
versitario español* [*Towards a Language Policy for the Internationalisation of Spanish
Universities: A Framework of Reference*]. Madrid: CRUE-IC. See https://is.muni.cz/do/
rect/metodika/VaV/vyzkum/hr4mu/CRUE_DMPL_14.10.16_EN.pdf.
Bergroth, M. (2006) Immersion students in the matriculation examination three years after
immersion. In S. Björklund, K. Mard-Miettinen, M. Bergström and M. Södergard (eds)
*Exploring Dual Focussed Education: Integrating Language and Content for Individual
and Societal Needs* (pp. 123–134). Vaasa: University of Vaasa, Centre for Immersion
and Multilingualism. See http://www.uwasa.fi/materiaali/pdf/isbn_952-476-149-1.pdf.
Biggs, J. (2003) *Teaching for Quality Learning at University: What the Student Does.*
Buckingham: Society for Research into Higher Education (SHRE) and Open University
Press.
Bonnet, A. (2012) Towards an evidence base for CLIL: How to integrate qualitative and
quantitative as well as process, product and participant perspectives in CLIL research.
International CLIL Research Journal 1 (4), 66–78.
Campbell, D.T. and Stanley, J.C. (1963) *Experimental and Quasi-experimental Designs for
Research.* Boston, MA: Houghton Mifflin.
Campbell Collaboration (2019) *Campbell Systematic Reviews: Policies and Guidelines.*
Version 1.4. doi:10.4073/cpg.2016.1
Coleman, J. (2006) English-medium teaching in European higher education. *Language
Teaching* 39, 1–14.
Contero, C. (2018) The key role of foreign language teachers in content and language inte-
grated learning at a university level. *International Journal of Learning in Higher
Education* 25 (2), 7–16.
Council of Europe (2001) *Common European Framework of Reference for Languages.*
Cambridge: Cambridge University Press.
Council of Europe (2007) *From Linguistic Diversity to Plurilingual Education: Guide for the
Development of Language Education Policies in Europe.* Strasbourg: Council of
Europe. See https://rm.coe.int/16806a892c (accessed 17 June 2020).
Coyle, D. (2005) *CLIL: Planning Tools for Teachers.* See https://www.unifg.it/sites/default/
files/allegatiparagrafo/20-01-2014/coyle_clil_planningtool_kit.pdf.
Cummins, J. (1984) *Bilingualism and Special Education.* Clevedon: Multilingual
Matters.
Dafouz, E. and Núñez, B. (2009) CLIL in higher education: Devising a new learning land-
scape. In E. Dafouz and M. Guerrini (eds) *CLIL across Educational Levels: Experiences
from Primary, Secondary and Tertiary Contexts* (pp. 101–112). Madrid: Santillana.
Dafouz, E., Camacho, M.M. and Urquia, E. (2014) 'Surely they can't do as well': A com-
parison of business students' academic performance in English-medium and

Spanish-as-first-language-medium programs. *Language and Education* 28 (3), 223–236. doi:10.1080/09500782.2013.808661

Delicado Puerto, G. and Pavón, V. (2015) La implantación de titulaciones bilingües en la Educación Superior: El caso de la formación didáctica del profesorado bilingüe de Primaria en la Universidad de Extremadura. *Educación y Futuro* 32, 35–63.

Doiz, A., Lasagabaster, D. and Sierra, J.M. (eds) (2013) *English-Medium Instruction at Universities: Global Challenges*. Bristol: Multilingual Matters.

Dörnyei, Z. (1997) Psychological processes in cooperative language learning: Group dynamics and motivation. *The Modern Language Journal* 81 (4), 482–493.

Escobar, C. (2013) Learning to become a CLIL teacher: Teaching, reflection and professional development. *International Journal of Bilingual Education and Bilingualism* 16 (3), 334–353.

Escobar, C. and Sánchez, A. (2009) Language learning through tasks in a content and language integrated learning (CLIL) science classroom. *Porta Linguarum* 11, 65–83.

Fernández-Costales, A. and González-Riaño, X.A. (2015) Teacher satisfaction Concerning the implementation of bilingual programs in a Spanish university. *Porta Linguarum* 23, 93–108.

Fortanet, I. (2008) Questions for debate in English medium lecturing in Spain. In R. Wilkinson and V. Zegers (eds) *Realizing Content and Language Integration in Higher Education* (pp. 21–31). Maastricht: Maastricht University.

Fortanet-Gómez, I. (2013) *CLIL in Higher Education: Towards a Multilingual Language Policy*. Bristol: Multilingual Matters.

Friedenberg, J.E. and Schneider, M. (2008) An experiment in sheltered sociology at the university level. In R. Wilkinson and V. Zegers (eds) *Realizing Content and Language Integration in Higher Education* (pp. 155–168). Maastricht: Maastricht University.

García, O. (2009) *Bilingual Education in the 21st Century: A Global Perspective*. Chichester: Wiley-Blackwell.

Gázquez Linares, J.J., Molero Jurado, M., Barragán Martín, A.B., Simón Márquez, M., Martos Martínez, A., Soriano Sánchez, J.G. and Oropesa Ruiz, N.F. (eds) (2019) *Innovación Docente e Investigación en Arte y Humanidades*. Madrid: Dykinson.

Halbach, A., Lázaro Lafuente, A. and Pérez Guerra, J. (2013) La lengua inglesa en la nueva universidad española del EEES. *Revista de Educación* 362, 105–132.

Hellekjaer, G.O. and Wilkinson, R. (2009) CLIL in higher education. *EuroCLIL*, Bulletin 7. See http://www.euroclic.net/index.php?inhoud=inhoud/bulletins/bulletin7/8.htm.

Kagan, S. (2001) *Brain-based Learning Smart Card*. San Clemente. CA: Kagan.

Karabinar, S. (2008) Integrating language and content: Two models and their effects on the learners' academic self-concept. In R. Wilkinson and V. Zegers (eds) *Realizing Content and Language Integration in Higher Education* (pp. 53–63). Maastricht: Maastricht University.

Klaassen, R.G. (2008) Preparing lecturers for English-medium instruction. In R. Wilkinson and V. Zegers (eds) *Realizing Content and Language Integration in Higher Education* (pp. 32–42). Maastricht: Maastricht University.

Kling, J. and Hjulmand, L.L. (2008) PLATE: Project in language assessment for teaching in English. In R. Wilkinson and V. Zegers (eds) *Realizing Content and Language Integration in Higher Education* (pp. 191–200). Maastricht: Maastricht University.

Koenraa, T., Hajer, M., Hootsen, G. and van der Werf, R. (2008) Towards a linguistically scaffolded curriculum. How can technology help? In R. Wilkinson and V. Zegers (eds) *Realizing Content and Language Integration in Higher Education* (pp. 64–73). Maastricht: Maastricht University.

Kontio, J. and Sylvén, L.K. (2015) Language alternation and language norm in vocational content and language integrated learning. *Language Learning Journal* 43 (3), 271–285.

Lasagabaster, D. and Ruiz de Zarobe, Y. (eds) (2010) *CLIL in Spain: Implementation, Results and Teacher Training*. Newcastle upon Tyne: Cambridge Scholars.

Lasagabaster, D., Doiz, A. and Sierra, J.M. (2014) *Motivation and Foreign Language Learning: From Theory to Practice.* Amsterdam: John Benjamins.

Lim, J.M.H. (2008) Analyzing recommendations for future research: An investigation into a hybrid sub-genre. In R. Wilkinson and V. Zegers. (eds) *Realizing Content and Language Integration in Higher Education* (pp. 131–154). Maastricht: Maastricht University.

Lorenzo, F., Trujillo, F. and Vez, J.M. (2011) *Educación bilingüe: Integración de contenidos y segundas lenguas.* Madrid: Síntesis.

Marsh, D. (2008) Language awareness and CLIL. In J. Cenoz and N.H. Hornberger (eds) *Encyclopaedia of Language and Education* (pp. 233–246). Dordrecht: Springer.

Marsh, D., Pavón, V. and Frigols, M.J. (2013) *The Higher Education Languages Landscape: Ensuring Quality in English Language Degree Programs.* Valencia: Valencian International University.

Martyniuk, W. (2008) CLIL – at the core of plurilingual education? In R. Wilkinson and V. Zegers (eds) *Realizing Content and Language Integration in Higher Education* (pp. 13–18). Maastricht: Maastricht University.

Mehisto, P. (2012) *Excellence in Bilingual Education: A Guide for School Principals.* Cambridge: Cambridge University Press.

Mehisto, P., Marsh, D. and Frigols, M.J. (2008) *Uncovering CLIL: Content and Language Integrated Learning in Bilingual and Multilingual Education.* Oxford: MacMillan Education.

Mellion, M.J. (2008) The challenge of changing tongues in business university education. In R. Wilkinson and V. Zegers (eds) *Realizing Content and Language Integration in Higher Education* (pp. 212–227). Maastricht: Maastricht University.

Meyer, O., Coyle, D., Halbach, A., Schuck, K. and Ting, T. (2015) A pluriliteracies approach to content and language integrated learning – mapping learner progressions in knowledge construction and meaning-making. *Language, Culture and Curriculum* 28 (1), 41–57. doi:10.1080/07908318.2014.1000924

Mohan, B. and Slater, T. (2005) A functional perspective on the critical theory/practice relation in teaching language and science. *Linguistics and Education* 16, 151–173.

Moore, P., Rubio-Alcalá, F.D. and Pavón, V. (2018) *Porta Linguarum. Special Issue 3: Addressing Bilingualism in Higher Education: Policies and Implementation Issues.* See https://www.ugr.es/~portalin/articulos/PL_monograph3_2018.htm.

Nikula, T. (2007) Speaking English in Finnish content-based classrooms. *World Englishes* 26 (2), 206–223. doi:10.1111/j.1467-971X.2007.00502.x.

OECD (2017) *Education at a Glance 2017: OECD Indicators.* Paris: OECD Publishing. doi:10.1787/eag-2017-en

Parks, S. and Black, H. (1992) *Organizing Thinking.* Pacific Grove, CA: Critical Thinking Books and Software.

Pastor, M.R. (2011) CLIL and cooperative learning. *Encuentro* 20, 109–118.

Pavón, V. and Gastaud, M. (2013) Designing bilingual programmes for higher education in Spain: Organisational, curricular and methodological decisions. *International CLIL Research Journal* 2 (1), 82–94.

Pavón, V. and Rubio-Alcalá, F.D. (2010) Teachers' concerns and uncertainties about the introduction of CLIL programs. *Porta Linguarum* 14, 45–58.

Pavón, V., Ávila-López, J., Gallego Segador, A. and Espejo Mohedano, R. (2015a) Strategic and organisational considerations in planning content and language integrated learning: A study on the coordination between content and language teachers. *International Journal of Bilingual Education and Bilingualism* 18 (4), 409–425. doi:10.1080/13670050.2014.909774

Pavón, V., Prieto, M. and Ávila-López, J. (2015b) Perceptions of teachers and students of the promotion of interaction through task-based activities in CLIL. *Porta Linguarum* 23, 75–91.

Pérez-Cañado, M.L. (2012) CLIL research in Europe: Past, present, and future. *International Journal of Bilingual Education and Bilingualism* 15 (3), 315–341.
Pérez-Cañado, M.L. (2016) Teacher training needs for bilingual education: In-service teacher perceptions. *International Journal of Bilingual Education and Bilingualism* 19 (3), 266–295. doi:10.1080/13670050.2014.980778
Pinter, A. (2006) *Teaching Young Learners*. Oxford: Oxford University Press.
Ramos-García, A.M. (2013) Higher education bilingual programs in Spain. *Porta Linguarum* 19, 101–111.
Ramos-García, A.M. and Pavón, V. (2018) The linguistic internationalization of higher education: A study on the presence of language policies and bilingual studies in Spanish universities. *Porta Linguarum (Special Issue 3: Addressing Bilingualism in Higher Education: Policies and Implementation Issues)*, 31–45.
Rubio-Alcalá, F.D., Arco, J.L., Ávila-López, F.J., *et al.* (2018) Quality assurance inventory for plurilingual programs in higher education (QAIPPHE). Unpublished presentation at the International Conference on Quality of Plurilingual Programs in Higher Education, University of Huelva.
Rubio-Alcalá, F.D., Arco-Tirado, J.L., Fernández-Martín, F.D., López-Lechuga, R., Barrios, E. and Pavón, V. (2019) A systematic review on evidences supporting quality indicators of bilingual, plurilingual and multilingual programs in higher education. *Educational Research Review* 27, 191–204. doi:10.1016/j.edurev.2019.03.003
Rubio-Cuenca, F. (2019) La innovación educativa en los programas de educación bilingüe de la Universidad de Cádiz. In J.J. Gázquez Linares *et al.* (eds) *Innovación Docente e Investigación en Arte y Humanidades* (pp. 629–640). Madrid: Dykinson.
Rubio-Cuenca, F. and Moore, P. (2018) Teacher attitudes to language in university bilingual education. *Porta Linguarum (Special Issue 3: Addressing Bilingualism in Higher Education: Policies and Implementation Issues)*, 89–102.
Saarinen, T. and Nikula, T. (2013) Implicit policy, invisible language: Policies and practices of international degree programs in Finnish higher education. In A. Doiz, D. Lasagabaster and J.M. Sierra (eds) *English Medium Instruction at Universities: Global Challenges* (pp. 131–150). Bristol: Multilingual Matters.
Serra, C. (2007) Assessing CLIL at primary school: A longitudinal study. *International Journal of Bilingual Education and Bilingualism* 10 (5), 582–602. doi:10.2167/beb461.0
Short, D.J. (2006) Content teaching and learning and language. In K. Brown (ed.) *Encyclopaedia of Language and Linguistics, Vol. 3* (2nd edn) (pp. 101–105). Oxford: Elsevier.
Slavin, R.E. (2016) Evidence and every student succeeds act. *Huffpost*, 19 April. See http://www.huffingtonpost.com/robert-e-slavin/evidence-and-the-essa_b_8750480.html.
Sloane, F. (2008) Through the looking glass: Experiments, quasi-experiments, and the medical model. *Educational Researcher* 37 (1), 41–46.
Smit, U. and Dafouz, E. (eds) (2013) Integrating content and language in higher education: An introduction to english medium policies, conceptual issues and research practices across Europe. *Aila review* 25, 1–12. Amsterdam: John Benjamins.
Soltero, S. and Ortiz, T. (2012) Discipline-based dual language immersion model in higher education (Position paper). Orlando, FL: AGMUS Ventures. See http://goo.gl/5HCviS.
Stehler, U. (2006) The acquisition of knowledge in bilingual learning: An empirical study on the role of language in content learning. *Vienna English Working Papers* 15 (3), 41–46.
Stryker, S. and Leaver, B. (1993) Teachers' concerns and uncertainties about the introduction of CLIL programs. *Porta Linguarum* 14, 45–58.
Toledo, I., Rubio, F.D. and Hermosín, M. (2012) Creencias, rendimiento académico y actitudes de alumnos universitarios principiantes en un programa plurilingüe. *Porta Linguarum* 18, 213–229.
Torres Menárguez, A. (2018) Why Spain's bilingual schools are full of teachers with poor English skills (trans. M. Kitson). *El País*, 18 December. See https://elpais.com/elpais/2018/12/17/inenglish/1545052143_282469.html.

Valcke, J. and Pavón, V. (2015) Transmitting complex academic information effectively: A comparative study on the use of pronunciation strategies for highlighting information in university lectures. In R. Wilkinson and M.L. Walsh (eds) *Integrating Content and Language in Higher Education: From Theory to Practice* (pp. 323–341). Frankfurt-am-Main: Peter Lang.

van de Pol, J., Volman, M. and Beishuizen, J. (2010) Scaffolding in teacher–student interaction: A decade of research. *Educational Psychology Review* 22 (3), 271–296.

Vinke, A. (1995) English as the medium of instruction in Dutch engineering education. Doctoral dissertation, Delft University of Technology.

Wächter, B. and Maiworm, F. (eds) (2014) *English Taught Programs in European Higher Education: The State of Play in 2014*. ACA Papers on International Cooperation in Education. Born: Lemmens Medien. See http://www.aca-secretariat.be/fileadmin/aca_docs/images/members/ACA-2015_English_Taught_01.pdf.

Wilkinson, R. (ed.) (2004) *Integrating Content and Language: Meeting the Challenge of a Multilingual Higher Education*. Maastricht: Maastricht University.

Wilkinson, R. and Walsh, M.L. (2015) *Integrating Content and Language in Higher Education: From Theory to Practice*. Maastricht: Peter Lang.

Wilkinson, R. and Zegers, V. (eds) (2008) *Realizing Content and Language Integration in Higher Education*. Maastricht: Maastricht University Language Centre.

Wode, H. (1999) Language learning in European immersion classes. In J. Masih (ed.) *Learning through a Foreign Language: Models, Methods and Outcomes* (pp. 16–25). London: Centre for Information on Language Teaching and Research.

Yang, W. (2014) Content and language integrated learning next in Asia: Evidence of learners' achievement in CLIL education from a Taiwan tertiary degree program. *International Journal of Bilingual Education and Bilingualism* 18 (4), 361–382. doi: 10.1080/13670050.2014.904840

Zegers, V. (2008) When European studies met English: A practitioner's view on content and language integrated learning. In R. Wilkinson and V. Zegers (eds) *Realizing Content and Language Integration in Higher Education* (pp. 228–236). Maastricht: Maastricht University.

8 Team Teaching: A Way to Boost the Quality of EMI Programmes?

David Lasagabaster

Introduction

Since Coleman (2006) stated more than a decade ago in his widely quoted state-of-the-art article that English was becoming the language of higher education in Europe, this trend has become even more noticeable not only in Europe but also in many other parts of the world (Byun *et al.*, 2011; Doiz *et al.*, 2013; Murata, 2019). The fact is that English-medium instruction (EMI) programmes are being adopted in higher education at an ever-increasing rate around the world. In this globalizing academic world, it is widely assumed that, by simply teaching content in English, students' English proficiency will significantly improve. However, there is ample evidence (Jiang *et al.*, 2019; Llinares *et al.*, 2012; Lyster, 2007) that mere exposure to the foreign language through a content-oriented approach will not equip EMI students with the appropriate language to make the most of their EMI experience. Students need language support so that they can successfully tackle the change of language of instruction from their mother tongue to English, which is why how to teach content and language is one of the main challenges that EMI teachers face.

At pre-university level the objective of achieving this integration is deeply entrenched in the beliefs of those involved in CLIL (content and language *integrated* learning) programmes, as this acronym habitually used in the literature clearly shows (Coyle *et al.*, 2010). Studies (Kong, 2014; Lo, 2015) confirm that the collaboration between content specialists and language specialists can lead to successful outcomes as a result of cross-curricular collaboration. However, at university level the need to focus on language has been overlooked (Lasagabaster, 2018), despite the fact that the lack of language support may have a detrimental effect on students' learning of the subject matter in English. Three main reasons explain this linguistic negligence. Firstly, it is worth noting that in most EMI contexts courses are almost exclusively taught by non-native English speaking teachers, who often deem teaching in the foreign language challenging and fraught with linguistic insecurities (Costa, 2012; Doiz & Lasagabaster, 2018). As a result, it does not come as a surprise that EMI teachers usually state that their language proficiency and lack of language training prevents them from dealing with language issues in their classes (Cots, 2013). Secondly, studies conducted in different contexts reveal that many EMI students do not have the necessary language skills to grasp abstract concepts or to actively participate in class (Airey, 2009; Doiz *et al.*, 2013; Jiang *et al.*, 2019), which is why many institutions do not identify language objectives, as they could discourage students from joining EMI programmes. Due to these linguistic hurdles, language objectives play second fiddle or, more habitually, none at all.

And thirdly, the desire and the rush to jump on the EMI bandwagon seem to have overshadowed some quality measures, teacher training being a very good case in point. In the Spanish context different studies (Halbach & Lázaro, 2015) concur that there is a lack of support concerning EMI teachers' training despite the dire need to equip them methodologically. This is also a global trend, as authors from such diverse contexts as China (Jiang *et al.*, 2019), Italy (Ackerley *et al.*, 2017), Korea (Byun *et al.*, 2011), Turkey (Sert, 2008) and Sweden (Kuteeva, 2019) also warn against the indolence of higher education institutions when it comes to teacher training. O'Dowd (2018) surveyed 70 European universities (located in Austria, Italy, Spain, Sweden, the Netherlands, Germany and France) in order to explore the training and accreditation of EMI teachers. He found that the training of EMI teachers was disregarded by many institutions and, in those cases where training was considered, very diverse criteria were defined and developed. Thus there was a clear lack of consensus concerning teachers' minimum level of English, which ranged from B2 to C2, whereas half of the universities completely omitted CLIL methodology and focused their training solely on communicative skills. More alarmingly, 30% of them did not provide any type of training courses (O'Dowd, 2018: 561). These data indicate that some measures need to be taken and it is at this stage that team teaching comes to the fore.

Exploring the Need for Collaboration

As a result of the widespread belief that content subjects taught in a foreign language provide students with the necessary language exposure and authentic communicative contexts, the vast majority of EMI programmes do not contemplate language learning objectives. However, research has recurrently shown how misguided this belief is (Coyle *et al.*, 2010; Jiang *et al.*, 2019; Lyster, 2007). With this in mind, many authors have called for 'the urgent need for increased collaboration between discipline experts and language specialists' (Schmidt-Unterberger, 2018: 539). Team teaching can become a doable option with a view to making language more visible in EMI classes. Since teachers can collaborate in different ways, the concept of teacher collaboration may sometimes be ambiguous (Lo, 2015). To avoid ambiguity, in this chapter team teaching is focused on the collaboration between English language teachers and content subject teachers in EMI university contexts. As a matter of fact, I have elsewhere defined team teaching in EMI contexts as 'collaborative work between a content lecturer and a language lecturer in an EMI programme in which the abilities of the team members complement each other to improve the learning results, so that the whole is greater than the sum of its parts' (Lasagabaster, 2018: 401).

In sharp contrast to the traditional perception of the teaching profession as an activity to be performed in privacy behind classroom doors that still pervades many contexts, team teaching aims to diminish the pedagogical solitude of the teaching profession in tertiary education while fostering reflection in teachers' teaching practices. In addition, the collaboration established through team teaching is conceived as a way to face the challenge of 'there not being enough: not enough time, not enough resources, not enough information and not enough diverse perspectives' (Tajino *et al.*, 2017: 4).

Studies have proven that a cogently implemented team teaching partnership can energize teachers while helping them to become more reflective practitioners by means of a meaningful dialogue between partners (Perry & Stewart, 2005), because teaching practice and reflection fuel each other (Escobar Urmeneta, 2013: 334). In addition, research indicates that collaboration is one of the most important components of academic and professional development (Shagrir, 2017).

The advocates of team teaching affirm that it is a means to tackle the perennial challenge of integrating both content and language objectives and that it will benefit the quality of EMI programmes. At the institutional level, this collaboration between members who work in the same institution enables not only their personal development but also the organization's development. In this vein, Shagrir (2017) contends the following:

> Those in roles that dictate institutional policy should take into account the advantages of collaborative work, the majority of which takes place within the institution for the benefit of faculty members' professional and academic development. To do this, they have to support collaboration and encourage persistence. Fruitful collaborations will lead to a consolidated staff that also investigates its work and is involved in the dynamics taking place in the institution. (Shagrir, 2017: 339)

However, it has to be acknowledged that collaboration between subject experts and language specialists often turns out to be challenging due to the boundaries between disciplines (Räisänen & Fortanet-Gómez, 2008; Wilkinson, 2018) and the lack of means devoted to its implementation. In fact, team teaching is not always easy to carry out due to the limited human resources and the scarce economic support found in many universities. Moreover, the lack of tradition of collaboration between language and content teachers in higher education (Carpenter *et al.*, 2007; Doiz *et al.*, 2013; Jiang *et al.*, 2019) appears as too high a hurdle, and this despite the benefits that such collaboration would entail (Lasagabaster, 2018; Schleppegrell & O'Hallaron, 2011). Efforts need to be made to overcome what could be labelled as the *two solitudes*, a term that I use to refer to the perceived lack of communication between language and content university teachers, as they seem to work in watertight compartments. Costa (2017: 87) points out that the language staff could 'act as facilitators and language advisors', as this could eventually lead content teachers to 'take up the role of content and language integrated teachers'. But what are EMI teachers' and student' beliefs about team teaching? In the following sections I will try to answer this question. But first, let us bring to light the importance of beliefs.

Teachers' and Students' Beliefs

Traditionally the literature has carefully examined teachers' beliefs due to their paramount role in everyday teaching and their impact on decision making. Beliefs 'can be defined as a complex set of variables based on attitudes, experiences and expectations' (Skinnari & Bovellan, 2016: 146). Since teacher beliefs usually exert substantial and enduring influence on teacher development (Martí & Portolés, 2019), they need to be brought to light in order to appraise them. As Borg (2003) points out, research has shown through a large body of studies that teacher cognition (what they know, believe and think) has an enormous effect on teachers' professional careers. It is at this stage that the label 'teacher language awareness' emerges, as it is the 'label applied to research and teacher development activity that focuses on the interface between what teachers know, or need to know, about language and their pedagogical practice' (Andrews, 2008: 287). Thus, teacher language awareness is a focal area of research within the larger domain of teacher cognition (Andrews, 2008: 293). Consequently, content teachers need to become aware of their language teaching beliefs, because these beliefs will more than likely affect their teaching. This is a question of the utmost importance when tackling team teaching, because the concerns of teacher language awareness are also relevant to EMI content teachers.

The first step would consist, then, in helping teachers reflect on their own beliefs and how they can have a bearing on their teaching and, consequently, on their students. EMI teachers should not constrain their role to that of content teachers, but they should also become critically aware of what their EMI teaching practices imply. Gebhard and Oprandy (1999) claim the need for teachers to make informed decisions about their teaching by investigating it through exploration and conversation, among other means. We believe that discussion groups may boost the self-exploratory process regarding their alleged roles when it comes to team teaching, as this may foster their reflection before they can proceed to explore their teaching.

As for students, their beliefs about the nature of language and language learning 'affect how learners make sense of their experiences and organise their learning' (Hüttner et al., 2013: 269). More often than not, students believe that language learning is characterized as using and being exposed to the language as much as possible, and these beliefs may have a strong impact on their views about team teaching. Reflection may also help in the students' case to make them think about how their beliefs and their attitudes towards team teaching (mis)match.

In practice, in many EMI contexts language learning goals are undefined, except perhaps for teaching specialized terminology (Costa, 2012). As mentioned above, this lack of explicit teaching of grammatical aspects may be due to teachers' lack of methodological training (Fortanet, 2010), as a result of which teachers believe that, just by receiving classes in English, university students will learn the foreign language. But it may also stem from the role assigned to EMI by teachers and students at university level, as both groups seem not to expect any specific attention to be paid to making transparent the ways in which grammatical aspects of language impact on subject learning. This is in sharp contrast to research in primary and secondary education, in which studies highlight 'changes in teacher self-perceptions on a journey towards a reconceptualization as content *and* language teachers' (Dafouz et al., 2016: 128, emphasis in original) and that separating content and language is artificial (Skinnari & Bovellan, 2016). Another possible reason for the differences observed between secondary education and university contexts may be that students (and to some extent teachers as well) attach less importance to English, as students' language competence is expected to be higher at tertiary level than at pre-university levels, while stakeholders are more concerned about content due to its increasing complexity (Lasagabaster & Doiz, 2016). Therefore, all these beliefs need to be revealed if the quality of EMI programmes is to be enhanced by implementing effective team teaching practices.

Last but not least, it has to be noted that research on the basic need for integration has explored EMI teachers' and students' beliefs mainly in primary and secondary education (Hüttner et al., 2013; Martí & Portolés, 2019; Tajino et al., 2017), and there have even been transnational comparative studies (Griva et al., 2014; Skinnari & Bovellan, 2016), whereas the number of studies centred on the tertiary level is rather limited (Dafouz et al., 2016; Escobar Urmeneta, 2013).

With this in mind, the current study aimed to unearth what linguistic issues EMI teachers and students usually find more problematic, in order later to explore their beliefs about whether team teaching should be implemented and, if so, how it could contribute to overcoming the linguistic hurdles they come across in their EMI classes.

The Study

In this section the context of the study (the two Spanish universities involved), the participants (EMI teachers and students) and the procedure followed to analyse the data will be described.

The context

This chapter is based on two previous publications (Doiz *et al.*, 2018, 2019). The study was conducted at two Spanish universities, the University of the Basque Country and the University of Cordoba. Both are young universities, the former having been established in 1980 and the latter in 1972. Both are public universities and whereas the University of the Basque Country is an officially bilingual university with more than 45,000 students, 5400 lecturers and around 1700 administration personnel, the University of Cordoba is monolingual and smaller with 18,000 students, 1400 lecturers and 750 administration personnel.

In both universities EMI is being implemented and it currently represents about 5% of available courses. Similarly, in both institutions EMI is considered to play a pivotal role in the internationalization process, as English is perceived as essential not only to attract international students, but also to equip local students with a key tool (the ability to use English proficiently in their different fields of specialization) for their future careers.

Both institutions have established that teachers need to have reached the C1 proficiency level of the Common European Framework of Reference for Languages (CERF), although the University of Cordoba also allows those with a B2 plus teaching experience to teach on EMI courses. The two universities offer training courses aimed at their EMI teachers with a view to improving their English proficiency and to providing them with essential knowledge and techniques.

Students are not required to certify their language proficiency, as they are expected to have reached at least a B1 level of competence after having passed the university entrance exam (also known as *Selectividad* in Spanish). Both universities have designed a plan to offer a number of EMI subjects in various degrees amounting to 30 credits so that students have a reasonable amount of EMI courses to choose from, rather than just a few subjects scattered in each degree. In this way, students will have the possibility of earning an EMI mention in their degree.

The participants

The sample was made up of 27 participants: 13 EMI lecturers and 14 EMI students. All the participants were either teaching or enrolled in three different degrees: history, education and veterinary science. The teachers had on average 18 years of teaching experience, although their teaching experience in EMI was more limited: three and a half years. This was due to the recent introduction of EMI programmes in both institutions. As for the students, only four had had any previous experience of content taught in English at pre-university level. Their English proficiency ranged from B1 to C1 on the CEFR. All the students except one Polish Erasmus student were local.

The procedure

Seven focus groups were organized, four at the University of Cordoba and three at the University of the Basque Country. Students and teachers participated in separate discussions, so that they felt more at ease and could speak openly. The focus groups were carried out in Spanish so that none of the participants would be constrained by English-related limitations and they could express their beliefs freely and without linguistic hurdles during the recorded sessions (the Polish student was proficient in Spanish). A researcher chaired each focus group and put forward a series of questions concerning team teaching, such as their attitudes towards it or the role that the language teacher should play in this collaborative endeavour.

A research assistant carried out the verbatim transcriptions of the focus groups which amounted to 69,434 words. Once the recordings were transcribed, three researchers (one of them being the author of this chapter) followed a coding procedure with notes for categorization which allowed them to extract the main ideas from the teachers' and students' responses about the main linguistic challenges they have to face in EMI and how team teaching could contribute to confronting them. The data was reread while contrasting and comparing ideas with a view to discovering patterns in the data. Firstly, keywords were detected and these keywords led to the establishment of categories. Each of the three researchers individually analysed the transcriptions and then compared and conferred on their analysis until a consensus was reached. When the three researchers agreed on the keywords and the labels of the subsequent categories, significant and illustrative quotations from the participants were translated into English.

The Results

The comparison of students' and teachers' beliefs and opinions about the linguistic challenges posed by EMI and the implementation of team teaching as a possible solution brought to light some parallels but also some interesting differences. The focus groups firstly dealt with the main challenges that students and teachers had to face in EMI settings. Whereas teachers were concerned with their more limited lexical resources in English, as they could not expand on ideas with the same fluency and richness as in their L1, students did not find their own lack of vocabulary so challenging. In fact, the latter affirmed that whenever they came across a word whose meaning was unknown to them, they simply looked it up in the dictionary (through their electronic devices) or directly asked the teacher for clarification.

Teachers found the language of instruction a handicap (they took it for granted that they knew their specialization well), whereas students were much more concerned about the content itself. In fact, some interesting reflections were found among the students. Some considered that their teachers' lack of linguistic security made content learning easier because the breadth and scope was more limited than had the subject concerned being taught in Spanish (or Basque in the case of the University of the Basque Country). Other students, however, had an opposite perception as they believed that their teachers' lack of the adequate English proficiency made content learning more complex because their explanations were not as detailed as they should be – a concern that was acknowledged by some of the EMI teachers themselves. Since students' perceptions of their EMI teachers' professional competence is highly influenced by their perceptions of their teachers' English proficiency (Dimova et al., 2015), this is an issue of the utmost importance and one that deserves attention in further research.

The concepts of vulnerability and immunity are worth considering at this stage. Vulnerability has to do with how teachers' emotional responses to the EMI environment affect their teaching practices (Song, 2016). The general trend among teachers is that, due to their linguistic insecurities, they sometimes avoid situations that they perceive as a potential threat, such as trying to explain a complex concept in different ways. Teachers feel vulnerable (the keyword 'insecurity' is mentioned several times in their discussions) because they consider that their linguistic resources are reduced and bemoan the fact that their fluency is negatively affected (Doiz & Lasagabaster, 2018). On the other side of the coin, most students seem to have developed immunity (Hiver & Dörnyei, 2017), that is, a defence system that protects them from the possible harmful impact of the EMI experience. Hiver and Dörnyei (2017) claim that immunity can turn out to be a powerful asset if it becomes a protective mechanism against challenging teaching and learning experiences such as EMI, and this seems to be the case among some of the students participating in this study. Despite their insecurities, they were able to overcome the feeling of vulnerability, which empowered them to feel less affected by it than their teachers.

There were clear parallels between the two groups regarding what language aspects they regarded as easier or more complicated. Reading and listening were thought to create few problems; however, writing and speaking were mentioned as the most difficult language skills. Both teachers and students found pronunciation a problem area. Spanish learners of English have traditionally labelled pronunciation as a thorny issue, although recent studies indicate that EMI may help to improve it (Richter, 2019). The participants found the pronunciation of technical words (such as 'sovereignty' in the case of the history teachers) particularly challenging. This does not come as a surprise, since previous studies in the Spanish context have also underscored that pronunciation is one of the skills more demanded by EMI teachers on teacher training courses and one of the students' main concerns (Doiz *et al.*, 2013). In this regard, the following two participants (one from each group) encapsulated the general feeling in the following terms: 'Spanish people fail at pronunciation, I would like to be helped with this' (Student 6, University of Cordoba, education); 'For us, speakers of Spanish, pronunciation is the most difficult aspect, but I think it is highly important. There are sounds that I cannot produce and there are words that I've never been able to pronounce correctly' (Teacher 4, University of the Basque Country, history).

Also in the pronunciation sphere, both teachers and students emphasized the difficulties they have to surmount when trying to understand some native speakers, whose accents they sometimes find abstruse. Nevertheless, in their discussion, reference was made to the international English they used in class, which did not cause any intelligibility and comprehensibility barrier. Although they did not use the term *English as a lingua franca*, because they were more than likely not acquainted with this concept, this seems to be what they referred to (Murata, 2019).

Therefore, it can be concluded that language teachers collaborating in team teaching should pay particular attention to writing and speaking skills, pronunciation playing a paramount role when working on the latter. Many of the participants highlighted that the difficulties they come across when understanding both teachers and students have a bearing on the quality of the learning process.

There was also widespread agreement concerning the role of the EMI content teacher, who is not a 'philologist' or 'linguist' and should try to avoid delving into linguistic issues. Although some teachers affirmed that they endeavoured to correct their students' mistakes on some occasions, the general belief was that this falls outside the EMI teachers' remit. The following quotations illustrate this point:

> In my case, I tell them the very first day that I am a teacher of history and not a teacher of English … that my job is to teach them history and not English. (Teacher 3, University of the Basque Country, history)

> I know I don't speak perfect English, I am not a philologist, I am the first one to make mistakes, but with this in mind I think that our obligation is to try to help students speak the best possible English. (Teacher 1, University of the Basque Country, history)

> I think that the teachers (EMI teachers) are not philologists, nor are they experts in language, so it is fine if they boost our good use of English but they shouldn't pay attention to grammatical aspects that are up to other type of professionals. That is my opinion. (Student 6, University of Cordoba, education)

> Yes, yes, I quite agree, they don't have to teach us English, but rather how to use the language to learn other contents. (Student 9, University of Cordoba, education)

> It is not the (EMI) teachers' job to pay heed to the language. (Student 3, University of the Basque Country, history)

Broadly speaking, however, the students were of the opinion that the EMI teachers' language-related corrections were positive if they were carried out on some specific occasions, although they did not deem important the language errors made by both teachers and students. Their main concern was that not much time should be allotted to corrections, because otherwise they might run the risk of not devoting the necessary time to content. In any case, the majority of them believed that language plays an ancillary role in EMI teachers' responsibilities. The only exception related to the specific vocabulary of each specialization, which all students affirmed that EMI teachers should highlight and elucidate.

When the participants were explicitly asked about their beliefs about implementing a collaboration between language and content teachers, both groups demonstrated very positive attitudes and affirmed that it would have a positive impact on the quality of the bilingual programmes:

> We have to admit that we are not using our mother tongue and we have certain limitations. Having the possibility of being assisted by a language specialist seems essential to me in order to contribute to carrying out *quality* teaching. (Teacher 3, University of the Basque Country, history, emphasis added)

> At the end of the day what we intend is to improve our students' linguistic competence, right? Then, with this objective in mind, it seems a great idea to me, I think it would be very positive for our students, but we would have to plan the classes in a different way. (Teacher 12, University of Cordoba, veterinary science)

> It would be good not only for us but also for the students, because someone has said before (earlier in our discussion) that we try to correct some expressions every now and then, but if a language teacher is in class, he should make these corrections. (Teacher 13, University of Cordoba, veterinary science)

EMI content teachers were willing to participate in team teaching, as they again and again underscored that they are not language experts or language teachers, and are not qualified to provide students with linguistic support (Doiz et al., 2019). These results tally with those obtained by Arnó-Maciá and Mancho-Barés (2015: 67) at the university of Lleida, in which not only was little attention paid to language in EMI course documentation in three different degrees (agronomy engineering, business and law), but classroom observations also confirmed that teachers' discourse was almost exclusively focused on content. In fact, the authors observed only 'a few episodes focusing on language usually arising out of lecturers' (perceived) low proficiency level or from covert/overt comprehension breakdowns'.

For their part, students considered that team teaching could help not only to improve their English proficiency, but also to learn the subject content in the different EMI subjects. The undergraduates highlighted three areas that would benefit most from this collaboration: written compositions, pronunciation and oral presentations. In this vein, it is worth noting that, although studies suggest that EMI contexts may favour the development of academic literacies (Arnó-Maciá & Mancho-Barés, 2015; Nightingale & Safont, 2019), our participants are well aware that focus on form is needed to achieve this objective. Their discussions reveal that both teachers and students believe that language support is needed, because mere exposure to academic language may not be enough:

> I think it would help us to further elaborate on specialized vocabulary that we find difficult to understand, because we would practice it with him (the language expert), who could even explain it to us with other words or synonyms, that is what we probably miss in the content classes. (Student 8, University of Cordoba, education)

> I think that this support is very important when it comes to learning how to write academic texts that do not look childish or that may seem to lack academic rigour. And of course when it comes to speaking too. (Student 7, University of Cordoba, education)

Some of the participants expressed concerns about team teaching. The most frequent issue had to do with *time limitations*, because if language teachers devoted part of the lessons to language issues, this would reduce the time available to cope with content. The following two quotations illustrate this point: 'I think that we normally need more time to go over the content, and we will lose valuable time that could be used for the content if another teacher participates' (Student 13, University of Cordoba, veterinary science); and '... provided it does not mean shortening my time in the lesson (laughs). This is crucial to me, but in principle, yes, I would do it' (Teacher 4, University of Cordoba, veterinary science).

A distinction between a weak version and a strong version of team teaching is frequently made in the literature (Tajino & Tajino, 2000). In the first option the teachers play a separate individual role; that is, each teacher takes charge of what falls within their specialization and each of them performs their job in class at different times. Thus, one of the teachers (the content teacher) assumes the leading role and the other (the language teacher) a subsidiary role. In the strong version, a concerted endeavour is pursued by the two teachers jointly and both teach at the same time in class. In this latter version both teachers share the leading role. Our results indicate that the weak version is definitively the one preferred and chosen by all our participants.

Another outstanding difference observed between both groups of stakeholders was the impact of having a language teacher in class. This presence did not represent any emotional load for the students, whereas it could spark nervousness and lead to insecurity (the idea of vulnerability again) among teachers. This feeling of apprehension was mentioned only by EMI lecturers, who seemed to believe that their professional performance might be put into doubt: 'On the one hand, I like the idea, but on the other I have to acknowledge that the presence of another person in class ... And I am also thinking about the students. I don't know, it can cause some ... I am a bit frightened' (Teacher 2, University of the Basque Country, history). Conversely, students do not consider this as an issue (despite Teacher 2's concern, they do not even mention this question), probably because they take for granted that teachers are there to help and to correct them whenever they make a mistake or are in need of help.

It is striking that no reference was made by any of the teachers to the demand for appropriate materials for their EMI students. This may be due to the fact that many of the teaching materials used in class are available in English. However, in some instances these materials need to be adapted due to students' language limitations and this is a task where the content and language teacher collaboration could bear fruit, but strikingly this question did not emerge during the discussions.

Another difference between teachers and students had to do with the profile of the language teacher. This was not of concern to students, whereas it spurred an interesting debate among EMI teachers. Some of them opined that the language lecturer should be a language expert, whereas other participants stated that s/he should also be a specialist in the field. The latter raised the possibility of collaborating with native English-speaking content teachers, whereas the former defended the idea that a language expert would be the best candidate, because s/he could easily put himself/herself in the students' shoes: 'if a lecturer from a different field comes to your classroom and he/she understands you, this means that the students understand you too' (Teacher 5, University of Cordoba, veterinary science).

Conclusion

Although 'quality teaching is a highly complex concept' (Torres *et al.*, 2017: 823), that is, in constant flux as a result of changes in society in general and education in particular, team teaching could play a significant role in developing quality bilingual practices in higher education. The benefits of collaboration between faculty members contribute not only to the professional development of the teaching staff but also to an institution's reputation, which is why institutions should 'create a culture of collaboration and enable faculty members to work in a collaborative environment' (Shagrir, 2017: 340). Team teaching can moreover help to provide the necessary tools to foster teachers' positive immunity and avoid negative vulnerability.

Experts in EMI agree on the fact that language plays a paramount role in content learning. However, research proves that 'a distinctive feature of a traditional EMI classroom at university is the absence of attention to language' (Richter, 2019: 60), and it is evident that this needs to be changed if students are to be exposed to quality language teaching in the EMI classroom. Whereas EMI students at pre-university level usually attend both CLIL content courses and regular EFL classes, this is not the case in many university contexts, where ESP courses have been drastically reduced or simply eliminated. Team teaching can help to boost and routinize collaboration between the different disciplines with the common objective of promoting both language and content learning. Unlike in other peer observation schemes in which there are unbalanced power relations (e.g. an expert teacher observing a novel teacher), the language and content teachers' collaboration can be carried out on an equal footing and, if conditions are clearly established from the very beginning (Lasagabaster & Sierra, 2011), it can help to foster teachers' development. And this should be an indispensable aim for any bilingual programme that intends to achieve the coveted 'quality label'.

Therefore, the answer to the question posed in the title of this chapter (Team Teaching: A Way to Boost the Quality of EMI Programmes?) can only be affirmative, as both teachers and students held a positive attitude towards team teaching. On the flip side of the coin, the participants also expressed some concerns. For example, our participants were concerned about the allocated class time for teaching language at the expense of the subject content, which might negatively affect content learning. This is just an indication that tensions may be generated, but they can be overcome if the goals and the procedure of the team teaching implementation are clearly stated.

We must conclude that the voices of the stakeholders collected in this study need to be taken into account, although it is not always easy to navigate the diversity of individual beliefs. The teachers' comments reveal a strong sense of commitment to the EMI courses and to the same standards being expected as in L1 courses, as they highlight the strenuous efforts that joining the programme demands from them (see also Doiz & Lasagabaster, 2018). Such commitment is worth praising and represents a key feature of quality bilingual education (de Graaff & van Wilgenburg, 2015), but they also believe that support from language experts should be an inherent part of the EMI classes. Therefore, institutions should think about new avenues that would facilitate collaboration between language and content teachers. Professional development should be an inherent part of any high-quality bilingual programme, which is why university departments and authorities should consider, for example, releases so that EMI teachers could work on course planning with their language colleagues, at least at the initial stages of EMI implementation. Cooperation is central when it comes to identifying linguistic needs and developing a plan to cater for these needs, something that has hitherto been overlooked by many higher education institutions (Halbach & Lázaro, 2015; O'Dowd, 2018).

Last but not least, it has to be noted that most of the researchers working in this field are applied linguists who are ardent advocates of the integration of content and language, but the stakeholders' voices must be heard if such integration is to be carried out successfully. A key objective of team teaching lies in the attempt to blur the binary division between disciplines. However, our results indicate that antagonistic relations (Jorgensen & Phillips, 2002, in Trent, 2010) emerge as our informants consider that it is not viable to be a content and language teacher simultaneously at university level and that there is a clear divide between the roles to be assumed by each of them.

According to our participants (both teachers and students), a rigid dichotomy should be maintained and the success of the collaboration will hinge on the content teachers' control over the team teaching endeavour and a clear-cut distinction of the roles to be played. The language teacher should therefore focus on language issues and the content teacher should almost exclusively concentrate on teaching content. Although at pre-university level researchers tend to state that 'teachers' beliefs about their respective roles as only content teachers or only language teachers limit students' language learning opportunities' (Tan, 2011: 325), at university level this divide turns out to be very hard to overcome. In fact, the relationship between EMI teachers' subject-matter learning cognitions and other aspects of cognition such as foreign language learning are very intricate. Since beliefs have a considerable impact on teaching and learning, as they are the glasses through which teachers see education and their everyday practice (Martí & Portolés, 2019), substantial discussions and concerted efforts may help to build synergies and lead to the development of joined forces which are core to the successful implementation of bilingual or multilingual programmes. Our results clearly indicate that there is much work to do as regards EMI teachers' language awareness. There is an urgent need to make content teachers aware of the fact that they are also language teachers, not in the traditional sense (i.e. teaching grammatical rules), but rather as facilitators of their students' linguistic scaffolding. The collaboration between the two solitudes should help to establish some basic language-related objectives and would undoubtedly help to underpin quality teaching.

Future studies should compare EMI teachers' and students' beliefs about the actual implementation of team teaching (in which teacher identities play a paramount role), as the real hands-on experience may help to change their perceptions and foster a less rigid collaboration between language and content teachers. The EMI field of research would also benefit from cross-national studies, as the contrastive discussion about the implementation of team teaching would be very much welcomed. This would allow us to delve into 'the variation of cultural and educational expectations of students and teachers with different backgrounds' (Dimova et al., 2015: 319), an urgent need at a time when EMI is spreading throughout educational systems the world over.

Acknowledgements

This work is supported by the Spanish Ministry of Economy and Competitiveness [Grant No. FFI2016-79377-P AEI/FEDER, UE] and the Basque Government [Grant No. IT904-16]. I would also like to acknowledge and give wholehearted thanks for the participation of my colleagues Aintzane Doiz (University of the Basque Country, UPV/EHU) and Víctor Pavón (University of Cordoba) in the completion of this study.

References

Ackerley, K., Guarda, M. and Helm, F. (2017) *Sharing Perspectives on English-Medium Instruction*. Bern: Peter Lang.

Airey, J. (2009) Science, language and literacy: Case studies of learning in Swedish university physics. Uppsala dissertations from the Faculty of Science and Technology, Uppsala University.

Andrews, S.J. (2008) Teacher language awareness. In J. Cenoz and N.H. Hornberger (eds) *Encyclopedia of Language and Education, Vol. 6: Knowledge about Language* (2nd edn) (pp. 287–298). New York: Springer Science + Business Media.

Arnó-Maciá, E. and Mancho-Barés, G. (2015) The role of content and language in content and language integrated learning (CLIL) at university: Challenges and implications for ESP. *English for Specific Purposes* 37, 63–73.

Borg, S. (2003) Teacher cognition in language teaching: A review of research on what teachers think, know, believe, and do. *Language Teaching* 36 (2), 81–109.

Byun, K., Chu, H., Kim, M., Park, I., Kim, S. and Jung, J. (2011) English-medium teaching in Korean higher education: Policy debates and reality. *Higher Education* 62 (4), 431–449.

Carpenter II, D.M., Crawford, L. and Walden, R. (2007) Testing the efficacy of team teaching. *Learning Environments Research* 10 (1), 53–65.

Coleman, J. (2006) English-medium teaching in European higher education. *Language Teaching* 19 (1), 1–14.

Costa, F. (2012) Focus on form in ICLHE lectures in Italy: Evidence from English-medium science lectures by native speakers of Italian. *AILA Review* 25, 30–47.

Costa, F. (2017). English-medium instruction in Italian universities: If we're gonna do it do it right – right? In K. Ackerley, M. Guarda and F. Helm (eds) *Sharing Perspectives in English-Medium Instruction* (pp. 77–93). Bern: Peter Lang.

Cots, J.M. (2013) Introducing English-medium instruction at the university of Lleida, Spain: Interventions, beliefs and practices. In A. Doiz, D. Lasagabaster and J.M. Sierra (eds) *English-Medium Instruction at Universities: Global Challenges* (pp. 106–127). Bristol: Multilingual Matters.

Coyle, D., Hood, P. and Marsh, D. (2010) *CLIL: Content and Language Integrated Learning*. Cambridge: Cambridge University Press.

Dafouz, E., Hüttner, J. and Smit, U. (2016) University teachers' beliefs of language and content integration in English-medium education in multilingual university settings. In T. Nikula, E. Dafouz, P. Moore and U. Smit (eds) *Conceptualising Integration in CLIL and Multilingual Education* (pp. 123–143). Bristol: Multilingual Matters.

de Graff, R. and van Wilgenburg, O. (2015) The Netherlands: Quality control as a driving force in bilingual education. In P. Mehisto and F. Genesee (eds) *Building Bilingual Education Systems: Forces, Mechanisms and Counterweights* (pp. 167–179). Cambridge: Cambridge University Press.

Dimova, S., Hultgren, A.K. and Jensen, C. (2015) English-medium instruction in European higher education: Review and future research. In D. Slobodanka, A.K. Hultgren and C. Jensen (eds) *English-Medium Instruction in European Higher Education: English in Europe, Vol. 3* (pp. 317–323). Boston, MA and Berlin: De Gruyter Mouton.

Doiz, A. and Lasagabaster, D. (2018) Teachers' and students' L2 motivational self-system in English-medium instruction: A qualitative approach. *TESOL Quarterly* 52 (3), 657–679.

Doiz, A., Lasagabaster, D. and Sierra, J.M. (eds) (2013) *English-Medium Instruction at Universities: Global Challenges*. Bristol: Multilingual Matters.

Doiz, A., Lasagabaster, D. and Pavón, V. (2018) Undergraduates' beliefs about the role of language and team teaching in EMI courses at university. *Rassegna Italiana di Linguistica Applicata* 2 (3), 111–127.

Doiz, A., Lasagabaster, D. and Pavón, V. (2019) The integration of language and content in English-medium instruction courses: Lecturers' beliefs and practices. *Ibérica* 38, 151–175.

Escobar Urmeneta, C. (2013) Learning to become a CLIL teacher: Teaching, reflection and professional development. *International Journal of Bilingual Education and Bilingualism* 16 (3), 334–353.

Fortanet, I. (2010) Training CLIL teachers at university level. In D. Lasagabaster and Y. Ruiz de Zarobe (eds) *CLIL in Spain: Implementation, Results, and Teacher Training* (pp. 257–276). Newcastle upon Tyne: Cambridge Scholars.

Gebhard, J.G. and Oprandy, R. (1999) *Language Teaching Awareness: A Guide to Exploring Beliefs and Practices*. Cambridge: Cambridge University Press.

Griva, E., Chostelidou, D. and Panteli, P. (2014) Insider views of CLIL in primary education: Challenges and experiences of EFL teachers. *International Journal for Innovation Education and Research* 2 (8), 31–53.

Halbach, A. and Lázaro, A. (2015) *La acreditación del nivel de lengua inglesa en las universidades españolas: Actualización 2015*. Madrid: British Council.

Hiver, P. and Dörnyei, Z. (2017) Language teacher immunity: A double-edged sword. *Applied Linguistics* 38, 405–423.

Hüttner, H., Dalton-Puffer, C. and Smit, U. (2013) The power of beliefs: Lay theories and their influence on the implementation of CLIL programmes. *International Journal of Bilingual Education and Bilingualism* 16, 267–284.

Jiang, L., Zhang, L.J. and May, S. (2019) Implementing English-medium instruction (EMI) in China: Teachers' practices and perceptions, and students' learning motivation and needs. *International Journal of Bilingual Education and Bilingualism* 22 (2), 107–119.

Kong, S. (2014) Collaboration between content and language specialists in late immersion. *The Canadian Modern Language Review/La Revue canadienne des langues vivantes* 70, 103–122.

Kuteeva, M. (2019) Researching English-medium instruction at Swedish universities: Developments over the past decade. In K. Murata (ed.) *English-Medium Instruction from an English as a Lingua Franca Perspective: Exploring the Higher Education Context* (pp. 46–63). London and New York: Routledge.

Lasagabaster, D. (2018) Fostering team teaching: Mapping out a research agenda for English-medium instruction at university level. *Language Teaching* 51 (3), 400–416.

Lasagabaster, D. and Doiz, A. (2016) CLIL students' perceptions of their language learning process: Delving into self-perceived improvement and instructional preferences. *Language Awareness* 25, 110–126.

Lasagabaster, D. and Sierra, J.M. (2011) Classroom observation: Desirable conditions established by teachers. *European Journal of Teacher Education* 34 (4), 449–463.

Llinares, A., Morton, T. and Whittaker, R. (2012) *The Roles of Language in CLIL*. Cambridge: Cambridge University Press.

Lo, Y.Y. (2015) A glimpse into the effectiveness of L2-content crosscurricular collaboration in content-based instruction programmes. *International Journal of Bilingual Education and Bilingualism* 18 (4), 443–462.

Lyster, R. (2007) *Languages Learning and Teaching through Content: A Counterbalanced Approach*. Amsterdam and Philadelphia, PA: John Benjamins.

Martí, O. and Portolés, L. (2019) Spokes in the wheels of CLIL for multilingualism or how monolingual ideologies limit teacher training. *English Language Teaching* 12 (2), 17–36.

Murata, K. (ed.) (2019) *English-Medium Instruction from an English as a Lingua Franca Perspective: Exploring the Higher Education Context*. London and New York: Routledge.

Nightingale, R. and Safont, M.P. (2019) Conversational style and early academic language skills in CLIL and non-CLIL settings: A multilingual sociopragmatic perspective. *English Language Teaching* 12 (2), 37–56.

O'Dowd, R. (2018) The training and accreditation of teachers for English medium instruction: An overview of practice in European universities. *International Journal of Bilingual Education and Bilingualism* 21 (5), 553–563. doi:10.1080/13670050.2018.1491945

Perry, B. and Stuart, T. (2005) Insights into effective partnership in interdisciplinary team teaching. *System* 33, 563–573.

Räisänen, C. and Fortanet-Gómez, I. (2008) The state of ESP teaching and learning in western European higher education after Bologna. In I. Fortanet-Gómez and C. Räisänen (eds) *ESP in European Higher Education: Integrating Language and Content* (pp. 11–51). Amsterdam: John Benjamins.

Richter, K. (2019) *English-Medium Instruction and Pronunciation: Exposure and Skills Development*. Bristol: Multilingual Matters.

Schleppegrell, M. and O'Hallaron, C.L. (2011) Teaching academic language in L2 secondary settings. *Annual Review of Applied Linguistics* 31, 3–18.

Schmidt-Unterberger, B. (2018) The English-medium paradigm: A conceptualization of English-medium teaching in higher education. *International Journal of Bilingual Education and Bilingualism* 21 (5), 527–539. doi:10.1080/13670050.2018.1491949

Sert, N. (2008) The language of instruction dilemma in the Turkish context. *System* 36 (2), 156–171.

Shagrir, L. (2017) Collaborating with colleagues for the sake of academic and professional development in higher education. *International Journal for Academic Development* 22 (4), 331–342.

Skinnari, K. and Bovellan, E. (2016) CLIL teachers' beliefs about integration and about their professional roles: Perspectives from a European context. In T. Nikula, E. Dafouz, P. Moore and U. Smit (eds) *Conceptualising Integration in CLIL and Multilingual Education* (pp. 145–167). Bristol: Multilingual Matters.

Song, J. (2016) Emotions and language teacher identity: Conflicts, vulnerability, and transformation. *TESOL Quarterly* 50, 631–654.

Tajino, A. and Tajino, Y. (2000) Native and non-native: What can they offer? Lessons from team teaching in Japan. *ELT Journal* 54 (1), 3–11.

Tajino, A., Stewart, R. and Dalsky, D. (eds) (2017) *Team Teaching and Team Learning in the Language Classroom: Collaboration for Innovation in ELT*. London and New York: Routledge.

Tan, M. (2011) Mathematics and science teachers' beliefs and practices regarding the teaching of language in content learning. *Language Teaching Research* 15, 325–342.

Torres, A.C., Lopes, A., Valente, J.M.S. and Mouraz, A. (2017) What catches the eye in class observation? Observers' perspectives in a multidisciplinary peer observation of teaching program. *Teaching in Higher Education* 22 (7), 822–838.

Trent, J. (2010) Teacher identity construction across the curriculum: Promoting cross-curriculum collaboration in English-medium schools. *Asia Pacific Journal of Education* 30 (2), 167–183.

Wilkinson, R. (2018) Content and language integration at universities? Collaborative reflections. *International Journal of Bilingual Education and Bilingualism* 21 (5), 607–615.

9 Understanding the Affective for Effective EMI in Higher Education

Maria Ellison

Introduction

Teaching has long been considered an 'emotional practice' (Hargreaves, 1998). All around the world, and across educational levels, teachers experience a barrage of emotions during their working day, and many of these are not their own, but the reverberations of others within the wider educational community – students, directors, guardians, administrative staff, policy makers, and so on. Education is life-determining, and cuts right at the heart of a nation. So, when we add to it another dimension – that of teaching and learning in another language – emotions are yet further charged. In most scenarios, this language is English. English-medium instruction (EMI), understood as 'The use of the English language to teach academic subjects in countries or jurisdictions where the first language (L1) of the majority of the population is not English' (Dearden, 2014: 4), is a global phenomenon. Yet in higher education it can be argued that 'English-medium' encompasses so much more. It has rapidly become the lingua franca for international communication, projects, publishing, researching and teaching, with a dramatic increase in recent years (Wächter & Maiworm, 2014). In Europe, this has been driven by supranational policy implementation under the conspicuous auspices of the Bologna Agreement which, despite promoting linguistic diversity, has somewhat paradoxically increased homogeneity, as it is 'hard to imagine European students learning the language of each of the countries in which they may be taking parts of their education' (Jensen & Thøgersen, 2011: 19). This is further reinforced by the fact that some countries with lesser spoken languages (e.g. Finland) would struggle to attract international students if it were not for EMI. Worldwide, EMI has been propelled by the dynamic forces of globalization and the internationalization strategies of higher education institutions (HEIs) (Knight, 2004). EMI is a visible indication of an institution's ability to internationalize, and part of national and institutional mission statements. English linguistic capital is thus seen as core currency in academia, and HEIs that now trade on it find themselves locked in embargoes or high-stakes 'trade' wars when it comes to the provision of quality programmes to attract international students and academic staff alike.

The reaction to EMI has been heated debates about linguistic imperialism and domain loss (Jensen & Thøgersen, 2011) with equally provocative language: 'Englishisation' (Phillipson, 2006); 'Englishising' (Costa & Coleman, 2013); 'Anglicization' and 'almighty English' (Ardeo González, 2013); and, yes, even 'killer language' (Coleman, 2006). The strong sentiment is also revealed through metaphor. Phillipson (2006: 13) likens it to the *parasitical cuckoo* 'in the European higher education nest of languages' which 'lives in murderous partnership with other ornithological species (…) threatening the life of other languages, or at least occupying the territories that traditionally have been their preserve'. Such a reaction is unsurprising when reports relay stakeholder concerns about threats to minority languages (Coleman, 2006) and the 'socially divisive nature of EMI' (Dearden, 2014: 2) and, in the 'heat of discussions', that it is 'incompatible with the national mission (…) to first and foremost educate their own citizens' amid claims of lower quality education and teachers 'unable to speak and write the language properly' (Wächter & Maiworm, 2014: 27). Along with this, the language still comes with too much cultural baggage and we have not yet come to a point where we can strip it back to the linguistic tool for operationalizing education. The lines are indeed still 'blurred' (Fortanet-Gómez, 2013: 169) and further distorted by 'highly diverse local realisations' of EMI which render it very complex indeed (Dafouz & Smit, 2017: 287).

Such complexity may be *understood* by policy makers, but it is surely *felt* by those entrusted with implementation – the lecturers at the 'interface between institution and internationalization' (Tange, 2010: 139). It is they who are 'most deeply affected' (Tange, 2010: 143). In many cases, little is done to support them by way of professional development programmes (Costa, 2015; O'Dowd, 2018), given this is often a short notice, supply-on-demand strategy. Lecturers are, more often than not, ill-prepared for such an undertaking, having entered the profession without any form of linguistic or methodological preparation for diverse international classrooms which bring the added challenge of students from different linguistic, cultural and methodological backgrounds. While this should be welcomed and harnessed as the stimulus for enriched intercultural exchanges, diverse perceptions on subject content and dynamic learning opportunities for all students, international and domestic, further demands are brought by the linguistic proficiency of students and the perceived need to make lecture content and materials less culturally specific (Tange, 2010; Vinke *et al.*, 1998). Lecturers may be 'expected' or 'persuaded' rather than willing to enter into EMI. Indeed, the prospect and ensuing practice may challenge their beliefs, identity and authority, which may leave them torn between their 'ideal' and their 'ought to academic self' (Doiz & Lasagabaster, 2016). For lecturers, EMI is high stakes, particularly as they are on the front line when it comes to quality assurance. Student assessment of lecturers is part and parcel of higher education evaluation practices. Incidents of poor language have been associated with professional ability, resulting in unfortunate outcomes which are seldom ignored by lecturers and have profound effects on their confidence and self-esteem.

Teacher emotion is a growing area of research (see Fried *et al.*, 2015, for a comprehensive account). However, there are few studies that deal directly with lecturer emotions, and fewer still with those in EMI. More often than not (and quite rightly), it is the emotions of students that have taken precedence. In this chapter, lecturers take centre stage, for it is they who firstly need to know their role in the play in order to guide the understudies through the performance. Here, we examine the 'affective dimension' of lecturers involved in EMI in higher education as an essential prerequisite to effective quality practice. The affective is understood in terms of emotions, attitudes and feelings (Arnold & Brown, 1999; Boud *et al.*, 1985; Damasio, 1994). Evidence of the types of lecturer emotions and their causes is drawn from studies that relate specifically to emotions, attitudes and feelings in EMI scenarios in higher education around the world reported in international journals (see, for example, Airey, 2011, for Sweden; Bradford, 2016, for Japan; Chen, 2018, for Taiwan; Tange, 2010, for Denmark). These are found to be similar and predominantly negative. Reflective practice is put forward as an essential component of professional development for EMI lecturers, providing them with the necessary agency to better understand and deal with the emotional demands of their own practice. Strategies for enhancing reflection such as reflective journals, collegial partnerships, observation and action research are proposed.

The Affective Domain: Understanding Teacher Emotion

It is said that the affective cannot be separated from the cognitive in studies of human behaviour, and that 'emotion is the combination of a *mental evaluative process*' (Damasio, 1994: 139, emphasis in original), yet research in education has preferred 'mind over matter' and anything to do with emotions is considered either too complex or too superficial. It has, one may even say, been given a somewhat *irrational* treatment. However, emotions can, quite literally, have profound negative effects on learning, not to say on teaching, which is why an awareness of them is crucial for optimizing quality educational experiences in any context. Damasio (1994) divides emotions into those that are primary (innate reactions) and secondary (associations with one's experience). Feelings comprise an awareness of emotional states as they unfold in the body. There are varieties of feelings and corresponding bodily responses to happiness, sadness, anger, fear and disgust. Feelings, Damasio (1994: 160) states, 'have a say on how the rest of the brain and cognition go about their business. Their influence is immense'. Emotions and feelings are inextricably linked to one's needs and purposes, and how these are met. Social, cultural and political factors influence emotions and the ways in which people express and manage them within and beyond professional communities such as teaching (Fried *et al.*, 2015). These authors present a complex, dynamic view of emotions which involves 'influences' (personal characteristics – beliefs, values, identity, appraisals and social, cultural, political factors), functions (information provision about oneself and others, giving quality to experience, influencing cognitive processes, regulating internal and external processes and providing motivation) and complexities (emotions evolve over time, are individual and unique). Awareness of these connections can affect the well-being of many people. Teachers need to be aware of how their personal and professional identities are shaped by, and are dependent on, the degree of the power and agency they are able to hold, and the role that emotions play in this (Zembylas, 2003). This casts them in a pivotal position as emotionally responsible agents who must be aware of their own emotions in order to be able to understand those of others (Arnold & Brown, 1999: 5).

Written in the late 1990s at the dawn of a new millennium and educational reform in the UK, Hargreaves' renowned article, aptly entitled 'The emotional practice of teaching', echoes loudly after over 20 years, and is just as relevant to those involved in implementing EMI, and cautionary to policy makers who may underestimate or ignore the role emotions play in affecting change 'in teaching and how teachers change' (Hargreaves, 1998: 385). Emotions are not usually on the agenda of reform, although in practice they are seldom far away from it. Drawing on literature from the sociological and social-psychological fields, Hargreaves (1998: 835) emphasizes four ways in which teacher emotions are embodied within the teacher–student relationship:

(1) Teaching is an *emotional practice* (and as such affects the behaviours and actions of all those involved which can relate to 'standards, success, achievement of and equity among students').
(2) Teaching and learning involve emotional understanding (recognizing and making sense of the emotions of others in relation to our own; interpreting or misinterpreting emotions as (in)appropriate).
(3) Teaching is a form of emotional labour (consciously preparing oneself to enact appropriate feelings for the work at hand).
(4) Teachers' emotions are inseparable from their *moral purposes* and their ability to achieve those purposes (and the feelings – positive or negative – that ensue when moral standards are/not reached).

Each of these points is determined to a greater or lesser extent by the specific contexts and conditions in which teachers work. These may enhance the relationship in a positive way or place barriers or restrictions on it, such as timetables and workloads with additional duties and further accountability, which place more demands on teachers and may prevent them from realizing personal and professional goals. This puts teachers' emotional well-being at risk and may lead to burnout or thrive-and-survive strategies (Fried *et al.*, 2015: 416) – now the focus of an increasing amount of literature related to teacher resilience.

Lecturer Emotion in EMI

It is possible to apply the above to EMI in HEIs, although this has its own layers of complexity, notably related to 'marketization', international rankings and the performance results of large numbers of students from increasingly diverse educational backgrounds, which are key drivers as well as indicators of success. This may make emotional understanding difficult to achieve. Jones (2017: 279) suggests that teachers in higher education may well 'internalize the external focus on measurable, market driven outputs and judge themselves against that criterion in a way which may lead them to feeling forced to perform in a personally inauthentic manner' which may be at odds with their moral purpose. Additional researcher and administrator roles further contribute to the dilemma, as well as the need to publish in English if one is to be recognized internationally. Add to this 'teach in English' in order to comply with the top-down internationalization strategy of the HEI, and the emotional labour is abundantly evident. Quinlan (2019: 1662) suggests that the extent to which Hargreaves' points can be applied to higher education depends to a large extent on whether lecturers identify themselves as *teachers*. This, she states, 'involves emotional attachment to the role which helps anchor who that person is and guides them in interpreting events and making meaning of their work and lives'. Lecturers in HEIs see themselves predominantly as researchers who teach. Traditional lecturing is to large numbers of nameless, faceless students, the emotions of whom are frequently unknown and inadvertently ignored. This is not to say that higher education is bereft of emotion. Lecturers *do* tend to be passionate about *their* fields and *their* particular disciplinary cultures, although not necessarily the field of didactics itself.

The emotions experienced by EMI lecturers and what triggers these are broadly similar across continents, although there are national and cultural idiosyncrasies pertaining to each context as to *what* and *how* emotions are revealed. These are particularly evident in qualitative studies that incorporate interviews, group discussions, open-ended questionnaires and written reflections which afford lecturers the opportunity to voice their feelings, and authors to add their own emotional interpretations of responses. Overall, negative emotions dominate, and positive feelings are much less pronounced and discussed. In this chapter, dominant emotions and their causes are divided into three categories: lecturer language, the international classroom and self-image.

Lecturer language and performance

Lecturer language proficiency is by far the area most discussed in the literature on EMI, and is the concern of course administrators and lecturers alike. High proficiency in English is a prerequisite and what lecturers themselves associate with pedagogic competence (Ellison *et al.*, 2017). To borrow Jones' (2017: 282) term, EMI lecturers can demonstrate 'pedagogic frailty', often caused by their limited understanding of the linguistic demands of their subject. This was experienced by Taiwanese lecturers in Tsui's (2018) study, with a subsequent decline in their self-efficacy. Language can indeed become a barrier, not just between the lecturer and students, but a psychological one within the lecturer themself. This is particularly problematic where lecturers lack linguistic flexibility accompanied by an ensuing lack of confidence, as noted in the early study of Dutch lecturers' performance by Vinke *et al.* (1998), where it was found that they struggled to express themselves clearly and accurately, to improvise, refine statements and express ideas. This put a strain on their delivery and subsequent quality of output. This is echoed by some of the Swedish lecturers in Airey's (2011) study who did not feel confident in making digressions or correcting students' English and struggled with fluency and pronunciation. Lecturers in this study claimed to move less, to use fewer gestures and were afraid of silence. In the international classroom where English is supposedly the neutral medium of instruction, lecturer input may be limited to concise academic discourse. A lack of confidence is noted by Werther *et al.* (2014), where inexperienced Danish lecturers, in particular, felt the strain and insecurity of being ill-equipped for EMI where the nuances disappeared from their performance. This is contrasted with more experienced lecturers who had spent time in English-speaking countries. The imbalance between academic language and 'casual' language was an issue in Tange's (2010) study. This can result in a reduced linguistic space with pedagogic consequences affecting classroom interaction. Lecturers' language proficiency is often the focus of course evaluation by students. Chen's (2018) study, conducted at a university in Taiwan, reveals novice EMI lecturers' frustration at student criticism of their pronunciation, which they felt was undermining their disciplinary ability as students associated it with their English language competence. This is in contrast to the more experienced lecturers who were 'immune from feelings of intimidation' (Chen, 2018: 8) because they relayed the attitude that speaking the lingua franca, the tool for communication, was not as important as having professional knowledge, a point also made by lecturers in the study of Doiz and Lasagabaster (2016) and those in the study of Tange (2010). Chen (2018) states that novice lecturers and their students viewed the

English language as a foreign language with the archetypal native-speaker benchmark, something that the author states is a perception further established by the prominence of international publishing in English which academics in Taiwan are required to do in order to be promoted.

The international classroom

In EMI settings where there are international students, the concept of educational culture becomes multidimensional (see Lauridsen & Lillemose, 2015). This incorporates a range of different cultures – national, linguistic, methodological and disciplinary – which calls for more tolerance and understanding, as well as a high degree of leverage and manoeuvring to avoid clashes between students' learning traditions (Tange, 2010) and teaching practices. HEI methodologies may differ according to national cultural contexts with varying degrees of power distance (Hofstede, 1986) and expectations of student autonomy and participation stemming from traditions adhered to in compulsory schooling. This may affect classroom atmosphere, mood and dynamics. This in turn requires an understanding of the students' previous educational culture and their affective repertoires (Pavlenko, 2013: 12). Bradford (2016) highlights the tension between Western-centric and local academic practices in her study of three universities operating EMI in Japan which could lead to a two-tiered system and hierarchical notions of EMI over Japanese-medium courses. In the study of Hung and Lan (2017), lecturer concerns and worries are related to their students' ability to grasp content, their language level and lack of active participation, and confidence and fear of making mistakes. For Vietnamese EMI lecturers in the study of Kim and Tatar (2017), English was a barrier to class participation, where 'home' students did not interact with international students. To compensate those students whose first language was Taiwanese, lecturers demonstrated 'cultural understanding' through code-switching. The variation in the English language trajectories of students contributes to a complex web which incorporates attitudes towards language learning and learning styles. Added to this is the communicative competence of students and the possible range of accents and acceptable pronunciations of English. On this point, I am reminded of a colleague who, during what she described as an 'incomprehensible presentation' by a foreign student, told the student that she could speak in English, to which the student replied, 'I *am* speaking in English'. This may be an extreme example, but it is not uncommon to experience difficulty in interpreting acts of communication that can lead to bewilderment or frustration. It also suggests the need for greater concentrated efforts on the part of both students and lecturers to interpret one another's version of English. This applies to written assignments and exams as well, and a possible 'leniency' with regard to quality. Lecturers also need to be conscious of their students' language needs, which requires a more heightened awareness of disciplinary literacy and support when entering the 'new' discourse community.

Cultural diversity was viewed by lecturers as both a challenge and a potential resource in Tange's (2010) study. Some felt overwhelmed while more experienced lecturers recognized the enriching potential as a 'platform for intercultural learning' (Tange, 2010: 147). Experience is noted as a key factor in the appreciation and management of culturally diverse classes, particularly where there are native-speaker students. This author also states that the responsibility for socializing international students into the HE setting lies with lecturers. Lecturers in this study relied on their 'cultural insight' from previous intercultural encounters with international students. The 'emotional and intellectual capacity' of the more experienced EMI lecturers in Chen's (2018: 8) study helped them make the most of those present in their classes. The impact of cultural diversity on novice lecturers in this study, however, was viewed as increased workload which involved adjusting materials to include more Asian examples. They also found student participation difficult to control. This is contrasted with experienced lecturers who embraced diversity as an opportunity to have lively discussions and learn about other cultures. Drawing on Fuller's development model of a teacher's career, Chen notes the novice lecturer's focus on the 'self', and the experienced lecturer's focus on the 'other' (their students). The novice lecturers felt increasingly at risk of having their teaching disrupted and their professional status threatened, which revealed their lack of 'experience' and an inability to be 'dispassionate'. However, in their study of the attitudes of Danish lecturers towards EMI, Jensen and Thøgersen (2011) indicate that younger lecturers who have more contact with EMI are likely to look upon it more favourably.

Self-image

In light of the above, and common to many studies, are lecturers' feelings about themselves and their self-image, which are often threatened by EMI. An overriding theme is of not being able to be themselves, especially when their linguistic competence in English prevents them from being extrovert, anecdotal, humorous, and even 'caring' and verbalizing or showing emotion (Airey, 2011; Tange, 2010; Werther et al., 2014). In Bradford's (2016: 350) study, Japanese lecturers of EMI were found to be 'examining their own identities and place within their faculties' and 'mindful of being perceived as outsiders imposing Western educational practices'. The affective side of EMI can have detrimental emotional side-effects (anxiety, inertia, frustration) or, at its worst, paralysis. The risks to self-esteem and reputation are huge. Lecturers do not want to admit to feelings of inadequacy (Werther et al., 2014). Indeed, to do so in some contexts would reveal an inappropriate degree of vulnerability. In Tange's study it was remarked that EMI had 'turned good lecturers into bad communicators' (Tange, 2010: 144). In this same study, the possibility of being demoted to less interesting courses as a result of poor language level was a genuine fear and consequent threat to status. It is therefore clear that support that helps lecturers to understand and manage the emotions that EMI can evoke within them is necessary so that they may retain the passion for their field while developing their professional identities and competences so as to provide quality learning experiences. These are the key constituents of affective professional development.

Affective Professional Development

In her study of EMI training programmes in Europe, Costa (2015: 129) states that there are two goals: 'training for better language competences; training for new teaching methodologies'. While these may be necessary, there is a need to provide opportunities for lecturers to become more self-aware of their capacity to develop, to better understand their identities as these are shaped by new experiences, and how these may lead to changes in their practice (Dafouz, 2018; Lauridsen, 2017). Training programmes that tell teachers what to do or simply emphasize the technical side of teaching are of limited effect. Lecturers should be guided to develop professional pedagogic understanding which they will have ownership over eventually. They need to learn about themselves and from their own practice in order to change. In other words, they need to be in control of their own self-development. Affective EMI lecturers need to understand their emotions and what triggers them. They need to be willing to confront these, to have their beliefs challenged and to ask themselves questions about their practice which enable them to (de)construct and (re)evaluate it. To do this, they need to adopt an attitude and state of 'mindfulness', 'wholeheartedness' and 'responsibility' (Dewey, 1933). This can be achieved through professional development programmes which incorporate reflection and reflective practice.

Reflection is the lens through which we may view our practice in order to effect change. For Stanley (1999: 111), 'reflection is necessary to explicitly identify, explore and utilise the role of emotion within teaching'. Reflective practice draws on the necessity to explore and question beliefs, motives and actions. It always leads to change, be this a more heightened awareness or a modification of practice, what Boud *et al.* (1985: 19) call 'new understandings and appreciations'. The essence of reflective practice is that it:

- involves examination of beliefs, values, assumptions, experiences;
- involves articulating/making explicit thoughts about practice;
- allows 'theories' to be re-evaluated and understood in a new light;
- is action-oriented;
- is transformative – of self and beyond (personal, social, political development and change).

(Adapted from Ellison, 2014: 131)

Reflection does not just happen; it is highly complex and can involve different types or levels which denote quality and depth. Ellison (2014: 139–142) identified four types:

- Type 0 – descriptive/behavioural, which is essentially habitual, unexamined behaviour;
- Type 1 – descriptive/analytical, frequently referred to as 'technical', which means applying theory without thought or reliance on personal experience, knowledge and skills which are unquestioned;
- Type 2 – dialogic/interpretative, which is where the teacher becomes open to other perspectives that help them to problematize, analyse, interpret and reshape their own practice; this is often the result of dialogue with the self as they deliberate, question and hypothesize about their practice in light of potential or actual outcomes; and
- Type 3 – critical/transformatory, characterized by reformulated perspectives and actions; moreover, it is an understanding of one's potential and responsibility to effect change amid the complexity of the educational environment.

In professional development programmes, it is important that lecturers become aware of these different types of reflection so that they can identify, monitor and guide themselves towards deeper reflexive practice. This, in turn, may well help them to nurture their students' potential to reflect. It is this combination of reflexive and meta-affective awareness that will transform the EMI teacher into an effective teacher who is in touch with the emotional practice of teaching.

Reflective practice is *affective practice*. It involves the cognitive act of thinking along with the emotional act of being, becoming and evolving. Affective reflective practice enables teachers to *understand* and *feel* teaching. As such, it is inextricably linked to personal and professional identity. This will help lecturers better understand their 'teacher self' and move from lecturer to teacher to facilitator of learning (Underhill, 1999: 126–132). Just as the fixed arm of the compass (the essence of what makes us) provides anchorage and stability, so the other arm circles to accommodate other identities and selves within its radius. EMI provides the necessary tension required for reflection before, during and on practice (Schön, 1983). For EMI lecturers for whom 'researcher' is a dominant identity, the act of investigating their own classrooms and the analytical and interpretative skills this requires and enhances will appeal to their researcher selves.

Operationalizing reflective practice for EMI teachers in HEIs

Operationalizing reflective practice is not easy. It is dependent on support which affords time, space, tools and opportunities to construct a collaborative, collegial environment of trust and confidentiality where reflection can take place. As Day (1993: 88) states, 'reflection is a necessary but not sufficient condition for learning. Confrontation either by self or others must occur'. It also needs to be systematic in order to provide the momentum for acting, reflecting, adjusting, de- and re-constructing which leads to change. This should be based on a pedagogy of reflection. Frequently, courses pay lip-service to reflection without actually incorporating practice that brings it about. Reflection needs to be understood before it is practised. Numerous models of reflective practice exist, all of which engage teachers in surfacing and examining their beliefs, values and experiences about their practice. Some of these (e.g. Boud *et al.*, 1985; Korthagen & Vasalos, 2005; Laravee, 2000) draw specific attention to the affective dimension of teaching. For these scholars, addressing negative experiences and the feelings associated with them which act as barriers to development, and replacing them with positive ones or utilizing them as drivers towards better practice is crucial to affective professional development. This may prevent further paralysis, thus leading to a new 'affective state' (Boud *et al.*, 1985: 20). Farrell (2020) puts forward a 'holistic approach' synonymous with a framework for reflecting on practice, which consists of five stages: philosophy, principles, theory, practice and beyond practice. The framework is flexible in that EMI teachers may reflect on each sequentially (theory-into-practice), the reverse (practice-into-theory) or on a single stage. The author suggests that the first of these may be the better route for novice EMI teachers, whereas more experienced EMI teachers may start by reflecting on their actual practice before considering theory. Reich and Müller (2016) engaged EMI lecturers at a university in Switzerland in reflexive exercises within workshops on a training programme. These exercises enabled lecturers to express their concerns about EMI and the emotions felt, which established domains for potential further reflection. The authors argue that lecturers should receive training in reflexive practices and the language of reflection.

Professional development programmes involving reflective practice require 'reflexive' course facilitators who know what reflection comprises, its types, and strategies and tools for supporting it. Surfacing and articulating reflection is difficult, particularly where practice has become routinized. It requires skill and patience which is why it is often likened to counselling. Ideally, a facilitator should have the necessary sensitivity to enable them to tease out that which may be tacit, and help lecturers revisit the emotions they felt during their teaching. They should know about EMI, and effective pedagogy which scaffolds the integrated teaching and learning of complex content with the academic lingua franca. In the former, this would also constitute subject-specific literacy, genre and cognitive discourse functions (Dafouz & Núñez, 2009; Llinares & Morton, 2017). For this they need to be aware of the content and pedagogic knowledge bases of both the disciplinary field and the language. Effective instruction, whether in the home language or in English, requires an understanding of how these knowledge bases fuse, as well as how students may communicate their understanding, which may mean changing the style of the traditional lecture from knowledge transmission to masses, to small group problem-oriented learning. This may amount to a paradigm shift which, coupled with new technologies and digital literacies as well as multimodal learning, is more in keeping with 21st century learners' ways of working. This clearly requires a reflection on disciplinary cultures, competences and commitment to active professional development and change. This is no mean feat, and urges lecturers to invest in, as well as reconceptualize, their own professional identities (Bonnet & Breidbach, 2017; Dafouz & Smit, 2017). Clearly, this is a lot to expect of an individual facilitator. Ellison *et al.* (2017: 64) suggest that this should be the undertaking of a team comprising 'language teaching and content teaching professionals who engage in constructive exchanges about the knowledge bases of their respective disciplines'. In addition, they should be conscious of the 'cultures' of the international classroom, and of the need to understand and foster effective intercultural communication.

Operationalizing reflective practice involves self-analysis. For EMI teachers, this should surface their roles and identities as researcher and teacher within their disciplinary cultures which have specific values, goals and ways of behaving and working. This is an essential starting point from which to deconstruct professional identity and practice. Thereafter, lecturers may be guided to reflect on specific aspects of their practice which triggers further reflection on ones they may choose themselves. Given the evidence from the studies mentioned in this chapter, EMI lecturers may be helped to reflect on their own language, methodology and intercultural competences, as well as those of their students and their needs within the multilingual classroom. They may do this through the use of various tools. This will involve some form of written or spoken reflection which may be individual or collective, public or private. What is important is that there is a choice from which people may find their preferred means, and that reflection is systematic so that lecturers are aware of their needs and how these may be fulfilled by themselves or with the support of others (see Ellison *et al.*, 2017, for an example of a needs analysis approach to professional development). If reflecting on one's own practice is too 'personal' for some, as may well be the case in some cultural contexts, the use of case studies and vignettes which include critical incidents may provide good alternatives (see Mann & Walsh, 2017; Richards & Farrell, 2005; Richards & Lockhart, 1996, for examples, although these do not relate specifically to EMI in higher education). Jones (2017) found in her pilot study using Novakian concept mapping with 'legal academics' in the UK, that some staff were more comfortable mapping the students' emotional journey, which she suggests 'would be likely to engender some discussion of the emotional aspects of teaching and thus promote a more open climate for discussion of emotion and well-being generally' (Jones, 2017: 282). This, in turn, may lead individuals to examine their own practice in private.

Other tools and techniques that may be considered for EMI lecturers are journals, critical/collegial partnerships, observation and action research, the merits of which are discussed below.

Reflective journals

It is said that writing is thinking; it gives shape to our thoughts. The act of articulating our words visually in enough detail to enable us to capture our actions and thoughts can help teachers develop a heightened sense of awareness of themselves. The permanence of writing means that it can be revisited and re-evaluated over time which affords the writer the opportunity to monitor their development. Reflective journals may be structured and guided by a course facilitator (see Bassot, 2016, for a reflective journal that combines explicit theory of reflection with the practice of reflecting) or more ad hoc where the writer may select their own format or write purely at will about whatever they choose and whenever they wish. The important thing to note is that the reflective journal should be visited regularly in order to provide systematic reflection on practice. One means of ensuring this is through a dialogue journal whereby the facilitator comments on and questions entries. This clearly means that it is not private, but it can be extremely useful in encouraging different types of reflection and maintaining momentum. Facilitators may also provide supportive comments and advice to lecturers. It also helps the facilitator to be aware of continuing needs and potential ways to address them.

Critical/collegial partnerships

Unless an individual's audio-recorded reflection is for themself alone, spoken reflection provides opportunities for interaction with others, whether colleagues, facilitators or a group of fellow course participants. This allows more perspectives to be heard which may shed new light on practice and support the reflective processes of others. This is particularly the case in what we may term 'critical partnerships'. Such partnerships may involve a course facilitator with a lecturer, or two lecturer colleagues who engage in discussion about an issue in their practice or in feedback on an observed 'lesson' (see Lauridsen & Lauridsen, 2018, for an example of effective 'supermentorship' involving structured observation and feedback). Issues that may be discussed are those that have had a significant impact on the lecturer's practice. Articulating 'critical incidents' will help the lecturer make assertions about their practice which may draw on prior experience and assumptions that have influenced it, as well as their own theories. Others present may help by providing their own perspectives. Such opportunities to air critical incidents encourage different types of reflection on practice leading to more self-awareness in those present, thus building a community of 'critical practitioners' (Richards & Farrell, 2005: 117). Regardless of the type of critical partnership, it should always be based on empathy and trust.

A further means through which to nurture collegial partnerships is cooperative development (CD; see Edge, 2002). This is a 'non-judgemental' dialogue involving two colleagues – one the 'Speaker', the other the 'Understander' – who jointly decide to reflect on an issue related to the Speaker's practice. The Understander, as the name suggests, is there to attempt to understand the issue without judging or advising, but rather by facilitating the flow of the Speaker's discourse in such a way that they come to a better understanding of the issue themselves (and possibly how to deal with it). The Speaker can talk about their issue in a non-defensive way, knowing that they are not being judged or evaluated by the Understander. Both Speaker and Understander are fully aware of their roles, pre-session. CD is enabled through a series of 'moves' (focusing, relating, goal-setting and trailing) which involve the Understander relaying back to the Speaker what they have said as closely as possible to their version of it. This is where the Speaker's reflection rebounds back on them, enabling them to hear their own 'voice' in the words of another (reflecting) (see Edge, 2002; 2007, for illustrations of practice). The non-judgemental attitude and role adopted by the Understander helps the Speaker make sense of their actions and reflect on them more deeply. CD develops the reflective capacity of both Speaker and Understander, and is empowering for both. The Speaker is helped to work through their own issue, and the Understander gains a sense of satisfaction that they have supported a colleague's self-development. The roles may be reversed, which further nurtures collegial relationships and bonds. CD could well be the precursor to lecturers developing partnerships with language teachers so that they may pool their expertise and experiment with teaching that involves them both.

Observation

Observation can take a variety of forms and involve numerous participants. One of these is structured observation by a field expert, course facilitator or 'informed' peer who will focus on specific, predefined aspects of the 'lesson'. They may design tools (rubrics or checklists) specifically for this purpose. These may include characteristics of the technical side of EMI (lecturer language – disciplinary and procedural – including question types and formulation, pronunciation, fluency and accuracy; methodology and management including coherence within lesson sequencing, appropriate balance of cognitive and linguistic demands, scaffolding of content and language, opportunities for student interaction), as well as personal communicative skills (posture, rapport, self-confidence, presence and enthusiasm). Observation provides the lecturer with the opportunity to have their practice seen through the eyes of another professional who may be able to capture the nuanced features that they may otherwise miss, which may, indeed, include many positives. The focus of the observation may also be decided by the lecturer themself having identified an area where they feel improvement is needed. Observation should be preceded by a discussion in which the lecturer provides an outline of their teaching–learning goals and predicted outcomes so that the observer can see if there is alignment between these and actual practice. It should always be followed by feedback, not only from the observer but also the lecturer. This provides opportunities for deeper reflection on practice, pooling of expertise, sharing of concerns, strategies and ideas *in situ*, as well as building collegiality (Richards & Farrell, 2005: 86).

Inter-faculty peer observation has become a common strategy for ongoing professional development in some HEIs. At the University of Porto, Portugal, for example, colleagues from different faculties may volunteer to take part in a series of structured observations of each other with subsequent feedback, the goal of which is to develop cross-disciplinary strategies and improve teaching methodology. This may be applied to EMI settings whereby lecturers from different faculties may observe each other. Such observations may help lecturers identify similar, or indeed different useful strategies for themselves and student engagement. It would be particularly beneficial if English language, English for academic purposes (EAP) and English for specific purposes (ESP) lecturers could observe lecturers from 'non-language' fields and vice versa (see Lasagabaster, this volume). In this way, disciplinary experts may notice strategies for drawing attention to and supporting the development of language, as well as tasks that promote language use. In turn, English language experts may gain an understanding of disciplinary content which may provide meaningful content or useful references for their language lessons. Needless to say, EAP/ESP lecturers who may have the same students would gain important insider knowledge of students' needs in such a context.

Observation may be greatly enhanced if it is accompanied by filming. This can, of course, be an effective substitute for observation which may be welcomed by those who, despite the collegiality of peer observation, may still regard it as intimidating and intrusive. Filmed 'lessons' may indeed be the only means by which a lecturer can 'see' their own lessons owing to lack of a human resources or timetabling issues which inhibit observation by others. Cameras can be mounted in strategic positions to capture as much or as little activity as is required. However, they cannot decide when to 'zoom in' or what to focus on; even a professional camera person would need to be instructed when to do this. These issues aside, the potential of filmed lessons to encourage and develop reflection cannot be underestimated. It is said that 'the camera never lies' and 'seeing is believing'. Through viewing films of their lessons, the lecturer will be faced with a reality which they may well have imagined differently – this is the objective, neutral view of the camera lens. Filmed lessons enable lecturers to spot the details, focus on specific aspects, back up an observer's comments and, importantly, help them monitor their own progress (Ellison, 2014: 164). Added to this, they may help to recall moments of 'reflection-in-action' as well as affective reflection as in '*How was I feeling at that point?*'.

Lecturers may self-select excerpts for collective analysis and interpretation of actions and events. These are powerful and sometimes uncomfortable means of gaining self-awareness, but may lead to crucial changes in posture and practice.

A further enriching dimension to classroom observation within professional development courses may be gained through micro-teaching. Here, lecturers teach a small part of a lesson to other course participants who may be from their own fields and faculties or from others. Micro-teaching allows lecturers the opportunity to experience lessons as students, and those teaching to receive informed student–lecturer feedback. Studies have revealed improvements in lecturers' methodological awareness of specific strategies to support input, but also lack of linguistic competence and weaknesses in terms of student involvement (Drljača Margič & Vodopija-Krstanović, 2018; Ellison *et al.*, 2017; Tsui, 2018).

Action research

Since a large part of lecturer activity is research oriented, it is appropriate to consider engaging them in researching their own practice. Action research (AR) is an enquiry-oriented approach to teaching. It is 'teacher-initiated classroom investigation which seeks to increase the teacher's understanding of classroom teaching and learning, and to bring about change in classroom practices' (Richards & Lockhart, 1996: 12). It involves teachers problematizing, investigating and improving their practice through cycles of planning, acting, observing and reflecting (Kemmis & McTaggart, 1988: 11). Outcomes can be empowering and emancipatory (Edge, 2001; Reason & Bradbury, 2008). Lecturers may well find such an approach to their professional development very appealing as they will be able to draw on their researcher competences while also developing and understanding their practice better. It may also bring them closer to understanding their students. Just as the goal of AR in pre- and in-service teacher education programmes is to 'give teachers ways of exploring their own classrooms' (Nunan, 1990: 62) and to 'internalise the fundamental aspects of the inquiry process' (Yost *et al.*, 2000: 44), so is it, too, in professional development programmes for EMI lecturers whose tendency is to research their disciplines and not their classrooms. Through AR, lecturers will come to understand integrated pedagogy and 'practitioner-researcher' classroom inquiry, which may further legitimize professional development for EMI.

Conclusion

In this chapter, we have come to an understanding of the emotional practice of English-medium instruction. EMI triggers many, often negative, emotions largely manifest in lecturers' linguistic and pedagogic performance within complex 'multicultural' classrooms. More often than not, lecturers are ill-equipped for such scenarios which leaves them with low self-esteem and doubtful of their ability to contribute effectively to the internationalization of their institutions. Amid change in education such as this, the affective dimension should never be ignored. HEIs would do well to heed Hargreaves' (1998) message that teaching is an *emotional practice*, which requires emotional *understanding*, *labour* and *moral purpose*. To ignore this would risk draining it of its passion and quality which affect the practice and livelihoods of so many.

As EMI continues to flourish around the world, HEIs need to take stock of their practices and ability to support those involved. For internationalization to be sustainable and demonstrably lead to high-quality education, HEIs need to accept responsibility for guiding new multilingual approaches to teaching and learning. It is unacceptable for institutions to expect their lecturers to change the medium of instruction without providing appropriate and relevant support. It is indeed unfair to expect lecturers to undertake EMI when their language skills are poor. Moreover, administrators should be cognizant of who they 'invite' to teach and set attainable standards for the lingua franca rather than conform to unrealistic native-speaker ideals. Short courses focused on the technical side of teaching are unlikely to provide sustainable solutions for long-term effectiveness. A better investment of time and human resources would be through professional development programmes which incorporate reflection and reflective practices so that lecturers can become more aware of themselves as teachers, and their beliefs and personal theories about teaching. Programmes should allow lecturers to invest in (Dafouz, 2018) and embrace other facets of their identity, which they may come to appreciate as part of personal and professional growth. This will be even more beneficial to an institution if it is nurtured with the support and guidance of reflexive facilitators within a collegial, non-judgemental environment, in which experience and expertise may be shared and channelled towards positive change. This will further engender autonomy, allowing those involved to become self-supporting and able to harness their own developmental momentum. Programmes focused on reflexivity – the awareness of the power of reflection – and reflective practices in enabling lecturers to be more conscious of their practice and how it can change, are preparing them for career-long learning which will be with them once the course is not. The benefits are 'therapeutic' and 'empowering', and have also led to better understanding of students' needs (Ellison *et al.*, 2017; Tsui, 2018).

In light of the above, there is also a need for more studies of professional development programmes which capture emotions through the reflections of those involved, and their long-term outcomes. For it is through these that we will learn more about the affective dimension of EMI. Only then, perhaps, may we be truly able to transform this endeavour into a powerful emotional force which can lead to better quality courses and practitioner well-being.

References

Airey, J. (2011) Talking about teaching in English: Swedish university lecturers' experiences of changing teaching language. *Ibérica* 22, 35–54.

Ardeo González, J.M. (2013) (In)compatibility of CLIL and ESP courses at university. *Language Value* 5 (1), 24–47.

Arnold, J. and Brown, H.D. (1999) A map of the terrain. In J. Arnold (ed.) *Affect in Language Learning* (pp. 1–24). Cambridge: Cambridge University Press.

Bassot, B. (2016) *The Reflective Journal*. London: Palgrave.

Bonnet, A. and Breidbach, S. (2017) CLIL teachers' professionalization: Between explicit knowledge and professional identity. In A. Llinares and T. Morton (eds) *Applied Linguistic Perspectives on CLIL* (pp. 269–285). Amsterdam and Philadelphia, PA: John Benjamins.

Boud, D., Keogh, R. and Walker, D. (eds) (1985) *Reflection: Turning Experience into Learning*. London: Kogan Page.

Bradford, A. (2016) Toward a typology of implementation challenges facing English-medium instruction in higher education: Evidence from Japan. *Journal of Studies in International Education* 20 (4), 339–356.

Chen, R.T.H. (2018) University lecturers' experiences of teaching in English in an international classroom. *Teaching in Higher Education* 24 (1), 1–13.

Coleman, J.A. (2006) English-medium teaching in European higher education. *Language Teaching* 39, 1–14.

Costa, F. (2015) English medium instruction (EMI) teacher training courses in Europe. *RiCOGNIZIONI Rivista di lingue, letterature e culture moderne* 4 (11), 127–135.

Costa, F. and Coleman, J. (2013) A survey of English-medium instruction in Italian higher education. *International Journal of Bilingual Education and Bilingualism* 16 (1), 3–19.

Dafouz, E. (2018) English-medium instruction and teacher education programmes in higher education: Ideological forces and imagined identities at work. *International Journal of Bilingual Education and Bilingualism* 21 (5), 540–552.

Dafouz, E. and Núñez, B. (2009) CLIL in higher education: Devising a new learning landscape. In E. Dafouz and M.C. Guerrini (eds) *CLIL Across Educational Levels* (pp. 101–112). London and Madrid: Richmond.

Dafouz, E. and Smit, U. (2017) A socio-linguistic approach to the multifaceted roles of English in English-medium education in multilingual university settings. In A. Llinares and T. Morton (eds) *Applied Linguistic Perspectives on CLIL* (pp. 287–306). Amsterdam and Philadelphia, PA: John Benjamins.

Damasio, A.R. (1994) *Descartes' Error: Emotion, Reason and the Human Brain*. New York: Avon Books.

Day, C. (1993) Reflection: A necessary but not sufficient condition for professional development. *British Educational Research Journal* 19 (1), 83–93.

Dearden, J. (2014) *English as a Medium of Instruction – A Growing Global Phenomenon*. London: British Council.

Dewey, J. (1933) *How We Think*. New York: Dover Publications.

Doiz, A. and Lasagabaster, D. (2016) The motivational self system in English-medium instruction at university. In A. Doiz and D. Lasagabaster (eds) *CLIL Experiences in Secondary and Tertiary Education: In Search of Good Practices* (pp. 127–159). Bern: Peter Lang.

Drljača Margič, B. and Vodopija-Krstanovič, I. (2018) Language development for English-medium instruction: Teachers' perceptions, reflections and learning. *Journal of English for Academic Purposes* 35, 31–41.

Edge, J. (ed.) (2001) *Action Research: Case Studies in TESOL Practice*. Alexandria, VA: TESOL.

Edge, J. (2002) *Continuing Cooperative Development: A Discourse Framework for Individuals as Colleagues*. Ann Arbor, MI: University of Michigan Press.

Edge, J. (2007) Developing the community of practice in the AMEP. *Prospect* 22 (1), 3–18.
Ellison, M. (2014) CLIL as a catalyst for developing reflective practice in foreign language teacher education. Unpublished doctoral thesis, University of Porto.
Ellison, M., Araújo, S., Correia, M. and Vieira, F. (2017) Teachers' perceptions of need in EAP and ICLHE contexts. In J. Valcke and R. Wilkinson (eds) *Integrating Content and Language in Higher Education: Perspectives on Professional Practice* (pp. 59–76). Frankfurt: Peter Lang.
Farrell, T.S.C. (2020) Professional development through reflective practice for English-medium instruction (EMI) teachers. *International Journal of Bilingual Education and Bilingualism* 23 (3), 277–286.
Fortanet-Gómez, I. (2013) *CLIL in Higher Education: Towards a Multilingual Language Policy*. Bristol: Multilingual Matters.
Fried, L., Mansfield, C. and Dobozy, E. (2015) Teacher emotion research: Introducing a conceptual model to guide future research. *Issues in Educational Research* 25 (4), 415–441.
Hargreaves, A. (1998) The emotional practice of teaching. *Teaching and Teacher Education* 14 (8), 835–854.
Hofstede, G. (1986) Cultural differences in teaching and learning. *International Journal of Intercultural Relations* 10, 301–320.
Hung, D.M. and Lan, L.T.D. (2017) Content lecturers' challenges in EMI classroom. *European Journal of English Language Teaching* 2 (1). See https://oapub.org/edu/index.php/ejel/article/view/479/1303.
Jensen, C. and Thøgersen, J. (2011) Danish university lecturers' attitudes towards English as the medium of instruction. *Ibérica* 22, 13–34.
Jones, E. (2017) Mapping the emotional journey of teaching. *Knowledge Management & E-learning* 9 (3), 275–294.
Kemmis, S. and McTaggart, R. (eds) (1988) *The Action Research Planner*. Victoria: Deakin University Press.
Kim, J. and Tatar, B. (2017) Nonnative English-speaking professors' experiences of English-medium instruction and their perceived roles of the local language. *Journal of Language, Identity & Education* 16 (3), 157–171.
Knight, J. (2004) Internationalization remodeled: Definition, approaches, and rationales. *Journal of Studies in International Education* 8 (1), 5–31.
Korthagen, F. and Vasalos, A. (2005) Levels in reflection: Core reflection as a means to enhance professional growth. *Teachers and Teaching: Theory and Practice* 11 (1), 47–71.
Larrivee, B. (2000) Transforming teaching practice: Becoming the critically reflective teacher. *Reflective Practice* 1 (3), 293–307.
Lauridsen, K. (2017) Professional development of international classroom lecturers. In J. Valcke and R. Wilkinson (eds) *Integrating Content and Language in Higher Education: Perspectives on Professional Practice* (pp. 26–37). Frankfurt: Peter Lang.
Lauridsen, K. and Lauridsen, O. (2018) Teacher capabilities in a multicultural educational environment: An analysis of the impact of a professional development project. *International Journal for Academic Development* 23 (2), 98–109.
Lauridsen, K.M. and Lillemose, M.K. (eds) (2015) *Opportunities and Challenges in the Multilingual and Multicultural Learning Space. Final document of the IntlUni Erasmus Academic Network project 2012–15*. Aarhus: IntlUni.
Llinares, A. and Morton, T. (2017) Content and language integrated learning (CLIL): Type of programme or pedagogical model? In A. Llinares and T. Morton (eds) *Applied Linguistic Perspectives on CLIL* (pp. 1–16). Amsterdam and Philadelphia, PA: John Benjamins.
Mann, S. and Walsh, S. (2017) *Reflective Practice in English Language Teaching: Research-Based Principles and Practices*. New York: Routledge.

Nunan, D. (1990) Action research in the language classroom. In J.C. Richards and D. Nunan (eds) *Second Language Teacher Education* (pp. 62–81). Cambridge: Cambridge University Press.

O'Dowd, R. (2018) The training and accreditation of teachers for English medium instruction: An overview of practice in European universities. *International Journal of Bilingual Education and Bilingualism* 21 (5), 553–563.

Pavlenko, A. (2013) The affective turn in SLA: From 'affective factors' to 'language desire' and 'commodification of affect'. In D. Gabryś-Barker and J. Bielska (eds) *The Affective Dimension in Second Language Acquisition* (pp. 3–28). Bristol: Multilingual Matters.

Phillipson, R. (2006) English, a cuckoo in the European higher education nest of languages? *European Journal of English Studies* 10 (1), 13–32.

Quinlan, K.M. (2019) Emotion and moral purposes in higher education teaching: Poetic case examples of teacher experiences. *Studies in Higher Education* 44 (9), 1662–1675.

Reason, P. and Bradbury, H. (eds) (2008) *The Sage Handbook of Action Research: Participative Inquiry and Practice* (2nd edn). London: Sage.

Reich, V. and Müller, A. (2016) Making the strange familiar – reflexivity and language awareness in the EMI classroom. In P. Studer (ed.) *Communicative Competence and Didactic Challenges: A Case Study of English-Medium Instruction in Third-Level Education in Switzerland* (pp. 21–38). Winterthur: ZHAW Zürcher Hochschule für Angewandte Wissenschaften.

Richards, J.C. and Farrell, T. (2005) *Professional Development for Language Teachers*. Cambridge: Cambridge University Press.

Richards, J.C. and Lockhart, C. (1996) *Reflective Teaching in Second Language Classrooms*. Cambridge: Cambridge University Press.

Schön, D.A. (1983) *The Reflective Practitioner: How Professionals Think in Action*. New York: Basic Books.

Stanley, C. (1999) Learning to think, feel and teach reflectively. In J. Arnold (ed.) *Affect in Language Learning* (pp. 109–124). Cambridge: Cambridge University Press.

Tange, H. (2010) Caught in the Tower of Babel: University lecturers' experiences with internationalisation. *Language and Intercultural Communication* 10 (2), 137–149.

Tsui, C. (2018) Teacher efficacy: A case study of faculty beliefs in an English-medium instruction teacher training program. *Taiwan Journal of TESOL* 15 (1), 101–128.

Underhill, A. (1999) Facilitation in language teaching. In J. Arnold (ed.) *Affect in Language Learning* (pp. 125–141). Cambridge: Cambridge University Press.

Vinke, A.A., Snippe, J. and Jochems, W. (1998) English-medium content courses in non-English higher education: A study of lecturer experiences and teaching behaviours. *Teaching in Higher Education* 3 (3), 383–394.

Wächter, B. and Maiworm, F. (eds) (2014) *English-Taught Programmes in European Higher Education: The State of Play in 2014*. Bonn: Lemmens.

Werther, C., Denver, L., Jensen, C. and Mees, I.M. (2014) Using English as a medium of instruction at university level in Denmark: The lecturer's perspective. *Journal of Multilingual and Multicultural Development* 35 (5), 443–462.

Yost, D.S., Sentner, S.M. and Forlenza-Bailey, A. (2000) An examination of the construction of critical reflection: Implications for teacher education programmes in the 21st century. *Journal of Teacher Education* 51 (1), 39–49.

Zembylas, M. (2003) Emotions and teacher identity: A poststructural perspective. *Teachers and Teaching* 9 (3), 213–238.

Index

Academic achievement 37, 141, 142, 156
Affective 7, 181, 189
Anxiety 105, 188

Benchmark(ed/ing) 5, 105, 118, 120, 187

Conceptualization 10, 15, 29, 102, 114, 167, 179
Content achievement 37, 38, 49

Efficiency 3, 12, 15, 24, 119
Emotional 109, 170, 181, 192
Employability 1, 15, 19, 20, 21, 23, 30, 41, 63, 147, 156
EU language policy 13, 14
European Association for Quality Assurance in Higher Education (ENQA) 59
European identity 10, 18, 22
Evidence-based practice (or practice-based evidence, or fact-based evidence) 77, 79, 86, 118, 138, 148

Globalization and glocalization 4, 54, 82

Hegemony 3, 11, 16, 25, 27

Identity 3, 4, 7, 12, 18, 22, 35, 54, 75, 107, 183, 197
Indicators 6, 8, 16, 47, 59, 72, 90, 113, 119, 125, 134, 141, 154, 185
Institutional challenges 96, 101, 102
International classroom 7, 77, 80, 186, 187, 192

International students 7, 35, 44, 56, 65, 75, 97, 147, 152, 168, 181, 187
Internationalization at home 4, 17, 21, 27, 28, 55, 69, 75
Internationalization of the curriculum 5, 27, 55, 74, 77, 82, 148
Inventory 6, 138, 152, 155

Language achievement 37, 96, 105
Language competence 16, 20, 24, 37, 82, 91, 130, 140, 167, 186
Linguistic diversity 3, 9, 14, 16, 23, 57, 85, 147, 181

Matrix xvi, 5, 6, 81, 115, 119, 120, 121, 127, 134
Mobility 2, 16, 20, 24, 47, 55, 60, 75, 89, 96, 116, 123, 137, 141, 147, 155
Mother tongue 20, 23, 35, 99, 100, 107, 147, 163, 172
Multilingual competence 23, 38

Nationalism 15, 114

Policy planning 10, 12, 17
Professional development xvi, 3, 5, 7, 74, 91, 107, 118, 124, 130, 175, 182, 189

Quality assurance xvi, 3, 6, 58, 116, 124, 133, 138, 152, 155, 183
Quality multilingual programmes 3, 5, 49, 59, 137, 197

Ranking(s) 3, 17, 27, 48, 125, 141, 185
Reflective practice(s) 7, 189–191, 197

Scaffolding 6, 43, 83, 132, 144, 151, 176, 194
SDG 5, 73, 74, 81, 90
Sustainability 6, 86, 91, 154, 156

Teacher training 39, 46, 64, 80, 99, 107, 123, 143, 151, 164, 171, 189

UNESCO 14, 37, 86, 91

For Product Safety Concerns and Information please contact our EU Authorised Representative:

Easy Access System Europe

Mustamäe tee 50

10621 Tallinn

Estonia

gpsr.requests@easproject.com